Popular Mechanics
WORKSHOP

Tables & Chairs

Tables & Chairs

Hearst Books
A Division of Sterling Publishing Co., Inc.
New York

POPULAR MECHANICS
WORKSHOP TABLE & CHAIRS

Produced by Spooky Cheetah Press, Stamford, CT
Design: Ray Leaning

Library of Congress Cataloging-in-Publication Data
Popular mechanics workshop : tables & chairs.
    p. cm.
  Includes index.
  ISBN (invalid) 1-58816-203-2
    1. Tables. 2. Chairs. 3. Furniture making. 4. Woodwork.
  I. Title: Tables & chairs. II. Popular mechanics (New York.
1959)
  TT197.5.T3P67 2003
  684.1'3--dc21   2003050867

10 9 8 7 6 5 4 3 2 1

Published by Hearst Books,
A Division of Sterling Publishing Co., Inc.
387 Park Avenue South, New York, N.Y. 10016

Popular Mechanics is a trademark owned by Hearst Magazines
Property, Inc., in USA, and Hearst Communications, Inc., in
Canada. Hearst Books is a trademark owned by
Hearst Communications, Inc.

www.popularmechanics.com

Distributed in Canada by Sterling Publishing
c/o Canadian Manda Group, One Atlantic Avenue, Suite 105
Toronto, Ontario, Canada M6K 3E7

Distributed in Australia by Capricorn Link (Australia) Pty. Ltd.
P.O. Box 704, Windsor, NSW 2756 Australia

Printed in China

ISBN 1-58816-303-2

Contents

Foreword

Tables and chairs represent some of the most challenging and rewarding projects a woodworker can tackle. Molding adds home value, and bookshelves are useful, but an Arts & Crafts dining room table is a showcase of skill and expertise, and a heirloom to be handed down generation to generation. We've selected all the projects in this book—from among the many that have appeared in the pages of *Popular Mechanics*—with that in mind. We've selected projects that are not only useful in the home, from a coffee table with built-in storage to a kitchen step stool that doubles as a chair, but that also enhance any room. These are truly handsome pieces of furniture. We've also taken pains to select pieces in a range of skill levels, so that there is something for everyone. You'll see the skill level listed at the beginning of each project, along with the relative expense of the project (low, moderate, or expensive) and the time the project should take the average woodworker to complete. But don't let the skill level deter you from any given project. An experienced craftsman may find a simpler project easier to do, but it will still be a beautiful addition to the home. A novice may need to be much more careful, and take a lot more time than we've estimated to tackle a more complex project, but it will represent a chance for him to grow his skills, knowledge, and experience. So choose the project that makes the most sense for your skills, home, and tastes. Then open the door to your workshop and step into your next woodworking adventure—courtesy of the experts at *Popular Mechanics*!

Joe Oldham
Editor-in-Chief
Popular Mechanics

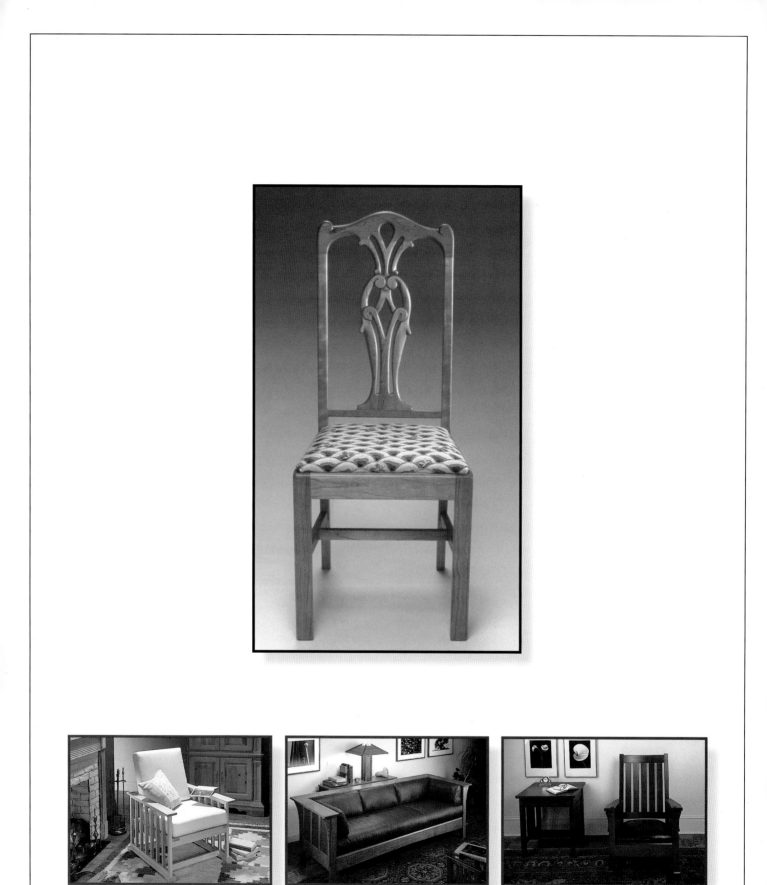

Chair Projects

Rock Star

This oversize rocker has classic lines and a comfortable leather seat.

There was a time, not so long ago, when rocking chairs could be found in just about every home. The gentle, soothing rocking motion brought a sense of peace and calm to anyone sitting in the chair. These old rockers were often the favorite seats in the house, and it is surprising how often our modern homes are furnished without one. The top of our rocker is stained with an aniline dye to bring out the mahogany's warm red tones, and finished with a traditional brushed varnish. The smooth finish and spacious, comfortable design ensure that the rocker is as much a joy to sit in and use, as it is to look at. And the solid construction ensures that your home will have a rocker for decades to come.

Key POINTS

TIME

Prep Time	10 hours
Shop Time	20 hours
Assembly Time	16 hours

EFFORT

Skill Level	advanced

COST / BENEFITS

Expense: **expensive**

- **Traditional home furnishing** that is enjoyable to use in any room.
- **Standalone style** makes this a portable, timeless addition to your furniture.

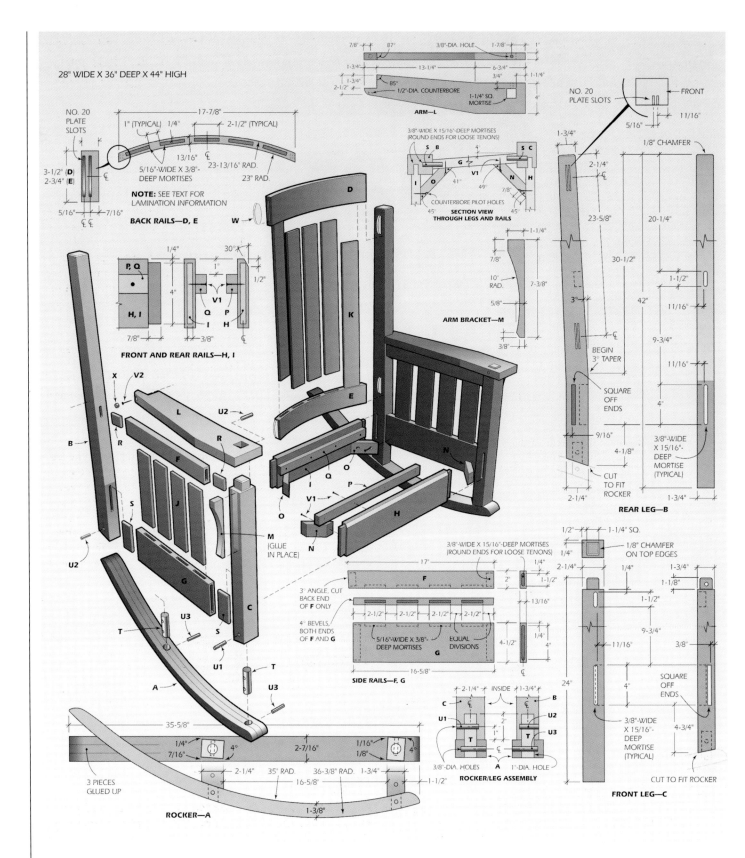

28" WIDE X 36" DEEP X 44" HIGH

BACK RAILS—D, E

NO. 20 PLATE SLOTS

3-1/2" (D)
2-3/4" (E)

5/16"   7/16"

1" (TYPICAL)   1/4"   2-1/2" (TYPICAL)
17-7/8"
13/16"
5/16"-WIDE X 3/8"-DEEP MORTISES
23-13/16" RAD.
23" RAD.

NOTE: SEE TEXT FOR LAMINATION INFORMATION

W

FRONT AND REAR RAILS—H, I

P, Q

H, I

7/8"   3/8"

1/4"   30°
1"
1/2"
4"
V1
Q   P
I   P   H

ARM—L

7/8"   87°   3/8"-DIA. HOLE   1-7/8"   1"
1-3/4"   13-1/4"   6-3/4"   1-1/4"
1-3/4"   3/4"
2-1/2"   85°
1/2"-DIA. COUNTERBORE
1-1/4" SQ. MORTISE   4"

3/8"-WIDE X 15/16"-DEEP MORTISES (ROUND ENDS FOR LOOSE TENONS)

S B   S C
G
I O   41°   49°   N H
COUNTERBORE PILOT HOLES
45°   45°
SECTION VIEW THROUGH LEGS AND RAILS

ARM BRACKET—M

1-1/4"
7/8"
10" RAD.
5/8"
7-3/8"
3/8"

NO. 20 PLATE SLOTS   FRONT
11/16"
5/16"

1/8" CHAMFER

1-3/4"
2-1/4"
23-5/8"
30-1/2"
42"
3°
BEGIN 3° TAPER
SQUARE OFF ENDS
9/16"
4-1/8"
CUT TO FIT ROCKER
2-1/4"

20-1/4"
1-1/2"
11/16"
9-3/4"
11/16"
4"
3/8"-WIDE X 15/16"-DEEP MORTISE (TYPICAL)
1-3/4"

REAR LEG—B

X V2
B
L
R
U2
R
F
J
S
U2
G
M (GLUE IN PLACE)
U3
T
U1
S
T
U3
A

D
K
E
Q
I   O
V1
N
P
O   N
H

3/8"-WIDE X 15/16"-DEEP MORTISES (ROUND ENDS FOR LOOSE TENONS)

17"
F
2"
3° ANGLE, CUT BACK END OF F ONLY
4° BEVELS, BOTH ENDS OF F AND G
2-1/2" 2-1/2" 2-1/2" 2-1/2"
13/16"
1/4"
5/16"-WIDE X 3/8"-DEEP MORTISES
EQUAL DIVISIONS
G
4-1/2"
16-5/8"
SIDE RAILS—F, G

1/2"   1-1/4" SQ.
1/4"
1/8" CHAMFER ON TOP EDGES
2-1/4"   1/4"
1-3/4"
1-1/8"
1-1/2"
9-3/4"
3/8"
11/16"
4"
SQUARE OFF ENDS
3/8"-WIDE X 15/16"-DEEP MORTISE (TYPICAL)
4-3/4"
CUT TO FIT ROCKER
FRONT LEG—C

35-5/8"
1/4"   4°   1/16"   4°
7/16"   1/8"
2-7/16"
2-1/4"   35° RAD.   36-3/8" RAD.   1-3/4"
16-5/8"
1-1/2"
1-3/8"
3 PIECES GLUED UP
ROCKER—A

2-1/4"   INSIDE   1-3/4"
C   B
U1   U2
2"
T   1"   T   U3
3/8"-DIA. HOLES   A   1"-DIA. HOLE
24"
ROCKER/LEG ASSEMBLY

The Arts & Crafts-style rocker that we created here is a synthesis of several traditional designs. The proportions of the chair are generous, both in seat size and in the massiveness of the chair parts, giving the feeling of a traditional armchair. The upholstered leather seat is soft and inviting, and the deeply contoured back provides comfortable support.

Although the techniques required to build this chair are beyond those of a beginning woodworker, a serious home craftsperson should not find this project too difficult. The chair is constructed of 4/4, 5/4, and 8/4 quarter-sawn white oak, which was the most common material used for Arts & Crafts furniture. If you have trouble locating quarter-sawn material, there are mail-order suppliers who will ship lumber anywhere in the country. Find them on the Internet or ask your local lumber supplier for sources.

Materials List

Key	No.	Size and description (use)
A	2	1⅜ x 2⁷/₁₆ x 35⅝" oak (rocker)
B	2	1¾ x 2¼ x 42" oak (rear leg)
C	2	1¾ x 2¼ x 24" oak (front leg)
D*	1	¹³/₁₆ x 3½ x 17⅞" oak (back rail)
E*	1	¹³/₁₆ x 2¾ x 17⅞" oak (back rail)
F	2	¹³/₁₆ x 2 x 17" oak (side rail)
G	2	¹³/₁₆ x 4½ x 16⅝" oak (side rail)
H	1	¹³/₁₆ x 4½ x 22¼" oak (front rail)
I	1	¹³/₁₆ x 4½ x 19⅝" oak (back rail)
J	8	⁵/₁₆ x 2½ x 10" oak (side slat)
K	5	⁵/₁₆ x 2½ x 21¼" oak (back slat)
L	2	1 x 4 x 21¾" oak (arm)
M	2	¹³/₁₆ x 1¼ x 7⅜" oak (corbel)
N	2	¹³/₁₆ x 1¾ x 4" oak (corner block)
O	2	¹³/₁₆ x 1¾ x 4" oak (corner block)
P	1	¾ x 1¼ x 20½" oak (cleat)
Q	1	¾ x 1¼ x 17⅞" oak (cleat)
R	4	⅜ x 1½ x 1¾" oak (loose tenon)
S	4	⅜ x 1¾ x 4" oak (loose tenon)
T	4	1"-dia. x 3⅜" oak dowel
U1	2	⅜"-dia. x 1¾" oak dowel (pin)
U2	4	⅜"-dia. x 1½ " oak dowel (pin)
U3	4	⅜"-dia. x 2" oak dowel (pin)
V1	16	1¼" No. 8 fh screws
V2	2	1½" No. 8 fh screws
W	8	No. 20 joining plates
X	2	½"-dia. x ½" dowel plug

Misc.: Yellow glue; 120- and 220-grit sandpaper; aniline stain; tung oil varnish; 0000 steel wool; paste wax.

* Laminated oak veneer.

Slats and Arms

Because the rockers are the heart of any rocking chair, they are the logical place to begin. Cut six pieces of ¹³/₁₆-in.-thick stock, each about 6 in. wide x 38 in. long. Apply glue to the mating faces of the boards, and assemble them into two blanks of three boards each. Clamp the blocks together until the glue sets.

It's important that the finished rockers have identical shapes with a smooth curve. The best way to ensure this is to work from a template. Transfer the rocker shape onto a piece of ¼-in.-thick plywood or hardboard. Then carefully cut the template to size with a band saw or sabre saw. Use a rasp or plane to adjust the template until it is perfect, then use it to trace the shape onto each rocker blank (**Fig. 1**).

Use a band saw to cut the bottom profile of each rocker, staying just to the waste side of the layout line. Clamp the blank between bench dogs, then use a sharp block plane to refine the profile. Cut the top profile of the rockers, then use a spokeshave to smooth the resulting curve (**Fig. 2**).

Legs and Rails

Cut blanks for the rear legs from 8/4 stock, then trace the leg profile on each blank and use the band saw to cut the legs (**Fig. 3**). Stay to the waste side of the layout line. Use a block plane to remove the saw marks and finish shaping the legs. Rip and crosscut the front leg posts to rough length as shown in the plan. Note that all legs will be cut to final length after assembly, because they must be fit to the curve of the rockers.

Lay out the mortise locations in the leg posts. The front

Fig. 1 *Glue up the stock for the rockers. Then make a template for the rocker shape and trace its outline onto the rocker blank.*

Fig. 2 *Cut the profile of the rocker on a band saw and clamp the rocker in a vise. Smooth the shape with a spokeshave.*

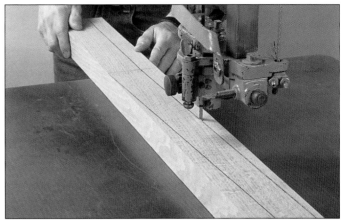

Fig. 3 *Make a template for the shape of the back legs and trace it onto the leg stock. Cut along the outline with a band saw.*

Fig. 4 *Lay out the mortises in the legs and use a plunge router with an edge guide and an up-cut spiral bit to make the cuts.*

Fig. 5 *Cut the tenons on the front and back seat rails using a dado blade in a table saw. Smooth the cuts with a sharp chisel.*

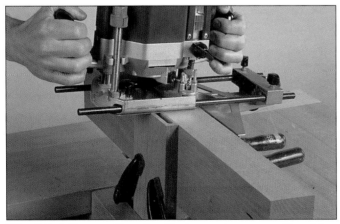

Fig. 6 *Cut the mortises for the loose tenons on the side rails using a router and edge guide. Clamp a block in place for support.*

Fig. 7 *Cut the loose tenons to size on the table saw. Then use a rasp to shape the ends of the tenons to fit snugly in the mortises.*

and back seat rails are joined to the posts by traditional mortise-and-tenon joints. Because the side rails join the posts at an angle, we used loose tenons to make these joints, simplifying the joint-cutting process and still yielding a strong connection between the parts.

The easiest way to cut the mortises is to use an up-cut spiral bit in the plunge router with an edge guide to register the cuts. Clamp a leg blank between bench dogs and make several passes to cut the mortises to finished depth (**Fig. 4**). These mortises are 1/16 in. deeper than the corresponding tenons to allow for excess glue at the bottom of the joint.

The mortises that house the loose tenons can retain their rounded ends since it is simple to shape those tenons to match. The mortises for the front and back rails, however, should be cut square at each end to match the normal tenon profile. Use a sharp chisel to make these cuts.

Cut the front and back rails to finished size, then use a dado blade in a table saw to cut the tenons on the rail ends (**Fig. 5**). After making the cheek cuts, readjust the blade height and cut the top and bottom shoulders on the tenons.

Next, cut the 30° chamfer along the top edge of the front seat rail using a table saw or a router with chamfer bit. Then rip the side rails to width and cut them to length with the appropriate angled cuts.

To cut the mortises for the loose tenons in the ends of the side rails, you'll have to provide an auxiliary support for the router base. Since the rail ends are cut at a 4° angle, you can rip the same angle along the edge of a piece of stock at least 2 in. thick x 4 in. wide x 16 in. long. Clamp this piece flush to the end of the rail (**Fig. 6**) to both support the router base and provide a registration surface for the edge guide. Make two or three passes to achieve the finished mortise depth.

Cut two lengths of 3/8-in.-thick stock for the loose tenons. Rip one piece 1 1/2 in. wide and the other 4 in. wide, then use the miter gauge on the table saw to cut the tenons to length. Note that the grain of the tenons must run perpendicular to the joint to provide adequate strength. Clamp each tenon in the bench vise, then use a rasp to shape its top and bottom ends to fit the mortise (**Fig. 7**).

Slats and Arms

Rip and crosscut 5/16-in.-thick stock for both the side and back slats. Then lay out the mortises for the slats in the side rails. Clamp a rail between bench dogs and use the router to cut the mortises. Be sure to support the router base by clamping two or three boards to the side of the rail. When you cut the end mortises, adjust the support boards so that they extend several inches past the end of the rail (**Fig. 8**). Square the ends of the slat mortises with a sharp chisel.

Use a dado blade in the table saw to cut the through tenons on the end of the front leg posts. Cut these tenons 1/4 to 3/8 in. longer than the finished dimension. Next, cut blanks for the chair arms from 1-in.-thick stock. Make a

Fig. 8 *Clamp the side rails to the bench to route the mortises for the side slats. Support the router with scrap blocks.*

Fig. 9 *Lay out the notch at the back of the arms that fits around the back legs. Using a backsaw, carefully cut out the waste.*

template for the arm shape from 1/4-in.-thick plywood or hardboard, then trace the shape onto the arm blanks. Use the band saw or sabre saw to cut the arms to shape (except for the notch that fits around the back leg post). Keep in mind that the cut that fits against the front side of the back leg must correspond to the angle of the leg. Clamp the arm in the bench vise and use a hand saw to make cuts (**Fig. 9**).

Lay out the through mortises in the chair arms, scribing the outlines of the mortise with a sharp knife. Next, drill a 1-in.-dia. hole through the arm—centered in the mortise—to remove most of the waste. Complete the mortise by chopping out the waste with a sharp chisel. Test the fit of the tenon in the mortise, and adjust as required.

Dry assemble a chair side, holding the parts together with clamps. Slip an arm over the appropriate through tenon and mark the tenon at the point that it protrudes through the arm (**Fig. 10**). Disassemble the side and cut the tenon 1/8 in.

Fig. 10 *Assemble each chair side, and mark where the leg tenon meets the arm mortise. Cut each leg ⅛ in. longer than the mark.*

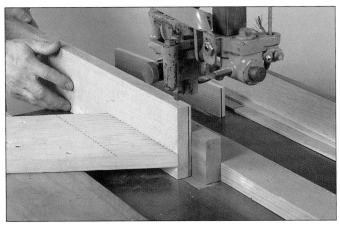

Fig. 11 *Use a band saw with a rip fence and fingerboard to cut the ⅛-in. oak strips for the outer layers of the back rails.*

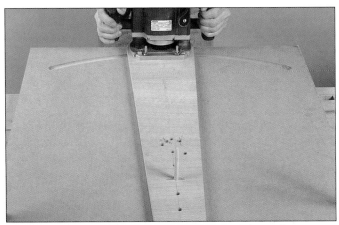

Fig. 12 *Make a trammel base and attach it to the bottom of your router. Use it to cut a pattern for the back rail bending forms.*

beyond the mark. Use a sharp chisel to chamfer the end of the tenon ⅛ in. on each side.

Back Rails

The back rails of the chair are formed by laminating strips of oak to achieve the necessary curved profile. The outer surfaces of the rails must match the quarter-sawn material of the rest of the chair, so these layers are sawn from a piece of quarter-sawn stock. Rip one piece of ¹³⁄₁₆-in.-thick stock 3¾ in. wide and one piece 3 in. wide. Then crosscut them both to 24 in. long. Clamp a tall fence to the band saw table to resaw ⅛-in.-thick strips, one from each side of both these boards (**Fig. 11**). When laminating the rails, place the smooth side of these strips toward the center of the rail to present a better gluing surface.

For economy, and to make the job easier, we used ¹⁄₁₆-in.-thick white oak veneer for the inner plies of the rails. The combination of two outer layers ⅛ in. thick and seven inner layers ¹⁄₁₆ in. thick yields a perfect ¹³⁄₁₆-in.-thick rail. (This veneer is available from a number of mail-order suppliers.)

The forms for gluing up the back rails are fabricated by stacking up five layers of ¾-in.-thick MDF (medium-density fiberboard) or particleboard. You'll need a panel at least 28 in. wide x 64 in. long. When cut, each set of forms should measure 24 in. wide x 12 in. long.

Begin by generating the appropriate curve, using our drawing as a guide. Then construct a trammel base for the router and install a ¹³⁄₁₆-in.-dia. straight bit in the router (**Fig. 12**). Measure from the inside edge of the bit to a point 23 in. down the trammel, and bore a ⅜-in.-dia. hole. Then place the trammel on the form stock, bore a corresponding hole in the form panel, and pin the two together with a short length of ⅜-in. dowel. Make a series of router passes along this arc until you have cut through the stock. Be sure to leave some material uncut at both ends of the arc so that the ¹³⁄₁₆-in. space is maintained. When the routing is done, cut the two

Fig. 13 *Cut the stock for the bending forms to rough size. Then cut it to finish size using the pattern and a flush trimming bit.*

arc shapes from the form stock. These two pieces will be the first layers of the male and female forms for your rails. Then trace these shapes onto the additional form material and rough-cut the other layers to within ¼ in. of the finished shape. Add one layer at a time to the form with screws, then use a flush cutting bit in the router to trim it to shape (**Fig. 13**). When all five layers are added to each form, place alignment lines across the forms to keep both sides properly oriented during glue-up. Apply two coats of wax to the inner surfaces of the forms to keep glue from sticking to them.

Use a short-nap roller to spread glue on the mating surfaces of all rail plies. Be sure not to leave any dry spots on the veneer faces. Place the veneer sandwich between the male and female forms and use clamps, both below and above, to squeeze the forms together (**Fig. 14**). Leave the rail clamped for at least 8 hours, then repeat the process for the second rail.

Use a cabinet scraper to smooth the band saw marks left on the faces of both rails. Then plane one edge of each rail flat and square to the face and use the band saw with a fence to rip the rails to width. Scrape or plane the cut edge to remove the saw marks.

The male gluing form can now be modified to act as a jig for sawing the rails to finished length. Cut the form to the finished dimension of the rails, which is 17⅞ in., making sure to center the arc in the middle of the form.

Screw a block to the back side of the form and add a holddown clamp to the top of this block. Then position the form along the table saw miter gauge, so that the end of the form aligns with the near side of the blade, and temporarily screw the form to the miter gauge. Place one of the rails on the form, secure it with the holddown clamp, and cut one end of the rail (**Fig. 15**). Then, reverse the rail in the form, aligning the cut end with the opposite end of the form, and make the second cut. Finish up the rails by laying out the back slat mortises. Use a ¼-in.-dia. bit in the drill press to bore out most

Fig. 15 *Use the inner bending form as a jig for cutting the back rails. Attach the form to a backer board and the saw fence.*

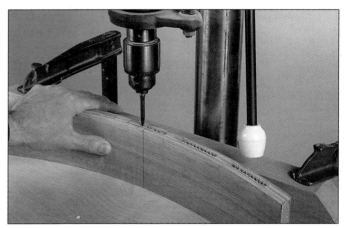
Fig. 16 *Lay out the slat mortises in the back rails, then remove the waste using a drill press. Finish the cut with a sharp chisel.*

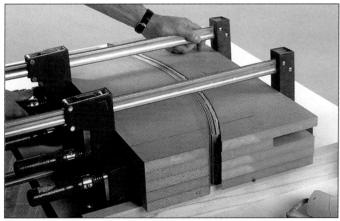
Fig. 14 *Apply glue to the pieces that make up the back rails. Then place them between the bending forms and clamp them tight.*

SHOP*Helper*

Trimming an errant miter cut can be frustrating because the saw tends to slip off the end of the wood piece. Accomplished carpenters trim to the line using a very sharp block plane, but if you lack the confidence for this, do the following. Place the just-cut pieces butted together in the miter box as they were before cutting. Clamp the pieces securely to the miter box so that they won't move, and make the trim cut. Using the second piece this way prevents the saw from slipping and ensures a neat trim cut.

Fig. 17 *Use the bending form to clamp the back rail assemblies to the bench. Then carefully cut plate slots in the rail ends.*

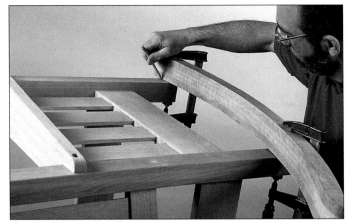

Fig. 18 *Assemble the chair pieces and clamp each rocker over the legs. Trace the proper cutting angle onto the legs.*

of the waste (**Fig. 16**). Then chop out the rest with a sharp chisel. Test fit each slat in its mortise.

Assembly

The back rails are joined to the rear leg posts by double joining plates. The same jig that you used to cut the rails can now be used as a holding jig to cut these plate slots. Fasten a rail in the jig and clamp the whole assembly to the workbench. Use spacer blocks under the plate joiner to properly locate the slots in the ends of the rail (**Fig. 17**). Lay out and cut the matching slots in the rear leg posts.

Use a sharp chisel to cut the ⅛-in. chamfer around the top ends of the rear leg posts. Then, sand all chair parts with 120-grit sandpaper, then 220-grit sandpaper. Begin assembly by joining the side rails to the slats. It is not necessary to glue the slats in place, but you should clamp the rail-slat assembly together to ease the next steps. Spread glue on the loose

tenons and in their respective mortises, then join the side rails to the front and back leg posts. Clamp the assembly together and check for square.

When the glue has set on these side assemblies, join the back rails to the back slats. Again, no glue is needed in these joints. Spread glue in the remaining leg mortises and on the front and back rail tenons. Also spread glue in the joining plate slots and on the plates themselves. Assemble the two sides to the rails, clamp together, and check for square.

Bore and counterbore pilot holes for fastening the arms to the back leg posts. Apply glue to the through tenons and arm mortises. Also spread glue along the top edge of the side arm rails. Fasten the arms to the posts with screws. Next, use a plug cutter in the drill press to cut matching plugs. Apply glue and tap the plugs in place to cover the screw heads.

Cut corner blocks to the size and shape specified in the

TECH *Tips*

Super Sanding
Final sanding is one of the most important phases in preparing a wood surface for finishing, and is almost your final chance to ensure that your hard work results in a beautiful piece of furniture. A top-quality finish demands a smooth, clean surface, and sanding is one of the easiest ways to achieve this. In addition, a complete sanding job creates a consistent surface quality on the entire piece, so the finish will appear uniform. Although some hand sanding is usually required, the bulk of the work is easily done with an orbital sander.

Because of the speed at which the pad of an orbital sander moves, you have some freedom when handling crossgrain construction. However, when hand sanding, always sand parallel to the grain direction. When the construction includes a crossgrain joint, such as in a frame around a panel, hand sand up to the joint line to avoid crossgrain sanding.

Work through progressively finer grades of sandpaper until you obtain a satin-smooth surface. If all tool marks and other blemishes have been removed, start with 100-grit sandpaper. For painted or other opaque work, a final sanding with 180-grit paper will suffice. Work to be stained or clear finished requires a final sanding with paper no coarser than 220 grit.

Fig. 19 *Cut the leg ends with a sabre saw, then reclamp the rockers in place. Scribe the legs where necessary to get a tight fit.*

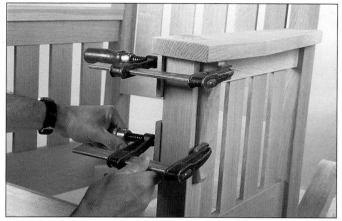

Fig. 20 *Cut the corbel brackets to size and finish sand them. Then glue and clamp them to the outside of the front legs.*

plans. Bore and counterbore pilot holes in the blocks, then apply glue to their ends and screw them in place, flush to the bottom edge of the rails.

Place the chair on its side on a padded table, then position one of the rockers over the ends of the legs and temporarily clamp it in place (**Fig. 18**). Scribe along the inner curve of the rocker to give the desired profile of the leg ends. Cut these legs to shape, then repeat the same process for the opposite chair side. Next, clamp one of the rockers to a pair of the cut legs. Because the curved rockers intersect the legs at an angle, the joint between the two may be slightly open. Use scribers to mark the leg for the necessary adjustment (**Fig. 19**).

Invert the chair over the edge of a padded table, then clamp the rockers in place over the leg ends. Mark guidelines along the rockers and legs, then bore the required holes through the rockers and into the leg ends for the connecting dowels. Cut pieces of 1-in.-dia. dowel for these joints, then

When using an orbital sander, it's especially important not to shift from a coarse paper to a fine paper and omit the intermediate grits. Otherwise, the orbital sander swirl marks from the coarse sandpaper will be nearly impossible to remove.

Final sanding inevitably embeds the pores of the wood surface with a fine dust that must be removed before applying the finish. A vacuum cleaner with a brush attachment will lift out most of the dust, but not all of it. To completely clean the piece and guarantee that all dust particles are removed, wipe the surface with a naptha-moistened cloth.

apply glue to both the holes and the dowels and drive the dowels into place. Lay out the two corbel brackets, then use a band saw or sabre saw to cut them to shape. Sand each smooth, then glue and clamp them in place (**Fig. 20**).

Bore holes for the ⅜-in.-dia. pins into the through tenon joints and into the leg-rocker dowel joints, as shown on the plans. Cut lengths of oak dowels for the pins, then apply glue to the holes, and drive the pins into place.

Finishing Up

We chose to have an upholsterer make up the chair seat cushion in brown leather. You have the option of having a spring seat made or using a foam cushion. If you opt for the spring seat, you will need to provide a cleat on the front and back rails to support the seat frame. Locate these cleats 1 in. down from the top edge of the rails. If you choose to use a foam cushion, you must provide a series of slats to support the seat. Fit the slats (½ or ⅝ in. thick), spaced approximately 1 in. apart, over the cleats and screw them in place. In either case, the top of the seat should be about 4 in. above the side rails.

To stain the chair, we used a water-soluble aniline dye. The color we chose is brown mahogany. Water-soluble dyes yield excellent color and clarity and are relatively easy to use, but they do raise the grain of the wood after application.

To prevent this problem, before staining, wipe the entire chair with a slightly damp sponge and let it dry thoroughly. The surface should become extremely rough to the touch. Lightly sand the chair with 220-grit sandpaper to knock off this rough grain, then dust off the chair before staining.

We finished our chair with three coats of a tung oil varnish. Simply wipe on each coat with a brush or rag, let it set for about 10 minutes and wipe off the excess. After overnight drying, repeat the process. When the final coat is dry, you can burnish the surface with 0000 steel wool and apply a coat of paste wax.

High Class

This elegant stool adds panache to your kitchen, and can even bring style to a family room bar.

Today's kitchen is more than just a room for cooking. These days it's more of a geographical region, less defined by walls than by what it contains—its appliances, cabinets, and, of course, the kitchen counter. In a way, the counter really reflects the nature of kitchen activity. From chopping to mixing to carving the roast, to having a cup of coffee and chatting with company, it's not the kind of work you do sitting down—at least, not in an ordinary chair. What you need is a chair that matches the stature of your counter— you need a kitchen stool. And this particular piece meets your needs in grand style. It's also useful at a phone station or for a high desk.

*Key*POINTS

TIME
Prep Time	10 hours
Shop Time	16 hours
Assembly Time	10 hours

EFFORT
Skill Level	intermediate

COST / BENEFITS
Expense: **moderate**
- **Comfortable seating** for working or just relaxing in the kitchen.
- Striking black finish and subtle lines make it a **piece of distinction.**

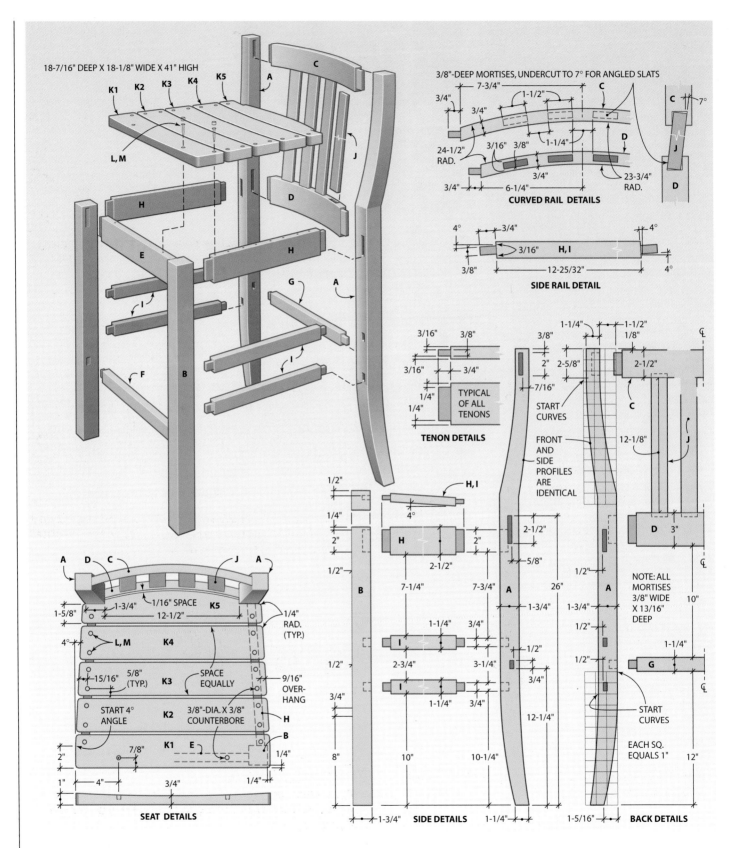

O ur kitchen stool design is perfect for all those quieter kitchen chores—like writing the grocery list. We built this handsome piece from sturdy maple and imbued it with an awesome ebonized finish for a modern look.

Making the Legs

Note that both the front and side profiles of each rear leg are the same. Make a precise template of this profile from ¼-in. plywood. Rip and crosscut 2¾-in.-square x 41-in.-long blanks for the rear legs.

If your stock isn't thick enough, glue up thinner pieces for the blanks. Then use the template to trace the leg shape onto the blanks. Cut 2-in.-thick stock to finished dimension for the front legs.

Lay out the rail mortises—except those for the top back rail—in the legs (**Fig. 1**). Then rout the mortises with a spiral up-cutting bit and edge guide (**Fig. 2**). Use a sharp chisel to square the ends. Cut the front and back profiles of a rear leg on the band saw. Save the waste pieces and tape them back onto the leg blank to support the piece while you cut the side profiles (**Fig. 3**). With both legs sawn to shape, use a spokeshave and cabinet scraper to remove the saw marks and carefully refine the profiles.

Materials List

Key	No.	Size and description (use)
A	2	2¾ x 2¾ x 41" maple (rear leg)
B	2	1¾ x 1¾ x 25" maple (front leg)
C	1	2¹/₁₆ x 2½ x 17" maple (upper curved rail)
D	1	1⅝ x 3 x 14" maple (lower curved rail)
E	1	¾ x 2½ x 15⅝" maple (upper front rail)
F	1	¾ x 1¼ x 15⅝" maple (lower front rail)
G	1	¾ x 1¼ x 14" maple (rear rail)
H	2	¾ x 2½ x 14⁹/₃₂" maple (upper side rail)
I	4	¾ x 1½ x 14⁹/₃₂" maple (lower side rail)
J	4	⅜ x 1½ x 12⅞" maple (back slat)
K1	1	1 x 3 x 18⅛" maple (seat slat)
K2	1	1 x 3 x 17¹⁵/₁₆" maple (seat slat)
K3	1	1 x 3 x 17½" maple (seat slat)
K4	1	1 x 3 x 17⅛" maple (seat slat)
K5	1	1 x 3 x 16¹¹/₁₆" maple (seat slat)
L	18	1½" No. 8 fh wood screw
M	18	⅜"-dia. x ⅜" maple plug

Misc.: 120-, 150-, 180-, and 220-grit sandpaper; 4/0 steel wool; jet black stain; retarder; sealer/finish.

Fig. 1 *Use a tape measure, square, and a mortise gauge to accurately lay out the locations of the mortises in the leg blanks.*

Fig. 2 *Rout the mortises with a spiral up-cutting bit and an edge guide. Take two or three passes with the router to avoid overloading the motor.*

Fig. 3 *After cutting the leg profile along one face, tape the waste back onto the leg to provide a base for the adjacent face cuts.*

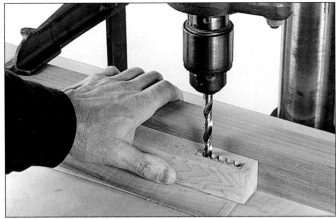

Fig. 4 *Begin the upper back rail mortises by boring a series of ³⁄₈-in.-dia. holes. Then finish the job with a sharp chisel.*

Fig. 5 *Use a dado blade to cut the tenons on the curved rail blanks. The blade height is different for the front and rear faces.*

Fig. 7 *Construct a jig for cutting the angled side-rail tenons on your table saw. The ramp holds the rails at a 4° angle.*

Fig. 8 *After removing most of the waste by boring holes, use sharp chisels to square the back-rail slat mortises.*

Now, lay out the mortises for the top rear rail joints on the inner surfaces of the rear legs. Because there isn't enough room for your router, use a drill press to bore a series of overlapping holes to remove most of the mortise waste (**Fig. 4**). Finish the joints with a sharp chisel.

Making the Rails

Rip and crosscut 2½-in.-thick stock to size for the curved rear rails. Then lay out the curved profile of each rail on the edge of its blank, including the location of the tenons. Install a dado blade in the table saw and use the miter gauge as a guide to cut the tenons (**Fig. 5**). Cut the rear face of each tenon first, then readjust the blade height to cut the front face. Finally, cut the shoulders at the top and bottom edges of each tenon. Use your band saw to cut the curved profile of the rear rails (**Fig. 6**), and smooth the surfaces with a spokeshave and scraper. Rip and crosscut ¾-in. stock to size

for the lower stool rails. The front and rear rails join the legs squarely so these are easy to cut with the table saw and dado blade. The side rails, though, join at an angle and have angled tenons. Although you could cut these joints by hand, we used a table saw jig for the work.

To make the jig, first screw a piece of ¼-in. plywood to the bottom edge of a 2½-in.-high fence to make a sliding table that's guided by your miter gauge. Then build a ramp to hold the rails at a 4° angle, screw the ramp to the sliding table, and clamp the jig to the table saw miter gauge (**Fig. 7**).

Use scrap stock to test your jig and determine dado blade height. Note that one face of each tenon is cut with the ramp sloped toward the blade and the opposite face with the ramp sloped away. Use a clamp as a stop block to position each rail for uniform cuts. Use the miter gauge without the jig to cut the 86° shoulders at the top and bottom of each tenon. Test fit the joints. If a tenon is too tight, carefully sand the tenon

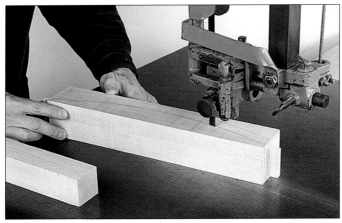

Fig. 6 *Band saw the curved shape of the rear rails. Finish the rails by smoothing them with a spokeshave and scraper.*

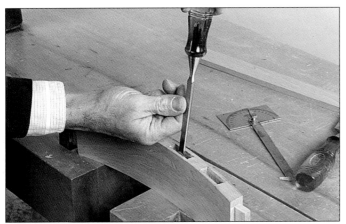

Fig. 9 *Use a chisel to undercut the opposite mortise faces in the top and bottom curved rails to accommodate the 7° slat angle.*

cheeks. If the fit is too loose, glue a veneer shim to the tenon.

Cut the back slats to finished size, and lay out the slat mortises in the curved back rails. Use the drill press to bore a series of holes in the rails to remove most of the waste from each mortise. Although the mortises are ⅜ in. wide, it is best to use a ¼-in. bit for the job. This allows you a little bit of flexibility in positioning the holes—a bonus when drilling into the edge of a curved rail.

Next, use sharp chisels to pare the walls and chop the ends of the mortises (**Fig. 8**). Study the drawing to see how the back slats sit at an angle to the rails. Use a chisel to undercut the front wall of the bottom rail and the back wall of the top rail to allow the slats to sit at the proper angle (**Fig. 9**).

Assembly
Carefully sand all stool parts with 120-, 150-, 180-, and 220-grit sandpaper. Begin assembly by joining the back slats to

Bandsaw Cutting

Most bandsaw cuts are made freehand, without the aid of a guide or fence. Freehand sawing is a two-hand operation. Use one hand to push the work into the blade, and the other to steer it along the line-of-cut. Before starting a curved cut, visualize the work being sawn along the cut line. This may help prevent interference with the saw's arm as the piece is maneuvered through the cut. Starting the cut from the other end of the line will often provide clearance for the piece. Try to avoid getting the blade trapped, forcing you to have to backtrack to free it. When you must backtrack, do so slowly to avoid pulling the blade away from the guides and off the wheels.

When executing an intricate cut, it's not usually possible to make the cut in a single continuous pass. Instead, make a series of shorter cuts to minimize backtracking. It's often easier to to bypass small, detailed areas and come back later, after a majority of the waste has been sawn away, and then finish them with short cuts.

When two curves meet to form an acute, inside corner, it's necessary to first make a cut through the waste area directly into the corner. Then cut along one of the curved lines and into the corner. Repeat the same cut along the remaining curved line to complete the cut.

When band sawing thin material, such as wood veneer, the underside of the material often splinters or forms burrs. This is caused by the clearance space around the blades as it passes through the slot in the table insert. To ensure smooth cuts, make an auxiliary worktable surface out of ¼-in. plywood or hardboard. Cut about halfway into the plywood panel and then secure it to the worktable with masking tape.

Fig. 10 *Begin stool assembly by joining the slats to the curved back rails. For our purposes, no glue is necessary in these joints.*

Fig. 11 *Join the back rails to the rear legs, and clamp. Compare opposite diagonals to check that the assembly is square.*

the curved rails (**Fig. 10**). Because the slats are held captive between the rails, you don't need to glue these joints.

Next, spread glue on the back-rail tenons and in the mating mortises in the rear legs. Join the rails to the legs and apply clamps to pull the joints tight. Compare diagonal measurements to check that the assembly is square (**Fig. 11**). Then join the front rails to the front legs and let the glue set. Finish assembling the stool base by joining the angled side rails to the front and rear leg subassemblies (**Fig. 12**). Stand the stool on a flat table to make sure that the legs rest evenly on the surface. If the stool rocks, adjust the clamps.

Cut 1-in.-thick stock to 3 x 18⅛ in. for the seat slats. Mark the curved profile on the edge of each slat. Use the band saw to cut the shape and smooth the surfaces. Cut the angled ends of each slat with your table saw or a miter saw, taking the finished length from the drawing. Cut the rear slat to fit between the legs and conform to the curve of the back rail.

Bore screw holes and ⅜-in. counterbores for attaching the slats to the rails, and install the slats with 1½-in. No. 8 fh screws. Use a plug cutter in the drill press to cut ⅜-in.-dia. plugs from maple stock. Spread glue in each screw hole and on the plugs, and install the plugs (**Fig. 13**). Let the glue set and then pare the plugs flush to the surface of the slats with a razor-sharp chisel. Sand the slats to 220 grit.

Finishing

Our finish is achieved by staining the wood, then applying a clear finish. The ebonized finish allows the wood grain to remain more visible than with paint. We used jet black stain. To ease application by brush or rag, add up to 10 percent retarder. For a deep black color, allow the first coat to dry for at least 1 hour, then apply a second coat. After drying, we applied three coats of sealer/finish. Brush each coat on the surface, let it set for about 20 minutes, then wipe off any excess. Let it dry overnight, then lightly sand the surface with 320-grit sandpaper. Apply the next two coats using the same technique. After the final coat has dried, burnish the surface to a satin finish with 4/0 steel wool.

Safety Sense

USING CHISELS SAFELY

Chisels are some of the most basic and commonly used woodworking project tools. But because they are so simple, it is easy to get lulled into the perception that they are not dangerous. The two basic rules for safe use of chisels are:

DO Always keep the chisel pointed away from you in use. This is so basic that woodworkers in a hurry often disregard it. But a chisel that slips can easily penetrate any soft tissue at which it is aimed.

DO Always make sure the chisel is razor sharp. If this seems counterintuitive, try using a dull chisel. The incidental grabbing makes duller blades unpredictable and consequently, a lot more dangerous (a dull chisel will cut you as quickly as a sharp one).

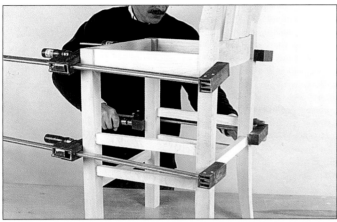

Fig. 12 *Join the rear and front subassemblies with the side rails. Set the stool on a flat table to check that the legs are even.*

Fig. 13 *Screw the seat slats to the rails and install the plugs. When the glue dries, pare the plugs flush to the seat surface.*

MATERIAL*Matters*

Common Glues
Finding the right adhesive can affect how fast you work, how strong your finished pieces are, and how easy assembly is. Choose wisely and you'll have enduring joints that can easily stand the test of time.

White glue. Most popular household glue, also known as PVA. A good general-purpose glue, it's meant for use on porous surfaces, including wood and wood products. It is non-toxic, odorless, and sets in less than 1 hour. It has poor moisture resistance.

Yellow glue. Also known as carpenter's glue, this is formulated for use on all types of wood and wood products. Water-based, it sets quicker and resists moisture better than white glue. This has good heat resistance, dries translucent, and is sandable so that it won't clog abrasive papers.

Hide glue. One of the oldest glues still in use, made from animal hides, hooves, and bones. It can be used on all types of wood and wood products. It is a long-setting glue, making it handy for when extra assembly time is needed. Although strong, it has poor moisture resistance.

Contact cement. This adhesive is used primarily to adhere plastic laminates and wood veneer to particleboard or plywood core. It is applied with a brush, roller, or spray gun. The cement is applied and left a few minutes until tacky, and the surfaces are then joined, bonding on contact. Available in solvent-based flammable, non-flammable, and water-based formulas. Water-based is least expensive and nontoxic, but takes up to 1 hour to dry.

Hot-melt glue. This comes in waxy sticks, and is applied with an electric glue gun. It sets almost instantly and can be used on nearly all materials. Hot-melt comes in several different formulas, including a wood tone glue. Don't apply to cold surfaces because it will form a very weak bond.

Resorcinal. A two-part resin that dries completely waterproof with what may be the strongest wood bond available. It dries reddish brown and should be used with eye protection and a respirator as protection against the catalyst dust.

Epoxies. These are available in two basic types: a 5-minute fast-set, and a slow-set. Epoxies are noted for their high strength and the ability to bond to a wide variety of materials. Fast-set epoxy is usually sold in a double-barreled syringe—one for hardener, one for resin. Mix thoroughly before using; it sets in about 5 minutes, but cures in 12 to 24 hours. Slow-set comes in separate containers and should be used when more assembly time is needed.

Plastic resin. This is a urea-formaldehyde powder that, when mixed with water, becomes a powerful wood glue that is both heat and moisture resistant. Although it has a long setting time—from 12 to 14 hours—it's a favorite of cabinetmakers because of its long pot life, strength, and nearly invisible glue line.

Sitting Pretty

Sit down to dinner on this beautiful dining chair right from your own workshop.

Of all the areas of woodworking, chairmaking stands out as a specialized field. Here, the skills of the joiner are paramount because chairs are subject to stresses not normally found in other pieces of furniture. It's not enough to simply make a strong chair. It must be light enough to be carried easily and shaped to accommodate a wide range of users. In addition, the chair design must complement its surroundings without sacrificing utility. This chair meets all those standards with admirable grace. The style has flair, but will mix with many styles of dining room furniture. As a standalone or at a table, it's a lovely piece of craftsmanship.

Key POINTS

TIME

Prep Time	8 hours
Shop Time	12 hours
Assembly Time	10 hours

EFFORT

Skill Level	intermediate

COST / BENEFITS

Expense: **moderate**

- **Elegant style** brings a flourish to any dining room, regardless of decor style.
- **Comfortable design** ensures that mealtimes will be enjoyable affairs.

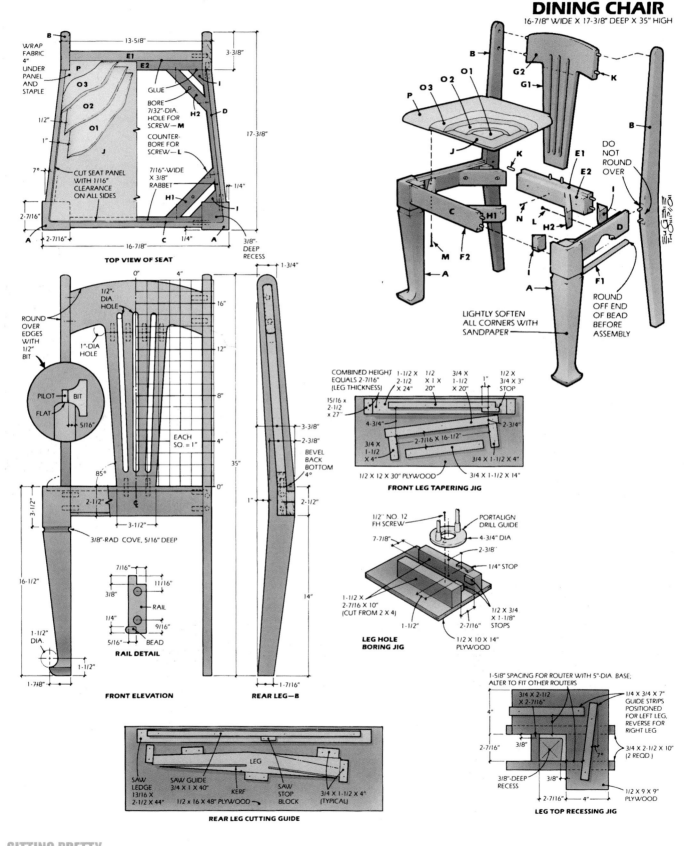

Our mahogany chair is constructed of $^{13}/_{16}$-in. stock and is designed to be made with portable power tools found in most home workshops. You'll want to make a full set. Although making six chairs may seem like an overwhelming task, by using our jigs and grouping similar operations together, you'll find it's not much more difficult than making just one.

Shaping the Legs

Our modified cabriole leg was designed as a companion to a standard Queen Anne dining room table, although the style goes perfectly well with more contemporary dining table designs. Begin the front legs by preparing the leg stock and routing a horizontal cove.

The inside radius found on the bottom of each leg is shaped by boring precisely placed 1½-in.-dia. holes. Construct the leg-hole-boring jig as shown in the drawing. Using a drill guide to ensure that the holes are square to the leg face, bore two holes at right angles to each other with a 1½-in.-dia. Forstner bit (**Fig. 1**). The spacing of the stop that positions the drill guide is based on the Portalign drill guide we used. If you're using a different guide, readjust the stop accordingly.

Cut the straight tapers—that begin at the horizontal cover and are tangent to the 1½-in. holes—most of the way with a circular saw (**Fig. 2**). Use the front leg-tapering jig to guide the saw and set the length-of-cut stop to end the cut just before the 1½-in.-dia. hole.

Finish the cuts with a sabre saw. Then mark the outside curves on the bottom of the leg and use your sabre saw to complete the profile.

Fig. 1 *Two 1½-in. holes create the inside curve on the front legs. Use a jig and drill guide for accurate positioning.*

Fig. 2 *Start the tapers with a circular saw guided by the tapering jig. Use a sabre saw to finish the cut and round the leg bottom.*

Materials List

Key	No.	Size and description (use)
A	2	2$^{7}/_{16}$ x 2$^{7}/_{16}$ x 16½" mahogany (front leg)
B	2	$^{13}/_{16}$ x 3$^{3}/_{8}$ x 35" mahogany (rear leg)
C	1	$^{13}/_{16}$ x 2½ x 12" mahogany (front rail)
D*	2	$^{13}/_{16}$ x 2½ x 12" mahogany (side rail)
E1	1	$^{13}/_{16}$ x 2½ x 12" mahogany (back rail)
E2	1	$^{13}/_{16}$ x 2$^{3}/_{8}$ x 12" mahogany (cleat)
F1*	2	¼ x $^{7}/_{16}$ x 12" mahogany (side bead)
F2	1	¼ x $^{7}/_{16}$ x 12" mahogany (front bead)
G1	1	$^{13}/_{16}$ x 5½ x 13$^{9}/_{16}$" mahogany (lower seatback)
G2	1	$^{13}/_{16}$ x 4½ x 12" mahogany (upper seatback)
H*	4	$^{13}/_{16}$ x 2 x 5" mahogany (corner brace)
I*	6	$^{13}/_{16}$ x 2 x 2" mahogany (corner block)
J*	1	$^{3}/_{8}$ x 14 x 16" plywood (seat)
K	26	$^{3}/_{8}$"-dia. x 1½" hardwood dowel
L	8	1" No. 10 fh screw
M	4	2½" No. 10 fh screw
N	3	6d common nail
O1	1	½ x 12 x 14" foam (bottom layer)
O2	1	½ x 13 x 15" foam (middle layer)
O3	1	½ x 14 x 16" foam (top layer)
P**	1	23 x 25" fabric

Misc.: 120- and 220-grit sandpaper; glue; ¼-in. staples and staple gun; Portalign drill guide; 1½-in.-dia. Forstner bit.

*Cut to fit.

**Fabric (style: Cardine, color: Parchment), approx. 3 yards required.

Fig. 3 *Rough cut the backs to shape and bore holes at the slot ends and the inside corners. Use a template to rout the finished profile.*

Fig. 4 *Rear leg cuts are guided with this jig. The stop keeps the circular saw from cutting too far. Finish with the sabre saw.*

Fig. 5 *Use a partially extended ½-in.-rad. rounding-over bit to round edges while leaving a corner on the rear legs and back.*

The inside radius of each leg can be smoothed with an appropriately sized drum sander mounted in an electric drill, or by hand with sandpaper wrapped around a large dowel. Use a block and sandpaper to clean up the outside foot surfaces and a pad sander on the flat tapered sides.

The Chairback

Cut the boards for the chairback upper sections about 1 in. oversize in width and exactly to length. The lower back section is cut 1 in. longer and wider than specified.

Bore ⅜-in.-dia. holes for the dowels that join the two sections as shown in the drawing. Be sure to place the holes so that the slots that must be cut later won't interfere with the joint. Apply glue sparingly to the holes and dowels, clamp up, and let dry overnight. After the clamps are removed, trim the bottom of the lower back section to length at a 4° bevel.

Next, make a cardboard template of the complete back outline and transfer the shape to each blank. Before cutting, however, bore 1-in.-dia. holes at the inside corners and ½-in.-dia. holes at the ends of the slots (**Fig. 3**). Then use your sabre saw to cut close to, but not on, the lines.

To make the backs completely uniform and minimize sanding, carefully cut a plywood template to guide your router and ½-in. straight bit around the slots and top section outline.

You'll need a template guide mounted on the router base for following the template. Measure the distance from the bit cutting edge to the guide and offset the template outline this amount. After trimming, clean up the outside edges of the lower section as close to the inside corner as possible with a hand plane. Finish up with sandpaper and block.

SHOP*Helper*

Belt-Sander Stop
When using a powerful belt sander, you must guard against the sander flinging the workpiece from your workbench. To do this, build an adjustable stop of ⅜-in. plywood. A good standard size would be 32 in. long x 2½ in. wide, with L-shaped cutouts centered top to bottom, about 8 in. in from each side. To make each cutout, drill out a ¼-in.-wide space, running lengthwise about 1⅜ in. long. Then cut a leg going up one side ¾", and a leg on the other side going up ⅜ in. Now attach the stop to your workbench apron with ¼-in. x 1-in. lagscrews and washers. Using the cutouts, the stop can be raised or lowered as you need to move materials across the surface or for sanding.

Cut the stock of the rear legs to 3⅜-in.-wide x 35-in.-long and construct the rear-leg cutting guide as shown in the drawing. By positioning the stock holding blocks and saw stop appropriately, you can make all four long cuts with your circular saw (**Fig. 4**). The block positions shown in the drawing hold the stock for the lower rear cut.

If the grain of the leg stock is not entirely straight, orient it so that it conforms to the final shape of the legs. Make the same cut on each piece before repositioning the blocks and stop. The back of the rear leg is finished by connecting the circular saw cuts with a straight cut made with our sabre saw. Complete the leg profile by rounding the leg top with the sabre saw and dress the edges smooth with a hand plane and sandpaper.

Our design calls for a rounding of the edges of the rear legs and back that softens the form but still leaves a corner to define the shape. Make this cut with a ½-in.-rad. bit mounted in the router. Adjust the bit depth so that the cutting edge protrudes only 5⁄16 in. beyond the base (**Fig. 5**). Then rout both sides of each leg and back.

Although we performed this operation on a router table, it can easily be done with a handheld router. Before routing the rear legs, however, temporarily attach a strip of wood 2⅞ in. long to the area where the side rails join. This prevents rounding over and ruining the mating surface.

Making the Joints

First, rip the stock for the chair rails and rear-seat support cleat to width, and cut the front and rear pieces to exact length. Before crosscutting the side rails, reset your circular saw to cut a 7° bevel and crosscut the stock so that it's 11²⁵⁄32 in. long as measured on one face.

Keep in mind that these beveled cuts must be parallel, making the overall length slightly greater than 11²⁵⁄32 in. Rout the ¼ x 5⁄16-in. rabbet for the bead trim on one edge of the front and side rails. Be sure to place this rabbet on the lower outside corner of the side rails. Then use a doweling jig to

Fig. 6 A dowel jig aids in positioning the ³⁄8-in-dia. holes. Use two 7° wedges to ensure the holes are square to the side rail ends.

Fig. 7 Nail down the stops to accurately position components when you are transferring dowel locations. Use the dowel centers to mark the holes.

Fig. 8 The front leg tops are recessed to receive the seat. After cutting all the right legs, reverse the stops for the left legs.

TECH *Tips*

End Grain Staining

Unless the end grain is given some special attention before you stain, it is certain to soak up so much stain that it almost turns black. To control the end grain absorption for a more even stain, use an artist's brush to apply undiluted boiled linseed oil to the end grain. Once this sealer coat is applied, apply the stain as usual. The treated end grain will absorb only a limited amount of stain.

Fig. 9 *Gluing the chair sides in pairs balances the clamping load. Assemble the backs and back rails while these dry.*

Fig. 10 *Apply slow-setting hide glue sparingly to the dowels and holes to allow sufficient time to get all the parts together.*

bore the dowel holes in the front and rear rail. Because the side rails are beveled, make two 7° wedges to position the doweling jig square to the ends (**Fig. 6**). Use the same technique with 4° wedges for the holes in the lower section of the chairback.

Prepare to transfer the hole locations to the front legs by first laying out a full-size outline of the frame and then nailing stops in place to position the pieces (**Fig. 7**). Next, use dowel centers to mark the front leg hole positions and use a

similar system for marking the rear leg joints. After all dowel holes are bored, nail and glue the rear rail cleat in place.

Next, rout the seat recess in the top of each front leg with a ⅜-in.-dia straight bit. Use the jig shown in the drawing for the left legs and simply reverse the stops to recess the right legs (**Fig. 8**). While your router is set up for a ⅜-in.-deep cut, rout the ⁷⁄₁₆-in.-wide rabbets on the top inside edge of the side and front rails. Finally, using a ⅛-in.-rad. half-round bit and a slotting bit, make up the bead trim. Install the beading in the

TECH *Tips*

Using a Handsaw
To saw accurately and safely, you must support and hold the work securely. If possible, hold the work with clamps or in a vise. Otherwise, use a pair of stable sawhorses at a height that provides a comfortable stance over the work.

Mark a clear cutting line. Start the cut by placing the heel of the blade (the teeth near the handle) on the edge of the wood on the waste side of the cutting line. Steady the blade against your thumb, then slowly draw the saw back once or twice to start the kerf. As soon as the cut has been started, move your hand away from the blade and make long, steady strokes. Keep your forearm and shoulder in line with the saw and cut slowly and surely.

When crosscutting, hold the saw at 45° to the work surface. When you near the end of the cut, slow down and shorten the length of the stroke. Grasp the waste piece with your free hand and finish the cut with short light strokes.

Ripping demands a steeper 60° angle. For fine work, leave more space between the cut and marked line to allow for a coarser cut that must be planed smooth.

Use a crosscut saw to cut plywood, but lower the angle to about 20° to minimize splintering.

If you find that the kerf closes behind the cut when ripping a long board, use a nail to keep the kerf open. Short work is best held in a vise for ripping. Reposition the work as the cut progresses so that the cut is near the vise.

Although the handsaw is a freehand tool, you can use guides to help improve accuracy. For consistent crosscutting, glue and screw together an L-shaped fence and clamp it to the work at the cutline. Adding a lip underneath that's square to the fence edge helps the guide ensure square cuts.

For guided rip cuts, use a straight length of 2 x 3 lumber. Clamp it in place next to the cutline.

Fig. 11 *Three bar clamps are all that's required to hold the completed assembly together. Let the glue dry overnight.*

Fig. 12 *Complete the frame by gluing the corner blocks in place. Diagonal braces, glued and screwed to the rails, provide rigidity.*

front and side rail lower rabbets as shown in the drawing. Use glue and brads to attach the molding and round the back end of the side rail bead where it terminates at the rear leg

Assembling the Chair

Begin by gluing together each front and rear leg with one side rail. Because this assembly is not flat and square, it's easier to clamp these side units in pairs (**Fig. 9**). Set each pair upside down on the edge of your worktable and use a single bar clamp and two boards to hold the parts together. While these are setting, glue the chair back to the rear rail.

When both assemblies are dry, join the side units to the chairback and front rail (**Fig. 10**). You should need only three bar clamps per chair for this operation. Before fully tightening the clamps, place the chair upright on a flat surface to ensure that the frame is not twisted. Then tighten

the clamps and let the glue dry overnight (**Fig. 11**). Excess glue that's squeezed out of the joints can ruin the staining and varnishing job. Apply glue sparingly to the holes and dowels and remove any excess after it's dry, using a sharp chisel and sanding carefully with a fine-grit sandpaper.

Because of the strains placed on chair frames, we added corner blocks and diagonal braces. Each chair requires three slightly different corner blocks and two different braces. Take the angles of each corner block and brace from an assembled chair and cut all similar pieces together to save time.

After cutting the braces, bore and countersink the screw holes for fastening to the frame, and the single hole for the seat-fastening screw. Then hold them in position and mark the pilot holes in the frames. Apply glue to the mating surfaces and letting the glue get slightly tacky. Then press each block in place. Use glue and screws when securing the braces (**Fig. 12**). Before installing the seat, finish sand the chair and soften all sharp corners. Then stain and varnish.

Our seat is constructed of a ⅜-in.-thick plywood base and three layers of ½-in.-thick foam rubber. Make a cardboard template of the seat base that leaves about ¹⁄₁₆ in. all around for fabric clearance. Then trace this onto the plywood and cut with a sabre saw.

Starting at the front edge, staple a roughly sized piece of fabric to the underneath side of the plywood. Keep the fabric taut as you go. Next, fasten the fabric at the back corners while holding it taut front to back and corner to corner. Finally, fold over the remaining fabric and staple it into place.

It's best to use upholstery fabric that's been treated to repel stains. If not, apply Scotch Guard spray or other waterproof stain repellent. You can use our fabric (noted in the materials list) or choose a fabric or special design that suits your own interior decorating scheme. Finally, fasten the chair's seat securely in place with four 2½-in. No. 10 fh screws to complete your assembly.

Bench Mark

This easy-to-build bench provides storage and a handy seat for mudrooms and halls.

Every home has an area set aside for boots, hats, scarves, gloves, and coats. You know the place: a separate room or even the alcove of an entry hall where all the winter outerwear and extra clothing seems to gather. And, regardless of whether it's the back porch or the front hall, there's a need for both storage and a sturdy, easy-to-clean place to sit down to lace up those boots. Our simple bench provides for both these needs, with a simple but pleasing style. It's constructed of solid poplar and birch plywood and is basic enough in construction to build in a weekend. And you don't need a lot of fancy equipment. We built the entire piece with hand tools and portable power tools.

*Key*POINTS

TIME
Prep Time	2 hours
Shop Time	6 hours
Assembly Time	6 hours

EFFORT
Skill Level	basic

COST / BENEFITS
Expense: **low**
- **Function** trumps form in this sturdy workhorse piece that's meant to "blend in."
- Only **basic skills** are needed for this quick-finish project.

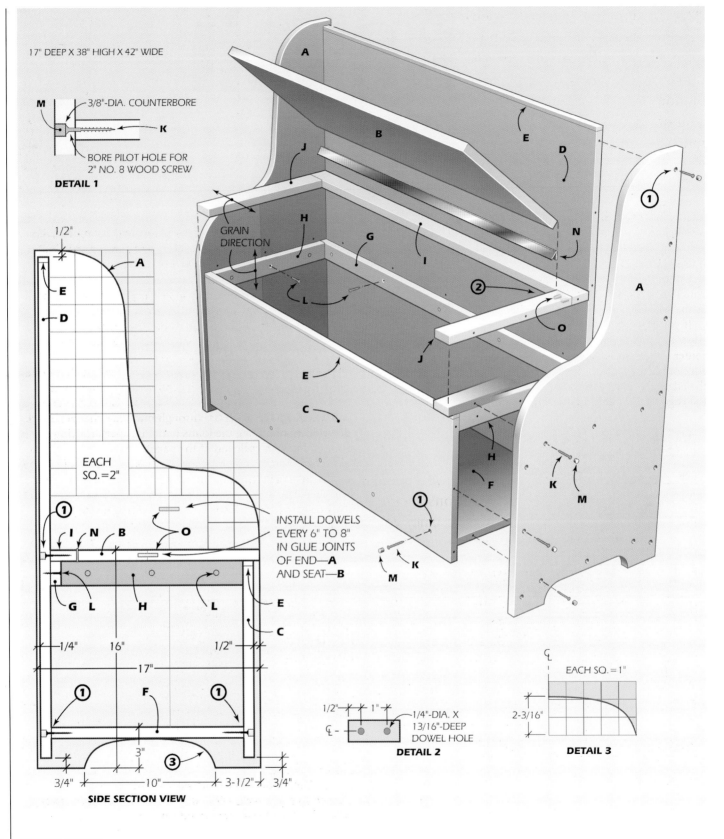

17" DEEP X 38" HIGH X 42" WIDE

M
3/8"-DIA. COUNTERBORE
K
BORE PILOT HOLE FOR
2" NO. 8 WOOD SCREW
DETAIL 1

A
B
E
D
J
N
H
G
I
O
2
L
A
J
E
C
H
F
1
K
M
K
M

GRAIN DIRECTION

1/2"
A
E
D

EACH
SQ. = 2"

1

INSTALL DOWELS
EVERY 6" TO 8"
IN GLUE JOINTS
OF END—A
AND SEAT—B

I N B O
G L H L E
C
1/4" 16" 1/2"
17"
1 F 1
3"
3
3/4" 10" 3-1/2" 3/4"

SIDE SECTION VIEW

1/2" 1"
1/4"-DIA. X
13/16"-DEEP
DOWEL HOLE
DETAIL 2

EACH SQ. = 1"
2-3/16"
DETAIL 3

Poplar lumber is generally available at home centers and lumberyards, and it's usually surfaced to a thickness of ³⁄₁₆ in. You'll probably find poplar sold, like other hardwoods, in random widths and lengths, so you'll need to do a bit of calculation to determine exactly how much material to buy.

Prepare the Panels

The bench ends and seat are made of edge-glued poplar boards. Based on the width of your stock, determine the number of pieces that you'll need for each panel. Be sure to crosscut the wood for the sides 3 or 4 in. longer than the finished dimension.

Cut the seat stock 12 in. longer than the finished seat. You'll use the extra length for support cleats and for the ends of the seat frame.

If you're hesitant to use a hand plane to true the mating edges of the boards in preparation for gluing, you can use a router with a straight bit and a straightedge guide. Clamp the edge guide to the work so the bit removes about ¹⁄₁₆ in. from the edge. Then run the router base along the guide to trim the edge straight and square (**Fig. 1**). Be sure to move the

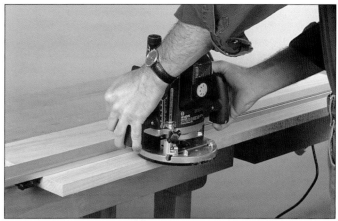

Fig. 1 *Use a router equipped with a straight bit to trim the board edges for joining. Guide the router against a straight strip clamped to the work.*

router from left to right to maintain proper control of the tool. Although a good glue joint is strong enough without any reinforcement, adding dowels makes it easier to align the board surfaces during construction. You might also use splines or a plate joiner to do the job.

Prepare for joining the boards by placing the stock for one panel on your bench so that the annual rings of adjacent boards are oriented in opposite directions. This technique will help keep the panel flat through humidity changes. Mark dowel locations along the joints 6 to 8 in. apart, starting about 3 in. from each end of the panel.

Using a doweling jig to guide the drill bit, bore ¹³⁄₁₆-in.-deep dowel holes (**Fig. 2**). Cut ¼-in. dowels into 1½-in.-long pieces and chamfer the ends of each piece with sandpaper. Note that the dowel pin length leaves room for excess glue that might otherwise keep the joint from closing tightly. Spread a bit of glue in each hole and tap the dowels into place (**Fig. 3**).

Materials List

Key	No.	Size and description (use)
A	2	¹³⁄₁₆ x 17 x 38" poplar (end)
B	1	¹³⁄₁₆ x 13⁷⁄₈ x 36¹⁄₈" poplar (seat)
C	1	¾ x 14¹⁄₁₆ x 40³⁄₈" birch plywood (front)
D	1	¾ x 36³⁄₈ x 40³⁄₈" birch plywood (back)
E	2	⅜ x ¾ x 40³⁄₈" poplar (edge band)
F	1	¾ x 14¾ x 40³⁄₈" birch plywood (bottom)
G	1	¹³⁄₁₆ x 1¾ x 40³⁄₈" poplar (cleat)
H	2	¹³⁄₁₆ x 1¾ x 13¹⁵⁄₁₆" poplar (cleat)
I	1	¹³⁄₁₆ x 2 x 40³⁄₈" poplar (frame)
J	2	¹³⁄₁₆ x 2 x 14" poplar (frame)
K	45	2" No. 8 fh screw
L	11	1¼" No. 8 fh screw
M	45	⅜"-dia. birch plug
N	1	36"-long 1½" piano hinge
O		¼"-dia. x 1½"-long dowel**

Misc.: sandpaper; latex primer; and paint.

**as required.

Fig. 2 *After marking the dowel locations, use a doweling jig to guide the drill. Place dowel holes every 6 to 8 in. along the mating edges.*

Fig. 3 *Apply a small amount of glue to the dowel holes. Tap 1¹/₂-in. dowels into the holes. Clamp the glued-up panel until the glue sets.*

Fig. 4 *Use a belt sander to smooth panel faces. Keep the sander moving evenly across the panel and let the weight of the sander do the work.*

Fig. 5 *After making a template of the bench end out of plywood or cardboard, clamp it to the end-panel blank. Carefully trace the outline.*

Fig. 6 *Clamp each end panel to your bench for cutting. Use a sabre saw and keep the kerf to the waste side of the cutline.*

Spread glue on the mating edges of the panel boards and join them. Use four or five clamps across the panel to pull the joints tight. Be sure to place the clamps and panel on a flat surface so the panel doesn't twist while the glue sets. After about 20 minutes, use a putty knife to carefully scrape off any squeeze-out from the joints, and then leave the pieces overnight so that the glue cures fully.

You can use a hand plane to clean off glue from an assembled panel and smooth any slight misalignment in the joint, but a belt sander is often faster and easier.

Clamp the panel to the workbench and use a 100-grit belt on the sander to smooth the surface (**Fig. 4**). Keep in mind that with a belt sander, it's easy to remove too much stock. Keep the sander moving along the panel surface and let the weight of the tool do the work.

After all panels have been assembled, make a template of the end-panel profile out of ¼-in. plywood, hardboard, or stiff

cardboard. After cutting it to shape, use a rasp, sandpaper, or knife to smooth and refine curves. Then clamp the template to one of the end blanks and trace the outline (**Fig. 5**).

Secure the panel to your workbench and use a sabre saw to follow the cutline (**Fig. 6**). Keep the saw kerf on the waste side of the line. Then use a spokeshave, rasp, or coarse sandpaper to remove the saw marks and refine the curved profile. Repeat the process for the opposite bench end.

Use a circular saw guided by a straightedge to cut the plywood panels to finished dimension (**Fig. 7**). Because a circular saw tends to chip out the top side of the cut, it's a good idea to cut the panel with the best side facing down.

Use the rip guide on your circular saw to cut two strips of ⅜-in.-thick poplar edge banding for the top edges of the front and back panels. Cut each strip several inches longer than the finished panel length. Spread glue on one of these strips and clamp it to the top edge of the bench front panel. Center the strip over the plywood edge so that you have an equal overhang on both faces and both ends. Clamp the strip every 3 in. to provide a good, tight joint. Completely scrape off any glue squeeze-out after 20 minutes and then let the glue set. Repeat this process for the back panel.

Use a block plane to trim the edge banding flush to the panel faces (**Fig. 8**). If you notice that the wood is tearing out, reverse your planing direction. Proceed carefully so that you don't cut through the thin veneer on the panel.

Use a small backsaw to cut the edge band flush with the panel ends (**Fig. 9**). Be sure to keep the saw square and fully support the tiny waste piece at the end of the cut so that it does not break off.

TOOL*Care*

Life Extension for Band Saw Blades

You probably haven't given much thought lately to the steel guide blocks in your band saw. However, they serve an important function. The four steel blocks keep the blade in line and free from twisting. This provides greater control during cutting and prevents the blade from wandering from the cutline. The problem, though, is that the blade regularly comes in contact with the blocks. This metal-to-metal contact produces friction, heat, and metal fatigue—all bad news for the blade. To prevent heat buildup and prolong blade life, you can replace steel guide blocks with Cool Blocks. Made of graphite-impregnated phenolic laminate, these handy blocks run cooler and won't dull or damage the blade. In fact, you can set Cool Blocks so that they lightly touch the blade for optimum control. The blocks come in a range of sizes and are usually sold in four-block sets, according to dimension. To install the blocks, you simply use a dollar bill as a spacer, slipping it in on either side of the blade. Push the block in until it lightly touches the bill. Install two blocks above the saw table, and two positioned below it.

Fig. 7 *Use a circular saw and edge guide to cut the plywood panels to exact size. Cut the panel with the good side facing down.*

Fig. 8 *After ripping the poplar edge banding and gluing it to the front and back panels, trim the banding flush with a block plane.*

Fig. 9 *Use a small backsaw to cut the edge bands flush with the panel ends. Support the waste side of the cut so that it doesn't break off.*

Assembly

Mark the outlines of the front, back, bottom, and seat on both sides of each bench end panel. Mark the outlines of the bottom on the front panel and both the bottom and seat frame on the back panel. You'll use the outside outlines for accurately locating screw holes, and the inside outlines for positioning the parts during assembly.

Bore screw clearance holes for No. 8 screws where required in the bench ends and front and back panels. Counterbore these holes for ⅜-in.-dia. wood plugs. If you use a combination drill and countersink (**Fig. 10**), you can accomplish this task in one step. Begin assembly by clamping the bottom panel to the front so the bottom is aligned with the inside layout marks on the front. Bore pilot holes into the edge of the bottom (**Fig. 11**), then fasten the two parts with 2-in. No. 8 screws. Next, clamp the back panel to the bottom, bore pilot holes, and fasten it in place.

Place ¾-in. scrap blocks underneath the front and back panels to provide the proper spacing, then clamp the bench ends in place. Carefully align the parts on the layout lines, bore pilot holes (**Fig. 12**), and attach the ends.

Rip a strip of poplar to 1¾ in. wide for the back seat support, cut to length, bore screw holes, and fasten it to the back panel. The side support strips must have grain running parallel to that of the bench ends. Cut these strips off the end of the bench seat blank and screw in place (**Fig. 13**).

Cut the seat frame pieces to size. As with side support strips, the grain of each end frame piece must run across its length. Cut these two pieces from the seat blank. Lay out dowel locations for each frame joint, then use the doweling jig to bore the holes. Apply glue to the dowel holes and mating edges, tap the dowels into place, and join the parts (**Fig. 14**). Use clamps to pull joints tight and check for square. Slide the seat frame into position, bore pilot holes into the edges, and fasten it in place. Cut the seat panel to

Fig. 10 *Mark outlines on both sides of the panels and bore the screw holes. A combination bit will bore the hole and plug the counterbore in one step.*

Fig. 13 *Cut the seat supports to size and screw them in place. Note that the grain of the side runs vertically to match the grain of the end panels.*

SKILL*Builder*

Handsaw Basics
It's easy to think that the only way to cut wood is with a power saw. After all, you want it done fast and you want it accurate. For many jobs, though, it may be nearly as fast to do the work by hand— and with accuracy that any circular saw user would envy.

Woodworking handsaws come in different varieties, but there are two that will handle most of your carpentry chores—a crosscut saw and ripsaw. They are similar in appearance, but different in the shape of the teeth.

Saws designed for cutting across the grain have beveled teeth filed to points that sever the wood fibers. Ripping, or cutting with the grain, requires a different tooth shape. The ripsaw has teeth that are filed straight across. Each tooth acts as a small chisel that plows away particles of wood.

Conventional saws also vary in blade length and tooth size. Typical blade lengths range from 15 to 26 in., the shorter blades being suitable for light work and confined spaces.

Tooth size is designated by the number of points per inch (ppi, or the points). A lower number means larger teeth—

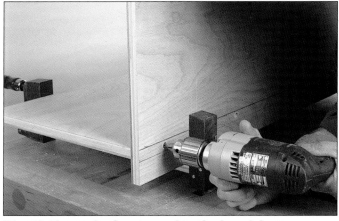

Fig. 11 *Clamp the front panel to the bench bottom. Position the parts accurately and then bore screw pilot holes into edge of the bottom.*

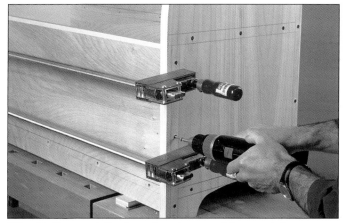

Fig. 12 *Support the bench subassembly on 3/4-in. blocks. Clamp a bench end in place, bore the pilot holes and attach with screws.*

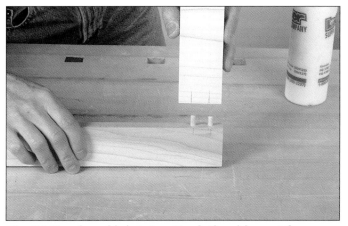

Fig. 14 *Use dowel joints to attach the side seat frame pieces to the back piece. When the glue has dried, screw the seat frame to the bench.*

Fig. 15 *After gluing plugs into screw hole counterbores, use a chisel to remove any excess. Sand the entire bench and soften all edges.*

and a faster and rougher cut. Ripsaws are available in 4½, 5½, 6, and 7 points, and crosscut saws are found in 8, 9, 10, and 12 points. A 5½-point ripsaw and an 8-point crosscut saw are good choices for general work.

Another feature common to both saw types is tooth set. Set refers to the amount that each tooth is bent away from the blade. By bending teeth alternately left and right, the saw kerf is made wider than the blade thickness, and allows the blade to move freely through the cut. Without set, the blade body would bind. Too much produces a rough cut. Quality blades are often taper ground—thinner at the back edge than along the tooth edge—so that set can be minimized for a finer cut.

finished size so there is a uniform ⅛-in. gap at each end of the seat when it is fit into the frame.

Use a common 48-in.-long piano hinge to mount the seat. Clamp it to the bench and cut to 36 in. long. Hold the hinge in place on the back edge of the seat and mark all screw holes. Bore ⅟₁₆-in.-dia. pilot holes for the screws, and then fasten the hinge to the seat. Lay the bench on its back and place the seat in the open position so that you can mark the hinge-screw locations on the back of the seat frame. Bore pilot holes and fasten the seat to the bench.

Use a small brush to apply glue to each counterbored screw hole, and tap a ⅜-in.-dia. plug in each hole. After the glue has set, use a sharp chisel to pare the plugs flush to the panel (**Fig. 15**). Sand the entire bench, finishing with 120-grit paper. Slightly soften all edges. We finished our bench by applying a latex primer, then sanding lightly and brushing on a semigloss latex topcoat.

Choice Seating

This lovely Chippendale-inspired dining room chair is a functional way to beautify your home.

The Chippendale design is considered one of the most elegant furniture styles, and this chair is a great example of why. In addition to great proportions and a comfortable sitting position, this cherry chair features a detailed, partially carved back. The easy-to-follow instructions and plans here are actually simpler than the final look would imply—the hand-carved back exhibits graceful scrolls and interlacing straps that seem daunting, but aren't. The backpanel, known as the splat, is joined to a top rail that has two scrolled ears. Although this project will take some time, you'll find the results are worth it.

*Key*POINTS

TIME

Prep Time . . . . **15 hours**
Shop Time . . . . **20 hours**
Assembly Time . . . . **12 hours**

EFFORT

Skill Level . . . . **advanced**

COST / BENEFITS

Expense: **moderate**

• **Stylish elegance** is the hallmark of this signature piece.
• The chair is distinguished by the **hand-carved back**, sure to draw attention.

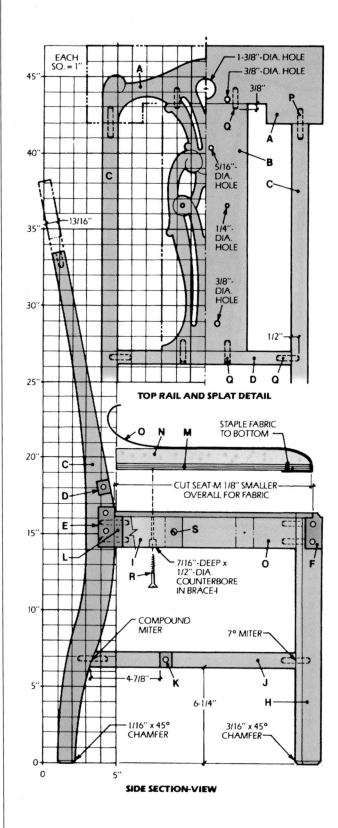

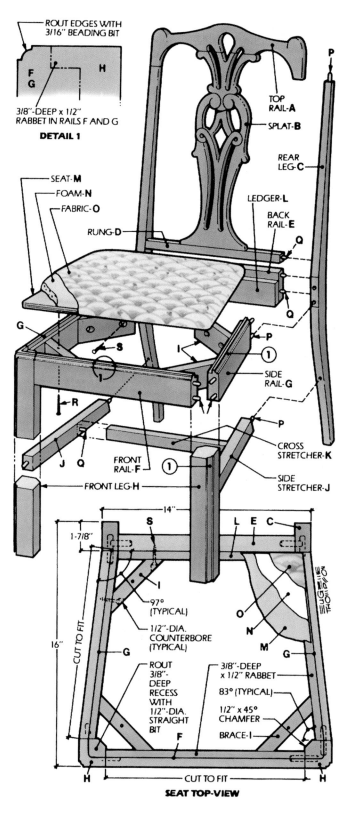

If you have not attempted wood carving before, don't be intimidated by this project. The moderate relief carvings shown are relatively easy and all that's required are a few basic carving tools and a little patience. The chair is made of cherry hardwood, except for the plywood seat panel. It's assembled using dowel-reinforced butt joints. The seat frame is strengthened by four corner braces screwed to the frame members.

Fig. 1 *Notch the top rail by elevating the blade slowly through the workpiece. Then make two cuts into the edge to drop out the waste.*

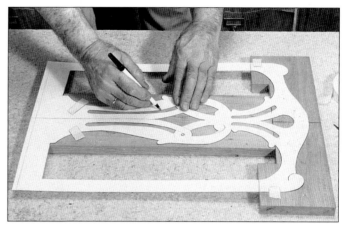

Fig. 2 *After making a full-size pattern of the splat and the top rail, use a ballpoint pen to transfer the pattern's shape to the workpiece.*

Splat and Top Rail Assembly

Start by cutting the splat and the top rail to the oversize dimensions given in the materials list. Cut a 1¼-in.-deep x 8¼-in.-long notch in the top rail (**Fig. 1**). Next, transfer a full-size pattern of the finished splat and top rail assembly from the drawing to heavyweight paper. Use a sharp knife to cut out the paper pattern. Place the pattern on the assembly and trace the cutting lines onto the workpieces (**Fig. 2**). Also, make centerline marks on the assembly to indicate dowel-pin locations.

Next, bore four ⅜-in.-dia. dowel-pin holes in the top rail—two for joining the splat and one dowel hole for each rear leg—and two in the top edge of the splat. Then, join the splat to the top rail using yellow carpenter's glue and two ⅜ x 1½-in.-long dowel pins (**Fig. 3**)

After the glue has dried, rough-cut the splat/top rail assembly to size on a band or scroll saw. Next, bore holes in the splat and top rail, as shown on the drawing, to establish the limits of the interior cutouts. Carefully cut away the

Materials List

Key	No.	Size and description (use)
A*	1	¹³⁄₁₆ x 5 x 16" cherry (top rail)
B*	1	¹³⁄₁₆ x 6 x 16¼" cherry (splat)
C	2	1¹⁄₁₆ x 5 x 33½" cherry (rear leg)
D	1	¹³⁄₁₆ x ¹³⁄₁₆ x 11⅞" cherry (rung)
E	1	1¹⁄₁₆ x 2⅝ x 11⅞" cherry (back rail)
F	1	1¹⁄₁₆ x 2³⁄₈ x 13¼" cherry (front rail)
G	2	1¹⁄₁₆ x 2³⁄₈ x 12⁹⁄₁₆" cherry (side rail)
H	2	1¾ x 1¾ x 16½" cherry (front leg)
I	4	¹³⁄₁₆ x 2 x 5" cherry (corner brace)
J*	2	¹³⁄₁₆ x 1 x 15" cherry (side stretcher)
K*	1	¹³⁄₁₆ x 1 x 14" cherry (cross stretcher)
L	1	½ x 2 x 11⅞" cherry (ledger)

Key	No.	Size and description (use)
M*	1	½ x 14 x 16" hardwood veneer plywood (seat)
N*	1	1 x 14 x 16" foam rubber (cushion)
O	1	20 x 22" upholstery fabric
P	18	⅜"-dia. x 2" hardwood dowel pin
Q	16	⅜"-dia x 1½" hardwood dowel pin
R	4	2" No. 12 fh screw
S	8	1¼" No. 12 fh screw

Misc.: Carpenter's and hide glue; 100-, 120-, and 220-grit sandpaper; oil-based cherry stain; satin polyurethane varnish.

*Trim to fit.

Fig. 3 *Use a doweling jig to bore ³/₈-in.-dia. dowel-pin holes in the splat and the top rail. Glue, dowel, and clamp the parts together.*

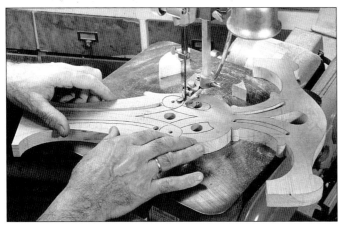

Fig. 4 *A scroll saw provides the easiest and most accurate means of making the cutouts in the chair back. The holes provide blade access.*

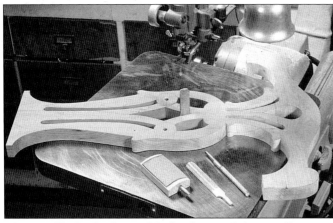

Fig. 5 *A file in the lower blade clamp of the scroll saw smooths away saw-blade marks. Tapered file tangs must be ground straight to fit.*

interior waste areas on a scroll saw (**Fig. 4**). A portable saber saw fitted with a narrow blade could also be used. Then use various shaped files and 100-grit sandpaper to remove saw-blade marks from the surfaces of the interior cutouts and from the outside edge of the assembly.

Here's a time-saving trick that you can use to effectively remove saw-blade marks: Place a small file in the lower chuck (blade clamp) of the scroll saw and power-file the surfaces smooth (**Fig. 5**). If the file has a tapered tang, grind it straight to fit it into the chuck properly.

Carving

Pencil in the outlines of the scrolls and interlacing straps. Next, use a sharp knife to make stop-cuts along the lines that separate the "raised" areas from the surfaces that will be carved to a lower plane (**Fig. 6**). Using a gouge, make shallow back-cuts up to the stop-cut lines (**Fig. 7**). Be careful not to cut deeper than the stop-cut lines, otherwise you may split the wood beyond the pencil outline. Use a skew or gouge to deepen the stop-cuts, then execute more back-cuts. Repeat this procedure until you've reached the desired depth. Once the specific details have been roughed out, use a wide, shallow gouge or a straight chisel to make long, sweeping cuts that form rounded, convex edges. As the carving nears completion, aim a lamp with a clear bulb across the work at a low angle (**Fig. 8**). This will highlight any areas that need additional work. The lamp is also helpful when making the final smoothing cuts with a gouge and bent chisel.

Finally, use 100-, 120-, and 220-grit sandpaper to sand the assembly smooth. Flexible emery boards are handy for sanding the shallow outside curves of the scrolls.

Rear Legs

Make a full-size paper pattern of the rear legs from the drawing. Then, trace the pattern onto the workpiece and cut

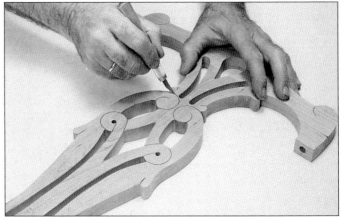

Fig. 6 *Outline the details of the carved splat using a sharp knife. These stop-cuts separate raised surfaces from the lower areas.*

Fig. 7 *Use a gouge to make shallow back-cuts up to the stop-cut lines. Don't cut deeper than the stop-cuts or splitting may occur.*

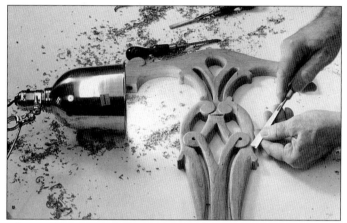

Fig. 8 *Shine a light across the carved surface to highlight rough spots that need additional work. Then finish sand the piece.*

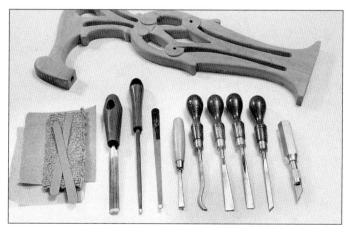

Fig. 9 *Tools used to carve the chair back (left to right): knife, skew, two gouges, spoon bit and bent chisels, files, and sandpaper.*

MaterialMatters

MANUFACTURED WOOD
Modern technology has given us many wonders, and among these stands the variants on nature's own tree products. But like all technological innovations, manufactured wood products cannot be adopted wholesale—they should be used in the right place and situation. Otherwise, they can detract, rather than help.

Traditional construction techniques have evolved to tolerate wood's natural peculiarities. Using the right forms of construction, such as frame-and-panel, several panels can be joined with little concern for the effects of wood movement. The lumber industry has taken this idea several steps further. The most common example is plywood.

Veneers, or thin layers of wood are glued together with the grain directions of adjacent layers oriented at right angles. This constrains swelling and shrinking. The veneers are produced by either rotary or flat slicing. Plywood with flat-sliced face veneers displays the same grain figure of solid wood and is the choice where a solid-wood look is desired. The edges are the challenge. They can be taped with a thin veneer of similar wood, covered with a thicker trim that's glued or clamped in place, or even mitered at the corners. Perhaps the best use of plywood is in combination with solid wood frames, making the most of both materials.

Particleboard—a composition of wood particles and glue compressed into panels—is available with veneer surfaces or its natural state. The type known as Medium Density Fiberboard (MDF) provides consistent density throughout the thickness of the panel. This makes for easily machined and painted edges. It is the obvious choice for uncluttered broad surfaces, such as contemporary painted furniture.

In solving some problems, however, manufactured panels have created others. The glue that holds the panels together is notoriously hard on cutting edges. Unless you enjoy frequent sharpenings, the use of a carbide-tipped blade is a necessity. And while these panels' 4 x 8 ft. size may be an advantage for large surfaces, they present a storage challenge. All of these panels are best stored by laying them flat on the floor. If you must stack them upright, make sure that they are as vertical as possible to avoid warping.

Fig. 10 *Trace a full-size paper pattern of the rear legs onto the workpiece. Then rough-cut both of the legs to size on a band saw.*

Fig. 11 *Sand flat the area where the side rails join the legs. Be sure that the sander's table is perpendicular to the sanding belt.*

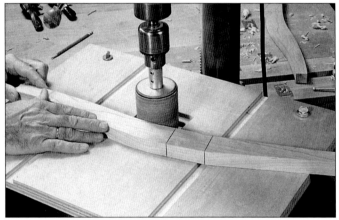

Fig. 12 *Finish sand the rear legs using a sanding drum fitted in a drill press. A portable belt sander could be used instead.*

Fig. 13 *For the doweling jig to sit square on top of the rear legs, the back must be cut parallel to the front surface.*

Tool*Care*

A FINE EDGE ON A SCRAPER
Scraper sharpening is one of those skills few woodworkers think of as a necessity—until their dull scrapers do damage. Follow some simple basic steps to keep scrapers in tune.

A properly sharpened scraper has a fine hook or burr that is shaped on the corners of both long edges of the tool. It's capable of removing that last, ultrathin shaving in preparation for finishing, or cleanly removing a bead of glue.

1. Begin sharpening your scraper by filing the two long edges straight and square with a smooth mill file. Then hold the scraper square to a fine flat stone and hone the long edges smooth. Hold the blade rigidly to achieve flat edges with

sharp corners. Remove the wire edge formed from edge-honing by holding the scraper perpendicular to the stone, and gently laying the scraper flat on it.

2. Next, hold the scraper flat on the edge of your bench so that its cutting edge overhangs the bench slightly, and put a drop of oil on the edge. Press the burnisher against one corner at a slight angle to the blade face. Then pull it across the edge to draw the corner out slightly.

out the two legs on a band saw (**Fig. 10**). Note that the section where the side rails join the rear legs must be perfectly flat. Smooth these areas on a stationary belt sander (**Fig. 11**). Remove blade marks from the remainder of the legs with a spokeshave, belt sander, and sanding drum (**Fig. 12**).

Another area of the legs that must be kept flat is 1½ in. of the upper back edge. This is necessary in order for the doweling jig to sit parallel to the straight front edge. Position the jig as shown (**Fig. 13**), and bore a ⅜-in.-dia. dowel-pin hole in the top of each leg.

Next, dry-assemble the rear legs to the splat/top rail assembly. Cut the rung (**D** in the materials list) that spans the legs along the bottom of the splat (**Fig. 14**). Then bore ⅜-in.-dia. dowel-pin holes in each end of the rung. Insert dowel center markers in each end. Place the assembly face down and position the rung to make dowel-pin location marks on the inside of each leg. Now bore dowel-pin holes in the legs where indicated by the dowel centers (**Fig. 15**).

Seat Rails

Next, cut the back rail and the two side rails. The front rail isn't cut until the front legs have been dry-fitted. Tilt the table-saw blade 7° to cut wedges. The wedges are needed to position the doweling jig parallel to the mitered ends of the rails. Tape the wedges to the rails as shown (**Fig. 16**), and bore dowel-pin holes. Be sure to locate the holes so that the dowel pins won't interfere with the back rail dowel pins or with the seat rabbet that will be cut later.

Install dowel pins in the ends of the back rail, bore holes in the legs, and dry-assemble the back rail to the rear legs. Next, rip a 1-in.-wide x 7° chamfer in a 1 x 3 x 5-in.-long scrap wood block.

Clamp the block to the outside of the rear leg as shown (**Fig. 17**). Bore ⅜-in.-dia. holes in the end of the side rail and insert dowel centers. Then, use the chamfered block as a

3. Secure the scraper in a vise and put a drop of oil on the edge. Position the burnisher on the edge and at right angles to the side surfaces of the scraper. Draw the burnisher toward you and across the edge to begin forming the hook. Gradually tilt the burnisher until it reaches a rough 85° angle with the scraper face.

4. After the first corner of one edge is burnished, you can shape the opposite corner and other edge in exactly the same way. When forming the hook, avoid using too much pressure—a light stroke will produce just enough hook for fine scraping.

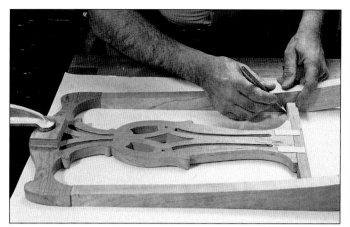

Fig. 14 *With the legs dry-fitted into the top rail, cut the horizontal rung to fit. Then, mark the legs to indicate the rung's position.*

Fig. 15 *Bore holes in the rung's ends and insert dowel centers. Transfer hole positions to the legs using a guide block.*

Fig. 16 *To bore dowel-pin holes in the side rails, use two 7° wedges to hold the doweling jig perpendicular to the mitered end.*

Fig. 17 *Clamp a guide block to the rear leg when transferring hole centers for the side rail. The guide block has a 7° chamfer.*

Fig. 18 *To transfer dowel hole centers from the side rails to the front legs, place a 7° wedge under the leg, as shown, for proper alignment.*

Fig. 21 *After joining the side stretchers with the cross stretcher, install this H-shaped piece to the front legs/seat rail assembly.*

guide to make dowel-pin location marks. Hold the side rail against the chamfered face of the block and slide the rail down to make hole centermarks in the rear leg.

Front Legs and Stretchers

Cut the two front legs to length, then locate dowel-pin holes using a 7° wedge as shown (**Fig. 18**). Bore the holes, insert dowel pins and dry assemble the chair parts.

Next, measure the distance between the front legs and cut the front rail to fit. Attach the front rail to the assembly and cut the stretchers (**J** and **K**) to fit (**Fig. 19**). Note that the rear of the side stretchers requires a compound miter cut.

Now disassemble the chair parts. Rout a ⅜-in.-deep recess in the top of each front leg with a ½-in.-dia. straight bit to accept the plywood seat panel. Also, chamfer the inside corners of the front legs.

Next, cut a ⅜-in.-deep x ½-in. rabbet in the front rail and

Fig. 22 *Once the glue has dried thoroughly, join the two main assemblies. Use slow-setting hide glue to gain more working time.*

Fig. 23 *Clamp the final assembly together with five bar or pipe clamps. Use two C-clamps to hold the ledger to the back rail.*

Fig. 19 *Dry assemble the chair and then scribe the side stretchers for a perfect fit. The cans and blocks support the stretchers at 6 in. high.*

the side rails for installing the seat panel. Then, rout the decorative edge on the seat rails and front legs with a ³⁄₁₆-in. beading bit (**see drawing detail 1**).

Final Assembly

Assemble the chair in two stages. First, using yellow carpenter's glue and ⅜-in.-dia. dowel pins, attach the rung to the splat. Glue and dowel one rear leg to the top rail, connect the rung and back rail, and then add the second leg (**Fig. 20**). Clamp the assembly together and allow the glue to dry.

During the second stage of assembly, it's advisable to use slow-setting hide glue so you won't have to rush. Glue and dowel the front legs to the side rails.

Next, join the side stretchers to the cross stretcher and attach the H-shaped assembly to the front legs (**Fig. 21**). Then glue the entire front leg assembly to the rear legs (**Fig. 22**). Tap the joints closed with a plastic or wooden mallet.

Fig. 20 *Start the final assembly by attaching the rung to the splat. Then install one rear leg, the back rail, and the second leg.*

Clamp the chair using five bar clamps (**Fig. 23**) until the glue dries. Also, glue and clamp the ledger (**L**) to the inside of the back rail to provide support for the seat panel. When the glue is dry, glue and screw the four corner braces in place.

Cut a ½-in. hardwood veneer plywood seat panel to fit in the rabbeted recess. Make the panel about ⅛ in. smaller on all edges to allow for the fabric.

Lay the fabric face down on a clean surface. Put the 1-in.-thick foam rubber padding and the seat panel on top of the fabric. Apply pressure to the panel until the padding is ¾ in. thick (**Fig. 24**). Then staple the fabric to the panel. When the pressure is released, the foam will expand and puff out the fabric. Screw the seat cushion in place after finishing the wood parts.

Apply three coats of satin polyurethane varnish. Sand lightly between coats. We tinted the first coat with a little oil-based cherry stain.

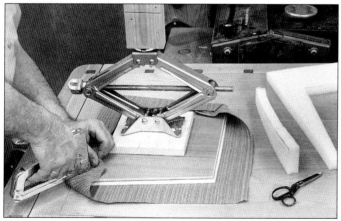

Fig. 24 *An auto jack is used to compress the seat cushion before stapling the fabric. The 2x4 is braced against a ceiling joist.*

TECH *Tips*

Precision Spacers
The most time-consuming part of cutting straight lines with a circular saw and guide is setting the guide so that the cut appears where you want it. The key to speed lies in making a spacer that defines the distance from the edge of the saw base to the inside of the blade. To make this spacer, first true the edge of a length of ¹⁄₄- to ¹⁄₂-in. stock and clamp it to a sawhorse. Then clamp a straight guide rail and cut the thin stock to get the spacer.

Two Good

This highly functional piece does double duty as a handy stepstool and a sturdy chair.

The common chair is such a simple structure that it's often called on to help with a variety of household chores. It's not unusual to see a chair used for a plant stand, as a small stepladder to change a bulb, or as a handy sawhorse when cutting a shelf to length. And how many times have you pulled over a kitchen chair so you could climb up and reach the top cabinet shelf? This design combines the requirements of both a simple kitchen chair and a multi-use stepstool in a neat little package that's not much more complicated to build than either separate piece. A simple pivot converts the chair to a 36-in. stepstool. The only thing better than a single, well-made piece of furniture, is two in one!

*Key*POINTS

TIME

Prep Time . . . . **6 hours**
Shop Time . . . . **8 hours**
Assembly Time . . . . **6 hours**

EFFORT

Skill Level . . . . **basic**

COST / BENEFITS

Expense: **low**

• **Useful convertability** makes this piece a durable kitchen workhorse.
• Simple construction and attractive finish make it a **wonderful first project**.

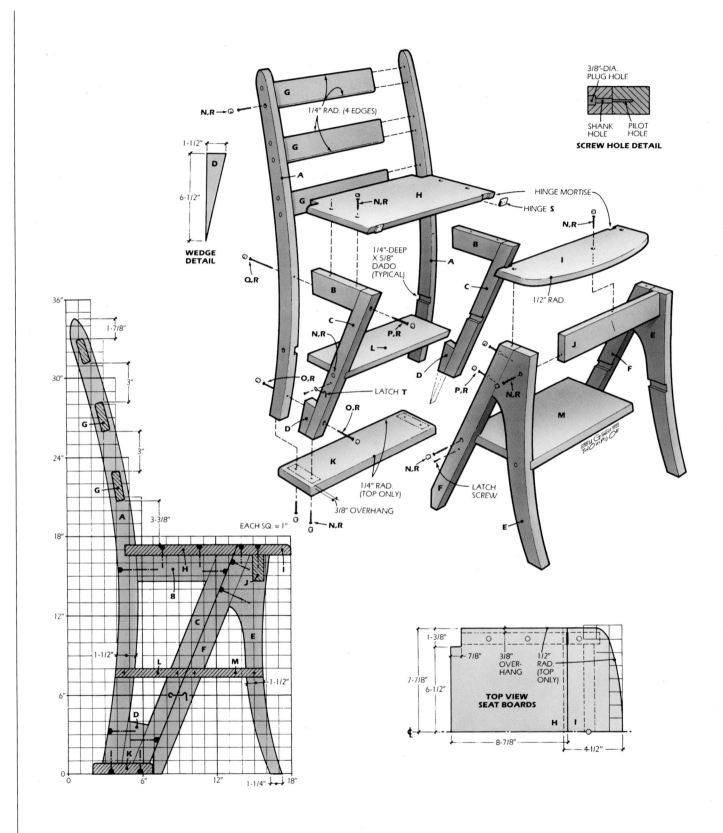

3/8"-DIA. PLUG HOLE

SHANK HOLE   PILOT HOLE

SCREW HOLE DETAIL

N,R

1/4" RAD. (4 EDGES)

G
G
A
G

1-1/2"

D

6-1/2"

WEDGE DETAIL

1/4"-DEEP X 5/8" DADO (TYPICAL)

N,R

HINGE MORTISE

HINGE **S**

H

I

N,R

B

C

A

1/2" RAD.

O,R

B

C

N,R

L

P,R

LATCH **T**

D

D

P,R

N,R

O,R

J

E

F

M

E

F

LATCH SCREW

N,R

K

1/4" RAD. (TOP ONLY)

3/8" OVERHANG

N,R

EACH SQ. = 1"

36"

1-7/8"

3"

30"

G

3"

24"

G

A

3-3/8"

18"

H

I

J

B

12"

C

E

F

1-1/2"

L

M

1-1/2"

6"

D

I   K

0

0   6"   12"   18"

1-1/4"

1-3/8"

7/8"

3/8" OVER-HANG

1/2" RAD. (TOP ONLY)

7-7/8"

6-1/2"

TOP VIEW SEAT BOARDS

H   I

8-7/8"

4-1/2"

Although this is an extremely traditional design, we've updated and simplified the joinery by using commonly available drywall screws, strong epoxy adhesive, and butt joints for convenient fitting and aligning of components. The whole piece is simple, useful, and lasting.

Starting Out

Begin construction by making patterns for the front and rear legs using ¼-in. plywood (**Fig. 1**). Draw a 1-in.-square grid for each leg on the plywood. Then transfer each point of intersection that the leg outline makes on the grid in the drawing to its corresponding position on your full-size grid.

To connect the points in a smooth curve, rip a 48-in.-long piece of scrap stock to ⅛ in. thick x ½ in. wide. Then drive small brads at the intersection points on your grid, hold the flexible strip against the brads, and trace the curve.

Cut out both leg patterns leaving ¼ in. extra on the bottom of the rear leg. Then, using these patterns, lay out a complete full-size side view of the chair as it is shown in the drawing

Materials List

Key	No.	Size and description (use)
A	2	⅞ x 5¼ x 33¾" oak (rear leg)
B	2	⅞ x 2 x 6½" oak (side rail)
C	2	⅞ x 1¼ x 17¹¹⁄₁₆" oak (rear support)
D	2	⅞ x 1½ x 3¼" oak (wedge)
E	2	⅞ x 4½ x 16⁹⁄₁₆" oak (front leg)
F	2	⅞ x 1¼ x 18⅜" oak (front support)
G	3	⅝ x 2¼ x 13¼" oak (slat)
H	1	¾ x 8⅞ x 15¾" oak (rear seat)
I	1	¾ x 4½ x 15¾" oak (front seat)
J	1	⅞ x 2 x 13¼" oak (front rail)
K	1	⅞ x 4⅞ x 15¾" oak (top step)
L	1	⅝ x 5¹³⁄₁₆ x 13¾" oak (step)
M	1	⅝ x 6⁷⁄₁₆ x 13¾" oak (step)
N	33	1½" No. 6 drywall screw
O	4	2" No. 8 drywall screw
P	6	2½" No. 8 drywall screw
Q	2	3" No. 8 drywall screw
R	45	⅜-in.-dia. plug
S	2	¾ x 1⅞" hinge
T	1	latch

Misc.: 150-grit sandpaper; epoxy adhesive; paste wax; stain finish polyurethane varnish.

Fig. 1 *Begin the leg templates by laying out a 1-in-sq. grid on ¼-in. plywood. Transfer the front and rear leg profiles as shown in the drawing.*

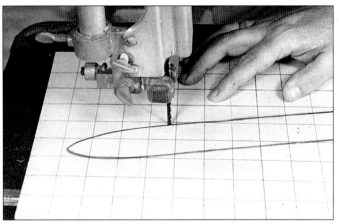

Fig. 2 *Carefully following the pattern outline, cut out the front and rear leg patterns with a band saw or a sabre saw.*

Fig. 3 *Draw a full-size layout of the chair using the leg patterns. Specifications for the remaining pieces are taken from this drawing.*

Fig. 4 *The trim angle for the middle support pieces is copied from the layout and transferred to the miter gauge for cutting.*

Fig. 5 *Use a tapering jig to cut bottom wedges at the required angle. A stop block behind the stock keeps work in place during the cut.*

(**Fig. 2 and 3**). This layout will enable you to accurately dimension and position the remaining components.

Keep in mind that the rear section pivots forward at the hinge position. The distance from the top of the rear leg to the seat should be equal to the height of the seat above the floor. This ensures that the rear leg tops will contact the floor when the unit is in its stepstool orientation.

Next, rip the ⅞-in.-thick rear leg stock to 6 in. wide and the front leg stock to 5 in. Crosscut these pieces slightly longer than their leg patterns. Transfer the pattern profiles to the stock and use a band saw or sabre saw to cut to the line.

Smooth the sawn edges with a drum sander or by hand with a spokeshave and sandpaper.

Rip the stock for the middle support pieces (**C and F on the drawing**) to 1¼ in. wide. Using your full-size layout as a guide for the support lengths, crosscut each piece slightly oversize. Use a sliding bevel gauge to copy the trimming angle. Then lay out and transfer this angle to the miter gauge on your table saw (**Fig. 4**).

Trim the rear support ¼ in. oversize in length at the appropriate angle and cut the front support to the exact length shown in your layout. The legs and supports of the rear side sections are connected by a rail (**H**) at the top and a wedge (**D**) at the bottom. We used a tapering jig (**Fig. 5**) to cut the wedges. If you don't have a tapering jig, you can cut a piece of scrap ¾-in. plywood to the required angle and guide this along the saw fence for cutting the wedges. Or, you can transfer the wedge shape from the layout and cut on the band saw.

Don't trim the points off the wedge bottoms because the entire rear section bottom will be trimmed after assembly. Cut the forward end of the upper side rails to the correct angle and transfer the line where they join the rear legs using your layout as a guide.

Band saw to the line. Lay the four parts that comprise each rear side assembly on the layout and check for proper fit and

alignment (**Fig. 6**). Repeat this alignment check for front side components.

Side Assemblies

When you're sure all side components match your full-size layout, you're ready for assembly. Clamp the pieces for one front side section in position on a corner of your worktable (**Fig. 7**) and mark the screw positions as shown in the drawing.

When boring for the screws, keep in mind that you'll need to bore three holes for each screw. First bore the ⅜-in.-dia. hole for the oak plug. Then bore the shank hole, followed by the actual pilot hole. The shank hole must be just larger than the outside diameter of the screw thread. You can buy special drill bits designed for boring all three holes at once to speed up the operation. After boring, screw the two front side pieces together without epoxy. Repeat this procedure for the remaining front section and two rear sections. When all four sections are screwed together, position each on the layout to make sure the parts are properly aligned.

If you're satisfied, remove the screws, apply epoxy to all joints, and reassemble. Then mark the bottom cutoff lines for the rear assemblies, set your miter gauge to the required angle as taken from the layout, and saw to the line (**Fig. 8**).

The Steps and Back

The steps (**L and M on the drawing**) are housed in dadoes cut in the side assemblies. Place each side section on the layout and transfer the step positions. Then lay a front and rear section—inside face up—on your worktable so that the marks for the steps align. Clamp a straightedge guide over the side to guide your router and ⅜-in.-dia. straight bit (**Fig. 9**). After the dadoes are cut, plane the stock for the steps to ⅝ in. thick, joint one edge on each, and crosscut to the specified length.

Take the exact width and bevel angle of each step off of

Fig. 6 *When all the side pieces are cut, place them on the full-size layout and check them for fit. Trim the components where necessary.*

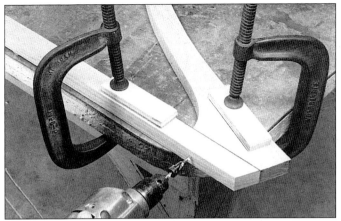

Fig. 7 *Clamp each side assembly to a corner of the worktable and mark and bore the plug, shank, and pilot holes for the screws.*

the full-size layout, and then trim the stock to width. Crosscut the back slat pieces and front rail to exact length and rip to width.

Before assembling the front and rear halves, construct a jig to hold the back slats in place. Temporarily tack two pieces of ¼-in. plywood together and trace the rear leg pattern on them (**Fig. 10**). Mark notches at the slat positions as shown on the layout and saw out the notches with a sabre saw. Separate the templates and clamp each to a rear section inside face.

Using bar clamps, dry assemble the rear side sections with the step, place the slats in the template notches and temporarily clamp. Then mark the screw positions and bore the plug, shank, and pilot holes for connecting the halves. Install the screws and check for proper alignment (**Fig. 11**).

Remove the screws from one side and apply epoxy to the mating surfaces. Refasten and repeat the procedure on the other side. After the rear section is completed, assemble the front halves, step, and rail in the same manner.

Seat and Top Step

Prepare the seat pieces by trimming two boards slightly wider than necessary and planing to ¾ in. thick. Crosscut to exact

Fig. 8 *The rear side bottom is trimmed after assembly. Use the table saw with a miter gauge set to the angle taken from the layout.*

Fig. 9 *Mark the lines for the dadoes that house the steps. Using a straightedge guide, rout the ¼-in.-deep x ⅝-in-wide dadoes.*

Fig. 10 *A ¼-in.-plywood template of the upper rear leg has notches to help in positioning the slats prior to boring screw holes.*

Fig. 11 *Dry assemble the units with drywall screws and check for a good fit. Then remove the screws, apply epoxy, and reassemble.*

length and cut to width following the dimensions and bevel angle shown in your layout.

Notch the rear seat board to fit between the rear legs. Transfer the front edge shape of the forward seat piece from the drawing to scrap ¼-in plywood and cut out. Trace this pattern on the seat stock, cut to the line, and smooth the sawn edge with a drum sander or sandpaper and block. Mark

the hinge positions and cut the hinge mortises with a dovetail saw and sharp chisel (**Fig. 13**).

Place each hinge in position on the rear seat piece and mark for the screw pilot holes (**Fig. 14**). After boring, it's a good idea to pretap the holes with a steel screw of the same size as the brass screws supplied with the hinges. This helps eliminate breaking the soft brass screws as they're driven into

TECH *Tips*

Applying a Wax Finish
Most factory-built furniture has a wax topcoat that adds a rich luster to the wood's surface while protecting the finish. It's important to maintain a protective wax finish on your furniture, including shopbuilt projects.

There are many liquid and spray-on furniture polishes available, but the one recommended by professional furniture finishers is old-fashioned paste wax. This is usually a blend of carnuba wax, beeswax, and turpentine. When applied and buffed properly, paste wax forms a surprisingly hard, durable, protective coating.

A waxed piece that has grown dull and flat can often be revived by simply buffing the surface with a soft, dry cloth. If this fails to restore the luster, then it's necessary to rewax.

1. Apply paste wax with a soft, water-dampened cloth. Spread on a thin, even coat and allow it to dry about 20 minutes. Don't over apply the wax. A thick, heavy wax coat will be nearly impossible to buff out.

2. Once the wax has dried, buff the surface by rubbing briskly—don't spare the elbow grease—with a soft, dry cloth. An electric polisher with a lamb's wool bonnet can also be used.

3. Stop buffing when the surface acquires a uniform, highly polished sheen. A simple thumbprint test will determine if more buffing is needed.

4. Push your thumb on the surface. If a clearly visible print is left, continue buffing.

5. Wait about one hour and then apply a second coat. Buff the second coat to a lustrous sheen.

If a piece of furniture has several coats of old, dirty wax, it's best to clean off the wax and start over again from scratch. Use naptha or mineral spirits on a soft cloth to remove built-up wax safely on pieces finished with varnish, shellac, or paint. On lacquered surfaces, use mineral spirits. Naptha may dull a lacquer finish. Once the surface is clean, apply two coats of wax.

Fig. 12 *Use a plug cutter to make the ³/₈-in.-dia. plugs. Glue them in place and trim them flush with a sharp chisel and fine sandpaper.*

Fig. 13 *Use a fine backsaw and sharp chisel to cut the hinge mortises. Then bore pilot holes and screw the hinges in place.*

the hard oak. Then lay the front piece on top and install the screws. Align front and rear assemblies and clamp together. Stand the entire unit up in its chair position using a ⅞-in-thick piece of stock in place of the top step (**K**) to support the rear section (**Fig. 15**).

Position the seat and bore the screw holes. If the dry assembly of the seat is correct, remove it, apply epoxy and reinstall. Then cut the top step to size, turn the chair upside down, and install.

Completing the Piece

Use a plug cutter to make enough plugs for all the screws, and glue the plugs in place (**Fig. 12**). Trim the excess with a sharp chisel. Then remove the hinges and hand sand the entire chair with 150-grit sandpaper. Clean up with a tack cloth and apply two coats of satin finish polyurethane varnish following the manufacturer's instructions. Apply a coat of paste wax and reinstall the hinges. Locate the screw positions for the hook and install.

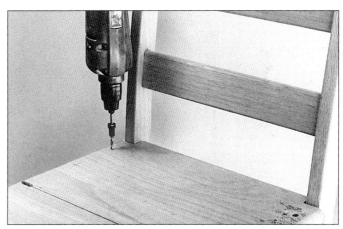

Fig. 14 *After clamping the front and rear units together, lay the seat in position and bore the holes for fastening the seat.*

TOOL*Care*

Clean Blade
To clean circular saw blades of resin using a minimum of solvent, try using a restaurant-style pizza pan (available at restaurant supply stores) as the holding container for the solvent. Buy a real aluminum pizza pan, not the disposable type, and you will be able to totally submerge your blades in a small volume of liquid.

Fig. 15 *Turn the chair upside down and position the ⁷/₈-in-thick top step. Mark and bore the hole for fastening with drywall screws.*

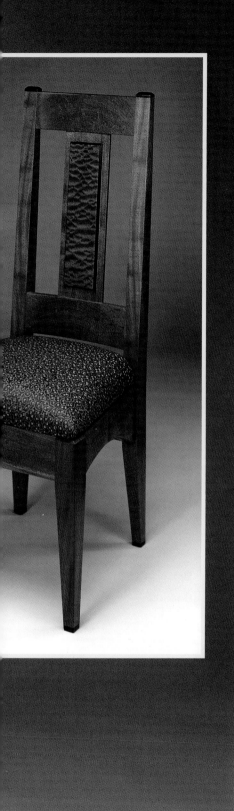

Pretty Perch

As part of a dining room ensemble or as a standalone furnishing, this chair holds it own.

Luxury often has a style all its own, and that is certainly the case with this one-of-kind chair. With big credit nods to both the Arts & Crafts and Art Nouveau design styles, we've created a contemporary design theme that's compatible with any decor. The detailing on this showstopping chair is subtle and refined, yet has no problem drawing attention to itself, a trait shared by the material of the chair. As we so often do for our signature pieces, we've chosen mahogany as the primary wood. But instead of the typical dark stain that is commonly used on pieces of this type, we have opted for a natural oil finish that gently darkens with use, turning a highly fetching golden, reddish brown.

*Key*POINTS

TIME

Prep Time	1 hour
Shop Time	3 hours
Assembly Time	6 hours

EFFORT

Skill Level	intermediate

COST / BENEFITS

Expense: **expensive**

- The **fabulous glowing finish** on this chair only gets better with time.
- Although formal, this piece is **at home in just about any decor.**

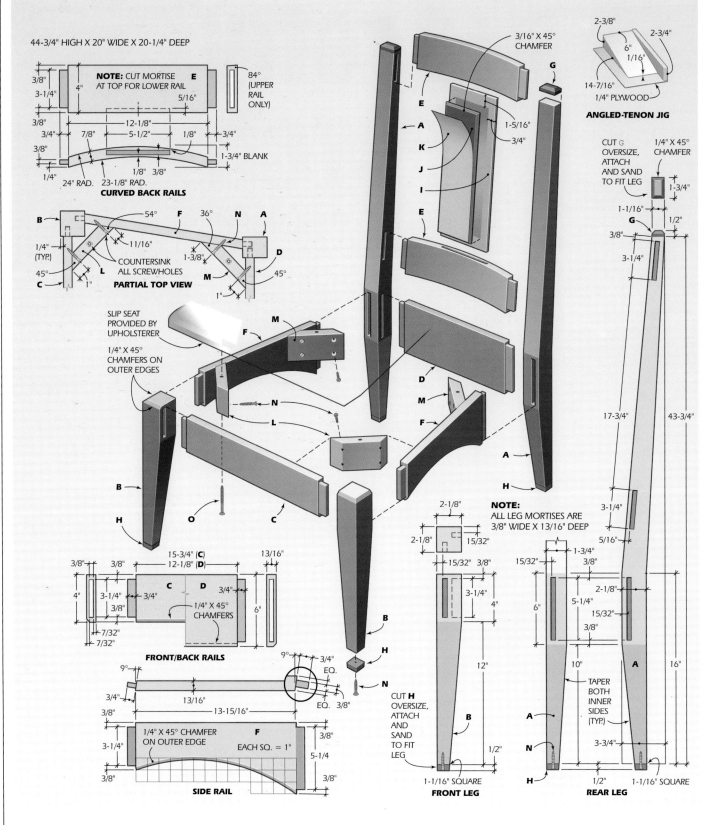

44-3/4" HIGH X 20" WIDE X 20-1/4" DEEP

NOTE: CUT MORTISE **E** AT TOP FOR LOWER RAIL

84° (UPPER RAIL ONLY)

3/8"
3-1/4"
4"
5/16"

3/8"
12-1/8"
3/4" 7/8" 5-1/2" 1/8" 3/4"
3/8"
1/8" 3/8"
1-3/4" BLANK
1/4"
24" RAD.   23-1/8" RAD.

CURVED BACK RAILS

2-3/8"
2-3/4"
6"
1/16"
14-7/16"
1/4" PLYWOOD

ANGLED-TENON JIG

CUT G OVERSIZE, ATTACH AND SAND TO FIT LEG

1/4" X 45° CHAMFER

1-3/4"
1-1/16"
G
1/2"

3/16" X 45° CHAMFER

G
E
A
K
J
I
E
1-5/16"
3/4"

E

B
54° F 36° N A
1/4" (TYP.)
11/16"
1-3/8"
D
45° L M
C 1" 45°
COUNTERSINK ALL SCREWHOLES 1"

PARTIAL TOP VIEW

3/8"
3-1/4"
54°

17-3/4"
43-3/4"

3/8"
3-1/4"
5/16"

SLIP SEAT PROVIDED BY UPHOLSTERER

1/4" X 45° CHAMFERS ON OUTER EDGES

F M
N
L
B
H
O
C
D
M
F
A
H

FRONT/BACK RAILS

15-3/4" (**C**)
12-1/8" (**D**)
13/16"
3/8" 3/8"
4"
3-1/4" 3/4"
C D 3/4"
3/8"
1/4" X 45° CHAMFERS
6"
7/32"
7/32"

9°
9°
3/4"
EQ.
3/4"
13/16"
3/8"
13-15/16"
EQ. 3/8"

1/4" X 45° CHAMFER ON OUTER EDGE F
EACH SQ. = 1"
3-1/4"
3/8"
3/8"
5-1/4"
3/8"

SIDE RAIL

2-1/8"
2-1/8"
15/32"
15/32" 3/8"

NOTE: ALL LEG MORTISES ARE 3/8" WIDE X 13/16" DEEP

15/32" 3/8"
3-1/4"
4"
6"
12
1/2"

CUT **H** OVERSIZE, ATTACH AND SAND TO FIT LEG

B
H
N
B

1-1/16" SQUARE

FRONT LEG

1-3/4"
15/32" 3/8"
2-1/8"
5-1/4"
15/32"
3/8"
6"
10"
A
N
H
TAPER BOTH INNER SIDES (TYP.)
3-3/4"
1/2"
16
1-1/16" SQUARE

REAR LEG

As if mahogany were not enough, we've used two highly attractive exotic woods to create tasteful decorative accents: wenge, a heavy, dense, dark wood, and pomele sapele veneer, a mahogany-like wood with a heavily quilted grain figure. Both of these materials are available through mail-order suppliers, and both are extremely unique and visually appealing. We had an upholsterer provide the slip seat for our chair. Find a local professional in the yellow pages under "Upholstery." The seat is your chance to add a highly personal touch to the chair by selecting a fabric that blends with your home's interior design scheme.

Start with the Legs

Begin by making a full-size template for the side profile of the rear legs from a piece of ¼-in.-thick hardboard or plywood. Use the template to lay out the legs on 1¾-in. stock, and cut to the waste side of the lines with a band saw (**Fig. 1**). Do not make the top and bottom cuts at this time—it's more accurate to make these cuts after final leg shaping.

Use a plane to smooth the sawn surfaces and refine the shape of the rear legs. Be sure to keep the planed surfaces square to the leg sides (**Fig. 2**). With shaping done, use a table saw and miter gauge to trim the top and bottom of each leg. Then rip stock for the front legs to 2⅛ in. square and crosscut these pieces to 16 in. long. Lay out all the mortise locations on the legs. To make this job more accurate, clamp two legs side by side and mark them together. Then use an edge guide and a spiral up-cutting bit to rout the mortises (**Fig. 3**). Make

Fig. 1 *Use a band saw to cut the rear leg shapes. Keep the saw kerf on the waste side of the layout line while cutting.*

Materials List

Key	No.	Size and description (use)
A	2	1¾ x 3¾ x 43¾" mahogany (rear leg)
B	2	2⅛ x 2⅛ x 16" mahogany (front leg)
C	1	¹³⁄₁₆ x 4 x 17¼" mahogany (front rail)
D	1	¹³⁄₁₆ x 6 x 13⅝" mahogany (rear rail)
E	2	1¾ x 4 x 13⅝" mahogany (back rail)
F	2	¹³⁄₁₆ x 6 x 15½" mahogany (side rail)
G*	2	½ x 1¹⁄₁₆ x 1¾" wenge (leg cap)
H*	4	½ x 1¹⁄₁₆ x 1¹⁄₁₆" wenge (foot)
I	1	⅜ x 5½ x 17⅝" mahogany (splat)
J*	1	⅜ x 4 x 15" wenge (panel)
K*	1	4 x 15" pomele sapele (panel veneer)
L	2	1 x 3 x 5⅛" maple (corner block)
M	2	1 x 3 x 5⁹⁄₁₆" maple (corner block)
N	20	1½" No. 8 fh wood screw
O	4	3" No. 10 fh wood screw

Misc.: Glue; wax paper; 120-, 220-, and 320-grit sandpaper; 4/0 steel wool; sealer/finish; slip seat provided by upholsterer.
* Finished dimension. Cut oversize and trim after assembly.

Fig. 2 *Smooth the cut surfaces with a hand plane. Be sure to keep the planed surface square to the adjacent faces.*

Fig. 3 *Rout the leg mortises with a spiral up-cutting bit. Another leg helps support the router while making these cuts.*

Fig. 4 *Use a sharp chisel to cut a ¼-in. bevel at the top end of a wenge blank. Then cut a leg cap from the blank.*

Fig. 6 *Use a dado blade to cut the rail tenon faces. Turn the stock on edge and readjust the blade to cut the tenon shoulders.*

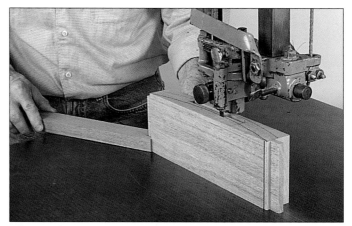

Fig. 7 *After cutting the curved-rail tenons and splat mortises, cut the inner curve on the back rails with a band saw.*

each mortise in two or three passes to avoid breaking the bit or overloading the router, and finish by chopping the ends square with a sharp chisel. Lay out the tapers on the front chair legs, use your band saw to cut the legs to shape, and plane the surfaces smooth. Rip a blank of wenge to 1⅛ x 1¹³⁄₁₆ in. and cut it about 8 in. long. Use a sharp chisel to carefully trim a ¼-in. bevel around one end (**Fig. 4**), and then cut a ½-in.-thick piece from the beveled end to produce a leg cap.

Repeat the process for the remaining leg cap. Apply glue to a cap and top end of a leg, position the cap (**Fig. 5**) and clamp it in place. When the glue dries, sand the cap edges flush and adjust the chamfer as required.

The final step of this part of the process involves cutting a wenge foot for each leg. Bore and countersink a pilot hole in each foot and securely fasten them to the legs with screws and glue. Sand the feet flush, and slightly soften the bottom edges so they won't chip.

Making the Rails

Cut ¹³⁄₁₆-in.-thick stock to size for the lower chair rails and use 1¾-in. blanks for the curved back rails. At this point you'll need to install a dado blade in the table saw, and use your miter gauge to cut the tenons on the front and back bottom rails (**Fig. 6**). Then you'll have to readjust the blade height and hold the work on edge to cut the tenon shoulders. When you're cutting the thicker back-rail tenons, you should note that the depth of the cut will be different on the front and back faces.

Mark the locations of the mortises in the edges of the curved rails, and rout the mortises before you cut the rails to shape. Square the mortises with a chisel.

Use your band saw to cleanly cut the inside curve of the rails (**Fig. 7**). Then clamp each piece to your bench and use a spokeshave to smooth the cut faces (**Fig. 8**). Return the rails to the band saw to cut the outer curved faces, and smooth

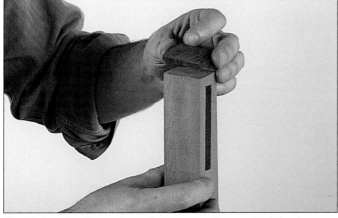

Fig. 5 *Apply glue, place the cap on the end of the leg, and clamp it. Sand the cap flush and adjust the chamfer as necessary.*

them thoroughly using a spokeshave or plane. To cut the angled side-rail tenons, first construct a jig for the table saw as shown in the Angled-Tenon Jig detail in the drawing. Build a ramp to support the rails at the 9° tenon angle, and screw the ramp to a ¼-in. plywood base.

Attach a solid wood back to the base behind the ramp and securely clamp the jig to the table saw miter gauge. Install a dado blade and then cut one side of each joint with the ramp sloping down to the blade (**Fig. 9**). Reverse the ramp to cut the other side of each tenon. Because the angle will raise the rail end high above the table, use a normal 10-in. blade and repeated cuts to finish each tenon.

Lay out the curved shape on the side rails and cut to the lines. Smooth the edges with a spokeshave and use a dovetail saw to cut the shoulders at the top and bottom of each tenon (**Fig. 10**).

Install a chamfer bit in your router, and bevel the bottom outside edges of the rails as shown in the drawing.

Fig. 8 *Use a spokeshave to remove saw marks on the inside face of the curved rails. Then cut the outside face and smooth.*

Fig. 9 *Build a ramp to support the side rails when cutting the angled tenons. Reverse the ramp for the opposite tenon faces.*

MATERIAL*Matters*

Putting Wood Waste to Use in the Garden
No form of wood in the workshop should ever go to waste. Whether you have a pile of superfine sawdust, chunks and pieces of project wood, or whole pieces, such as pushsticks, there's a way to put it to use.

Sawdust makes great mulch for the garden. A 2-in. layer around soft-leaved plants will prevent slug or snail damage. Sawdust also increases soil acidity to a modest degree, aiding plants such as rhododendrons that need slightly acidic soil. Sawdust can also be composted along with other yard waste.

Small chunks of softwood are great as filler in the bottom of potted plants. They are lightweight, so they don't make the container heavy, and they will absorb water, releasing it

slowly to give plant roots a continual source of moisture. Large end pieces can be chipped with tree branches to make a great mulch—but use a metal detector to insure there are no nail ends or other pieces of metal in the wood.

The exception to these uses is dust or scraps from treated wood or manufactured panels such as plywood or MDF. Remnants from treated wood may contain chemicals that will pollute the soil, and can leach into water sources.

The Veneered Panel

Cut the back splat to size and check that it fits snugly in the back-rail mortises. Use your band saw to resaw a blank of wenge just slightly thicker than ⅜ in. for the decorative panel core. Plane the sawn surface smooth to finished thickness. Leave it at least 1 in. oversize both in width and length.

The simplest way to cut veneer is with a veneer saw. This is a small saw with fine teeth that are beveled on only one side. Hold the flat side of the saw against a straightedge guide while you make several passes to cut through the veneer (**Fig. 11**). Apply light pressure so you don't tear the veneer at the edges. Cut your veneer to the exact size of the wenge blank.

Use a foam roller to apply the glue to the wenge blank (**Fig. 12**). For this small veneered panel, use regular yellow glue—for a larger panel, slower-setting glue is recommended. Cover the entire surface with glue, but don't spread so much that it pools. Place the veneer on the glued face, aligning its edges with those of the wenge. Place a sheet of wax paper over the veneer and sandwich the blank between cauls of ¾-in. plywood. Apply clamps, working from the center toward the ends (**Fig. 13**). Allow the glue to set for a few hours before removing the clamps. Let the panel dry overnight.

Trim the veneered panel to finished size and bevel the edges with a router. Sand the back splat and panel with 220-grit sandpaper and lightly mark the position of the panel on the splat with a pencil.

Apply a light coat of glue on the mating surfaces, then position the panel and clamp it to the splat.

Assembly

Sand all the parts, finishing with 220-grit sandpaper, and join the splat to the curved rails (**Fig. 14**). You don't need glue at these joints since the splat is held captive between the rails. If the joints are excessively loose, though, use a drop of glue in each mortise to keep the splat from rattling. Wrap the ends of the rails with masking tape where they join the legs to keep glue from drying on the wood surface (**Fig. 15**).

Spread glue on the back-rail tenons and leg mortises. Join

Fig. 10 *Clamp a side rail in your vise and use a dovetail saw to cut the shoulders at the top and bottom ends of each tenon.*

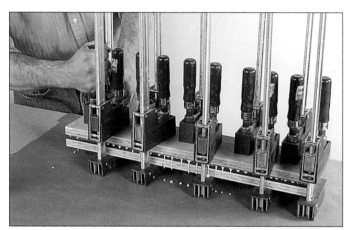

Fig. 13 *Starting at the center, apply clamps along the panel. A modest amount of glue will squeeze out along the edges.*

the rails to the legs and add clamps to pull the joints tight (**Fig. 16**). Then, join the front rail to the legs.

Complete the base by joining the front and back leg subassemblies to the side rails. Stand the chair on a flat table so that all the legs rest evenly (**Fig. 17**). Make the 1-in.-thick corner blocks, bore and countersink pilot holes for mounting them, and bore holes for attaching the seat. Then screw the blocks to the chair rails.

Finishing

We used sealer/finish for our chair. Apply it with a brush or rag and let it soak in for about 30 minutes. Use a lint-free rag to wipe off the excess and let it dry overnight. Lightly scuff the surface with 320-grit sandpaper and dust off before applying a second coat using the same technique. After overnight drying, apply the third and final coat. Rub the dried finish with 4/0 steel wool to give it a soft, satin shine.

SHOP *Helper*

Edge-gluing boards can be a frustrating exercise as you clean drips off the face of the boards. You can make it easier by crafting a guide to fit around the glue bottle's spout. Use a coping saw to cut into a ¾-in. PVC coupling, leaving a ¾-in. quarter-round "lip." Dab PVC cement on the inside of the coupling, slide it onto the glue bottle, and let dry. Now the lip functions as a "fence" to prevent glue from going over the edge of the piece you're working on.

Fig. 11 *Use a veneer saw, guided by a straight piece of wood, to cut the veneer. Finish the cut in several light passes.*

Fig. 12 *Use a foam roller to spread glue on the wenge panel. The glue must cover the surface, but shouldn't pool.*

Fig. 14 *Begin assembly by joining the splat to the back rails. You don't need to use glue unless the joints are loose.*

Fig. 15 *Protect the sanded parts from glue squeeze-out during assembly by applying masking tape at the rail ends.*

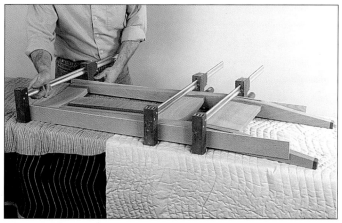

Fig. 16 *After applying glue to the mortise-and-tenon joints, clamp the rear legs to the rails to pull the joints tight.*

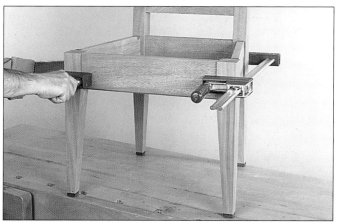

Fig. 17 *Join the front and rear subassemblies to the side rails. Stand the chair on a flat table and check that all legs rest evenly.*

Ottoman Empire

An Arts & Crafts chair and ottoman provides the perfect place to put your feet up and take a break.

The elegant ottoman and chair we present here are fine examples of the American Arts & Crafts furniture style, also sometimes called the Mission or Morris style. This type of furniture evolved from a movement in England in the late 19th century, in which craftsmen rejected the heavy ornamentation and shoddy construction of mass-produced Victorian furniture. Gustav Stickley, an American furniture designer and manufacturer went to England in the late 1890s and returned home with great enthusiasm for the new design trends. Once you spend a relaxing evening in the comfort of this duo, it will be easy to see why. Whether you're watching TV or reading, this is the place to do it.

*Key*POINTS

TIME
Prep Time . . . . **1 hour**
Shop Time . . . . **3 hours**
Assembly Time . . . . **6 hours**

EFFORT
Skill Level . . . . **intermediate**

COST / BENEFITS
Expense: **expensive**
- This wonderful addition to a den or comfortable living room features the perfect combination of **rugged good looks** and **wonderful comfort**.

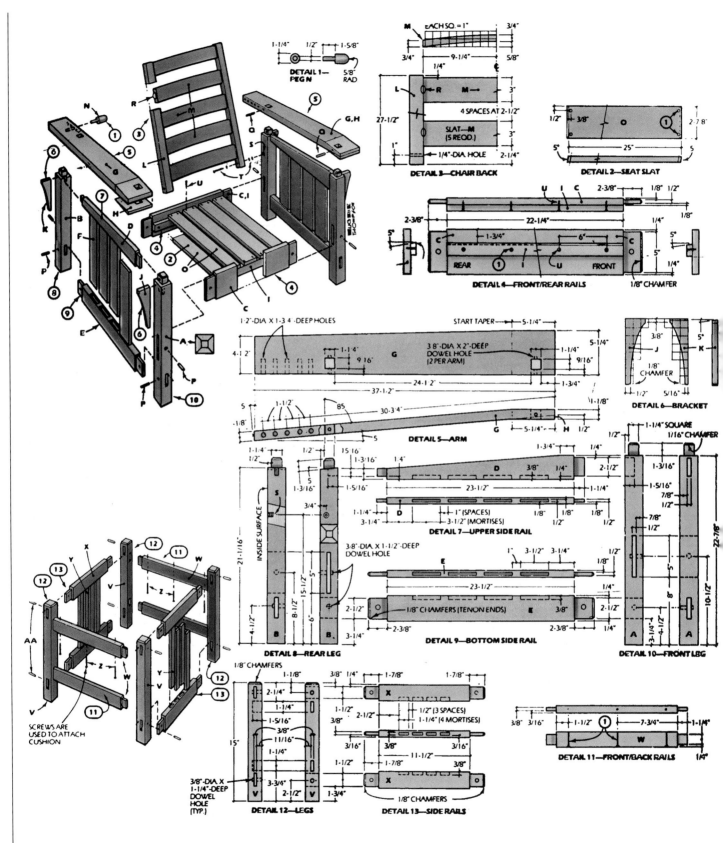

DETAIL 1—PEG N

DETAIL 3—CHAIR BACK

DETAIL 2—SEAT SLAT

DETAIL 4—FRONT/REAR RAILS

DETAIL 5—ARM

DETAIL 6—BRACKET

DETAIL 7—UPPER SIDE RAIL

DETAIL 8—REAR LEG

DETAIL 9—BOTTOM SIDE RAIL

DETAIL 10—FRONT LEG

DETAIL 11—FRONT/BACK RAILS

DETAIL 12—LEGS

DETAIL 13—SIDE RAILS

SCREWS ARE USED TO ATTACH CUSHION

Characteristic of Stickley's works are heavy, unornamented, rectilinear forms with through-tenon construction. Most of his pieces were built from quarter-sawn white oak, and then upholstered in brown leather. Our pieces are faithful to the originals, including the chair's adjustable back with five different reclining positions. Whether you are reading, watching TV, or taking a well-earned Sunday nap, you're sure to find a comfortable spot that's just right for you.

Making the Chair Parts

Begin by making the legs. The best way to display the oak's unusual grain is to construct the legs so that the grain is visible from all sides. We assembled the leg from four beveled pieces glued to a solid square core.

Begin by ripping slightly oversize slats from ¾-in.-thick stock. Set the table saw blade at 45°, and carefully rip the slat edges so that the piece has a width of 2¼ in. across its face.

Do not cut the slats to finished length yet. Rip the core pieces slightly oversize, then joint their surfaces. Dry assemble each leg to check the joints.

Lay out the four facing pieces and the core piece for a leg and apply a thin film of glue to all the joint surfaces (**Fig. 1**). Apply the glue sparingly. Too much glue will result in a sloppy fit and will make the parts hard to clamp. Assemble the leg with masking tape, and clamp the assembly until the

Fig. 1 *Each leg is an assembly of four beveled pieces glued to a core. Spread a thin film of glue on each bevel and each core.*

Fig. 2 *Tape the leg assembly together, then position closely spaced clamps around the entire assembly and let the glue set.*

Materials List

Key	No.	Size and description (use)
A	2	2¼ x 2¼ x 24¹/₁₆" white oak (front leg)
B	2	2¼ x 2¼ x 22¼" white oak (rear leg)
C	2	¾ x 5½ x 27" white oak (rail)
D	2	¾ x 3 x 26" white oak (rail)
E	2	¾ x 3 x 28¼" white oak (rail)
F	8	½ x 3½ x 14⅝" white oak (slat)
G	2	1⅛ x 5¼ x 38" white oak (armrest)
H	2	½ x 5¼ x 5¼" white oak (wedge)
I	2	¾ x 1½ x 22¼" white oak (ledger)
J	2	¾ x 2½ x 8" white oak (front arm bracket)
K	2	¾ x 2⁵/₁₆ x 8" white oak (rear arm bracelet)
L	2	1⅛ x 1¾ x 27½" white oak (backrest side)
M	5	1⅜ x 3 x 18½" white oak (backrest slat)
N	2	1¼-dia. x 3⅜" white oak (backrest peg)
O	6	¾ x 2⅞ x 25½" white oak (seat slat)
P	8	⅜-dia. x 1½" white oak (dowel peg)
Q	4	⅜-dia. x 2" white oak (dowel peg)
R	10	No. 20 joining plates
S	2	¼-20 threaded insert
T	2	¼-20 x 2¼" brass rh machine screw and 6 brass washers
U	28	1¼" No. 8 fh screws
V	4	1¾ x 1¾ x 15" white oak (legs)
W	4	¾ x 1¾ x 18" white oak (rails)
X	4	¾ x 2 x 15¼" white oak (rails)
Y	8	⅜ x 1¼ x 10⅛" white oak (slats)
Z	6	2¼" No. 8 fh screws
AA	8	⅜-dia. x 1¼" white oak (dowel peg)

Fig. 3 *Using a miter gauge, cut the tenon on the leg with a dado blade in the table saw. Bevel the tenon end with a chisel.*

Fig. 4 *Cut the leg mortises with a plunge router. To provide adequate support for the router, clamp two legs together.*

glue sets (**Fig. 2**). Next, use dado blades in the table saw to cut the tenons at the top of the front legs. Use a stop block on the miter gauge to guarantee accuracy in the cuts. Butt the

workpiece against the block. Cut the tenon slightly oversize and then pare it smooth using a sharp chisel (**Fig. 3**). Accuracy is important here because the tenon end is exposed,

MATERIAL *Matters*

Drying Wood
Freshly cut wood contains a high percentage of the water it needed in its cells to remain alive. Because of the structure of wood, it will hold onto that water for quite some time. The trick is to get the water out without degrading the quality of the wood, or causing problems later, after the wood has been used in a piece of furniture. There are two basic ways to bring lumber to a moisture content that will ensure that it won't move or distort significantly after the project is completed. The simplest is to let it dry naturally in the air.

To effectively air-dry lumber, boards are typically stacked with evenly spaced sticks placed in between the layers to allow for effective air circulation. The time it takes for complete drying depends on the moisture content of the wood and the relative humidity of the air in the space in which the drying is done. To ensure success in working with the wood, final drying must take place in an environment with the same humidity of the location that will house the final project. Don't be tempted to speed up the process by bringing green wood directly into your house: the wood will dry too quickly, causing checks and cracks.

Kiln-dried wood has been subjected to an accelerated drying process. Unfortunately, if kiln drying is done too quickly, it can cause problems. Case-hardening occurs when the outside of the board dries first, and becomes rigid. When the inside dries, it stretches as it conforms to the rigid outer shell. This internal stress becomes apparent when the board is ripped—

the saw kerf will immediately close behind the cutting edge and bind on the blade. It also means that removing any stock from only one face will cause the board to warp as the stress is relieved. In extreme cases, case-hardening can cause internal cracks called honeycombing.

No matter what wood you buy, how dry the dealer says it is, and regardless of how much you pay for it, the wood will move (shrink, cup, crook, bow, or twist) if it hasn't been dried to the same moisture level that it will eventually attain. Even after your wood has been dried adequately, it will continue to move with seasonal changes in humidity.

The easiest way to determine the moisture content of your wood is to check it with a moisture meter. The most common type measures the resistance of the wood to electric flow and translates the data into a moisture-content percentage. For the headaches they save, these are excellent investments.

Fig. 5 *Attach an extension fence with a stop to the miter gauge, and cut the tenon shoulders on the front and back rails.*

Fig. 6 *Securely attach an auxiliary fence to the table saw's rip fence, and then use a shopmade tenoning jig to cut the tenon cheeks.*

so don't remove more than the thickness of a light shaving.

The tenons on the rear legs have a shoulder that is not 90° to the tenon, so it is simpler to cut these joints by hand. Clamp a leg blank in a vise and make the vertical cheek cuts using a dovetail saw. Then, holding the legs flat to the benchtop, saw the tenon shoulders. Finish the tenons by shaving them smooth with a chisel.

Lay out the mortises on the chair legs. Note that the only leg mortises that are not through mortises are for the top side rails. For the through mortises, cut half the mortise depth from one side of the leg using a plunge router. Then turn over the workpieces and complete the cut. This requires that the top and bottom limits of the mortises be accurately marked. Also, the router edge guide must be placed on the same leg face when cutting both sides of the joint.

Clamp two legs together on the workbench to provide a stable support for the plunge router. Make a series of increasingly deep passes with the router until you have cut slightly more than half the mortise depth. Do not cut the mortise in a single pass. White oak is too tough a material to do this. Turn over the legs and complete the cut (**Fig. 4**). Cut the ends of the mortise square with a chisel.

Next, rip and crosscut the front, back, side rails, and side slats to finished dimension. Lay out the tenons on the end of each rail. Begin cutting each joint by making the shoulder cuts using the table saw and miter gauge (**Fig. 5**). Attach an auxiliary fence to the miter gauge to do this, and attach a clamp on the fence to act as a stop. Butt each workpiece securely to the fence and stop to make the shoulder cut. Next, cut the tenon cheeks using a shopmade tenoning jig on the table saw (**Fig. 6**).

Mark the slat mortises on the side rails, and cut the mortises in a series of shallow passes until you have arrived at the depth shown in the plans. As was done with the legs, provide a stable base for the router by clamping two rails to

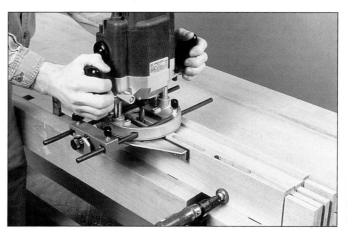

Fig. 7 *Cut the slat mortises in the side rails using a plunge router. Again, clamp two rails together to support the plunge router.*

Fig. 8 *Cut a wedge for each arm, and glue it to the arm. After the glue has set, saw the top of the arm to produce the flat surface.*

Fig. 9 *Fasten an arm to the workbench, and support it at a slope. Cut the through mortise for the leg tenon using a chisel.*

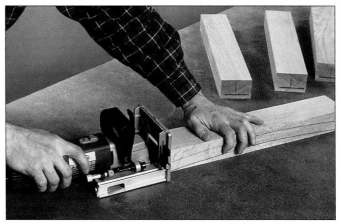

Fig. 10 *Mark the curve on the backrest slats, and mark the biscuit location. Cut the biscuit slots using a plate joiner.*

the bench (**Fig. 7**). Again, use the edge-guide attachment on the plunge router, and square the cuts with a chisel when you're done. Mark the tape on each side top rail, and cut the taper on the band saw. Cut just to the waste side of the line. Remove the saw marks from the surface and work down to the taper line using a hand plane.

Select two pieces of 5/4 stock for the arm blanks and cut them to rough size. Lay out the wedge shapes on a piece of 5/4 stock and cut out the wedges using the band saw. Feed the workpiece into the blade slowly to avoid burning it. To disguise the wedge, and make it appear that the arm is made from one piece of wood, it's important to get a good glue joint here. To ensure this, plane or sand the cut surface of the wedge so that it is smooth and flat. Glue and clamp the wedge to the arm. After the glue has set, cut the flat on the top of the arm using the band saw (**Fig. 8**). Proceed slowly to minimize burning. Clean off the saw marks by sanding or

using a hand plane.

Mark the location of the through mortises in each arm. Note that the angle of the rear leg mortises is not perpendicular to the adjacent arm surfaces. Bore a 1-in.-dia. hole in the center of each mortise to remove most of the waste. Clamp an arm to the workbench with support blocks under the workpiece to hold it at a slope. Cut the mortises to shape using a sharp chisel and work from both sides of the arm to prevent splintering where the mortise exits (**Fig. 9**).

Sand all parts before assembling the chair because it will be impossible to sand them afterward. Use 120-grit and 220-grit sandpaper, and dust off thoroughly between each grit. This should leave only minor touchup sanding after the chair is assembled. Also, ease all sharp corners with a finely set block plane or sandpaper before assembling the pieces.

Cut the backrest sides and backrest slats to dimension. Make a plywood template for the slat's curved shape, and

TECH *Tips*

Centerline Scriber

One of the more common challenges woodworkers face in a variety of projects is finding and marking the exact centerline of a piece of lumber. There is a trick that can help you do this.

You will find the center of boards quickly with this simple scriber. It's a very basic apparatus—an example of simplicity being the best workshop principle—made from a clean piece of wood (such as 1x2) and three nails.

The nails are hammered into the board, and must be in a direct line, with one at each end and one close to the middle of the board. The middle one must be centered exactly between the outer two. The center nail should penetrate the other side of the board just enough to scribe, while the other two go all the way through. Hold the scriber flat on the board to be marked, and adjust so that the outside nails are riding the edges of the board. Then pull to scribe.

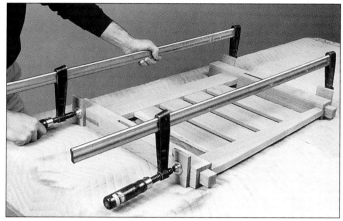

Fig. 11 *Glue and clamp the side slats to the side rails. Then glue and clamp this subassembly to the front and back legs.*

Fig. 12 *Glue and clamp the armrests to the side assemblies. Use scrap blocks to prevent marring and to spread the clamp pressure.*

trace the shape onto each blank.

Place the backrest sides and slat blanks flat on the worktable. Place the parts together in their appropriate positions and mark the location of the joining plate slots on each part. Hold the plate joiner and the workpiece firmly against the table. With the plate joiner held on the mark, make the plunge cut (**Fig. 10**).

Cut the inside curve on each slat using the band saw, then clamp each piece between bench dogs and use a cabinet scraper to remove the saw marks. Cut the outside curve on

Fig. 13 *After the side-arm assembly is complete, use a doweling jig to bore the holes for the backrest peg in each arm.*

Fig. 14 *Glue and clamp the side assemblies with the front and back rails. For adequate pressure, use two clamps at the front and back.*

Fig. 15 *Bore holes and install the threaded inserts in the rear legs. Lubricate the inserts with wax before installing them.*

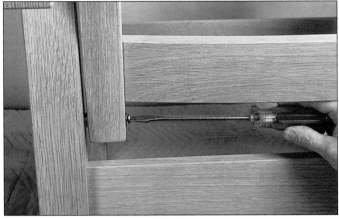

Fig. 16 *Drive a machine screw through the backrest side and into the insert. Use three washers between the leg and the side.*

the slats, and use either the scraper or belt sander to remove the saw marks. Locate and bore the holes in the backrest sides for the screws that mount the backrest to the chair base. Sand the backrest parts with 120- and 220-grit sandpaper, carefully easing all sharp edges. Dust off the parts and test fit them. Glue and clamp them together using biscuits at each joint.

Assembly

Begin assembly by gluing and clamping the side slats to the top and bottom side rails. Then glue and clamp each of these subassemblies to the front and back leg posts (**Fig. 11**). The bottom side rails have through tenons. To prevent glue from getting on the tenon end, apply glue sparingly on the tenon cheeks only. Next, glue and clamp an armrest to the side assembly (**Fig. 12**). Again, the top tenons on the legs go through the armrests. Therefore, apply glue only on the tenon cheeks. Before you move on to the next assembly, bore holes in the

armrest for the backrest pegs (**Fig. 13**), and bore the hole for the dowel peg that is driven through the arm into the leg tenon.

Join the side assemblies by gluing and clamping them together with the front and back rails (**Fig. 14**). Now cut the seat slats and ledger strips, and bore and counterbore pilot holes in the ledger strips and slats. Go ahead and install the ledgers and slats.

Using the doweling jig, bore holes in the rear legs and the backrest for the threaded inserts (in each rear leg) and the machine screw (through the side of the backrest).

Bore the peg holes at each of the remaining joint locations that have an exposed tenon. Using just a little glue, install an overlength peg at each joint. After the glue has set, pare the peg flush with a sharp chisel.

Lubricate the threaded inserts with a little paste wax and drive an insert into each back leg (**Fig. 15**). You can find these inserts at lumber yards, hardware stores, or larger home

Safety Sense

ON GUARD
Recently, machine guard violations topped the Occupational Safety and Health Administration's (OSHA) list of the most cited offenses for those workplaces with woodworking facilities. If this is a major problem among craftsman who make their living from working with wood, it is almost certainly endemic to those who do woodworking as a pastime. The irony is that removing or modifying guards is one of the most dangerous

things you can do in a workshop—and yet is one of the easiest situations to avoid because it has nothing to do with moving quickly or being tired (the major causes of serious workshop injuries).

Not only should you never remove or modify equipment guards, you should regularly inspect the guards on your machines to ensure that they are properly affixed and that they are not damaged in any way.

Fig. 17 *Bore and counterbore pilot holes for attaching the ottoman's slip seat. Use the drill press or a doweling guide to do this.*

Fig. 18 *Begin the ottoman assembly by gluing and clamping the side rails to the slats. Then glue and clamp this to the legs.*

centers. Complete the assembly by installing the backrest. Separate the backrest sides from the legs with three brass washers (**Fig. 16**).

The Ottoman

The construction of the ottoman uses the same techniques as the chair, but the legs are cut from solid 8/4 stock.

Cut the parts to dimension, then mark and cut the mortises and tenons.

Before proceeding to assembly, remember to bore and counterbore pilot holes through the top side rails (**Fig. 17**). The ottoman's seat is attached to the rails by screws driven through these holes.

Begin assembling the ottoman by gluing and clamping the slats to the front and back rails, then glue and clamp this subassembly to a pair of legs (**Fig. 18**). Bore and install pegs at the joints, then glue and clamp these subassemblies spanned by the remaining rails (**Fig. 19**).

You can now proceed to finish the two pieces. To achieve an authentic Arts & Crafts appearance, we used American walnut stain. We also used retarder to prevent lap marks.

Next, we carefully applied three coats of natural Danish oil finish. Apply the oil generously with a rag or brush, let it sit for about an hour, then wipe it off. Allow the oil to dry overnight between coats. After the last coat was thoroughly dry, we buffed the finish with 4/0 steel wool and polished with a soft cloth.

To complete the chair and ottoman in the most authentic manner, as well as to impart a luxurious touch, we had the cushions upholstered in leather.

Leather is expensive and special techniques are required to work it. For this reason, we went to a professional upholsterer to have the cushions made. To do this, it's best to bring the separate furniture pieces to the shop so that everything can be made to fit properly.

Fig. 19 *Join the ottoman side assemblies by gluing and clamping them with rails. One clamp should provide sufficient pressure.*

TOOL*Care*

New Life for Abrasives
Sanding discs and belts are some of the most commonly used equipment in the workshop, so preserving them can save a significant amount of money. A small block of acrylic plastic, such as Plexiglas or Lucite, when passed lightly over a moving sanding disc or belt, does a good job of removing embedded gum and pitch from the abrasive surface. Clogged sanding surfaces can be renewed this way several times before you have to replace them.

Reserved Seating

Oak, leather, and a truly classic design combine to make this the best seat in the house.

Of all woodworking's many facets, chair making is especially demanding. Along with a facility for joinery and finishing, a good chair maker must combine the skills of a structural engineer and the sensitivity of an ergonomics expert. Following the principles of Arts & Crafts furniture, our dining chair features straightforward, yet elegant and functional design. Mortise-and-tenon joinery and rectilinear components simplify construction. The finishing processes aren't that difficult to master, nor will you need to maintain the finishes. And you'll find that a complete set of dining chairs isn't that much harder to make than just one. Once you have a machine or tool set up to cut a particular part, it's not hard to keep cutting.

*Key*POINTS

TIME
Prep Time	1 hour
Shop Time	4 hours
Assembly Time	4 hours

EFFORT
Skill Level	intermediate

COST / BENEFITS
Expense: **moderate (per chair)**

• Signature **Arts & Crafts** style sets this chair apart, and makes it an ideal partner for a table with the same design style.

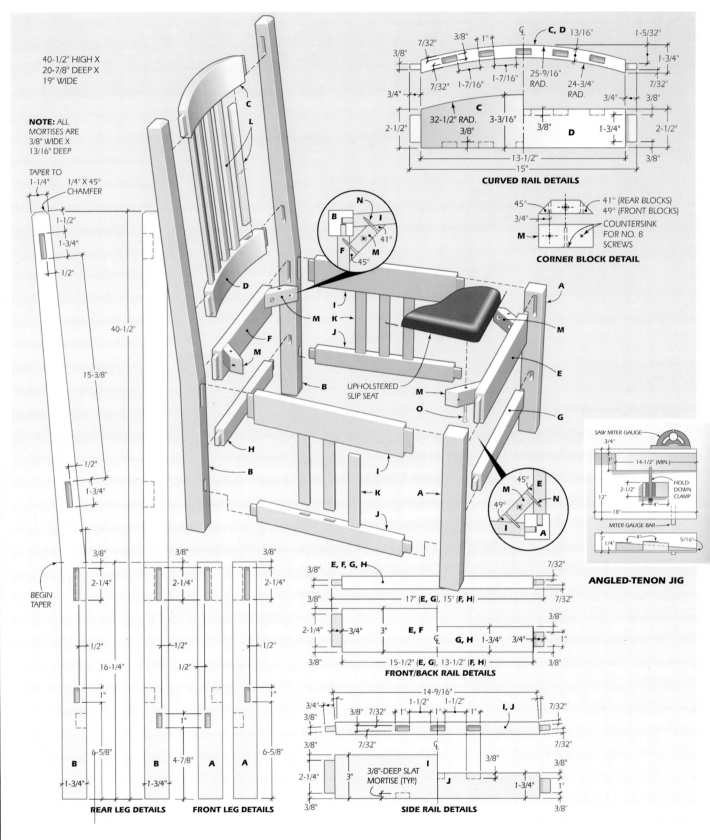

40-1/2" HIGH X
20-7/8" DEEP X
19" WIDE

NOTE: ALL
MORTISES ARE
3/8" WIDE X
13/16" DEEP

TAPER TO
1-1/4"
1/4" X 45°
CHAMFER

1-1/2"
1-3/4"
1/2"

C
L
C

40-1/2"

15-3/8"

1/2"

1-3/4"

BEGIN
TAPER

3/8"
2-1/4"

3/8"
2-1/4"

3/8"
2-1/4"

1/2"
16-1/4"

1/2"

1/2"

1"

1"

1"

1"

6-5/8"
B

B
4-7/8"
A

A
6-5/8"

1-3/4"

1-3/4"

REAR LEG DETAILS   **FRONT LEG DETAILS**

CURVED RAIL DETAILS

7/32"   3/8"   1"   C   C, D   13/16"   1-5/32"
3/8"   1-3/4"
7/32"   1-7/16"   1-7/16"   25-9/16" RAD.   24-3/4" RAD.   7/32"
3/4"
2-1/2"   32-1/2" RAD.   C   3-3/16"   3/8"   D   1-3/4"   2-1/2"
3/8"   3/8"
13-1/2"
15"

45°   41° (REAR BLOCKS)   49° (FRONT BLOCKS)
3/4"   COUNTERSINK
M   FOR NO. 8
SCREWS

CORNER BLOCK DETAIL

B   N   I
F   M
45°   41°

A   M   I
K   J

UPHOLSTERED
SLIP SEAT

M   O

E
G

A   K   A   J

M   45°   E   N
49°   I   A

SAW MITER GAUGE
3/4"
3"   14-1/2" (MIN.)
HOLD-DOWN
CLAMP
2-1/2"   4"
12"
18"
MITER GAUGE BAR
3"
1/4"   4"   5/16"

ANGLED-TENON JIG

3/8"   E, F, G, H   7/32"
3/8"   17" (E, G), 15" (F, H)   7/32"
3/8"
2-1/4"   3/4"   3"   E, F   G, H   1-3/4"   3/4"   1"
3/8"   15-1/2" (E, G), 13-1/2" (F, H)   3/8"

FRONT/BACK RAIL DETAILS

14-9/16"
3/4"   1-1/2"   1-1/2"   I, J   7/32"
3/8"   3/8"   7/32"   1"   1"   1"   1"
3/8"   7/32"
3/8"   I   3/8"
2-1/4"   3"   3/8"-DEEP SLAT   J   1-3/4"   1"
MORTISE (TYP.)
3/8"   3/8"

SIDE RAIL DETAILS

Our chair features an upholstered seat, so that you have the opportunity to coordinate the chair with your decor. You might choose a fabric for the seat, or go with the traditional leather as we did. We had an upholsterer supply the seats for a set of chairs. The chairs are constructed of 4/4 and 8/4 quarter-sawn white oak. If you do not have access to a planer, have your supplier surface the material to thicknesses of 13⁄16 in. and 1¾ in.

Making the Parts

Begin construction by ripping and crosscutting stock to size for the front legs. Then cut two 4x4 2-in. blanks for the rear legs. Make a cardboard template for the rear legs and trace around it to transfer the shape to each blank. Saw to the waste side of the line with a band saw or sabre saw, and use a sharp plane to trim each leg square and to finished dimension (**Fig. 1**).

Clearly mark the mortise locations on all the chair legs. To make this job easier, clamp several legs together with the ends held even and mark across them using a straightedge or square as a guide.

Install a ⅜-in.-dia. spiral up-cutting bit in your router, and use an edge guide to carefully rout the mortises in the legs

Materials List

Key	No.	Size and description (use)
A	2	1¾ x 1¾ x 16¼" oak (front leg)
B	2	1¾ x 3¾ x 40½" oak (rear leg)
C	1	1¾ x 3 3⁄16 x 15" oak (top rail)
D	1	1¾ x 2½ x 15" oak (bottom rail)
E	1	13⁄16 x 3 x 17" oak (top front rail)
F	1	13⁄16 x 3 x 15" oak (top back rail)
G	1	13⁄16 x 1¾x 17" (lower front rail)
H	1	13⁄16 x 1¾ x 15" oak (lower back rail)
I	2	13⁄16 x 3 x 16¼" oak (top side rail)
J	2	13⁄16 x 1¾ x 16¼" (lower side rail)
K	6	⅜ x 1 x 7¾" oak (side slat)
L	5	⅜ x 1 x 15⅜" oak (back slat)
M	4	13⁄16 x 1½ x 3⅝" (corner block)
N	8	1½" No. 8 fh wood screw
O	4	2¼" No. 8 fh wood screw

Misc.: Medium fumed oak aniline dye; sealer/finish.

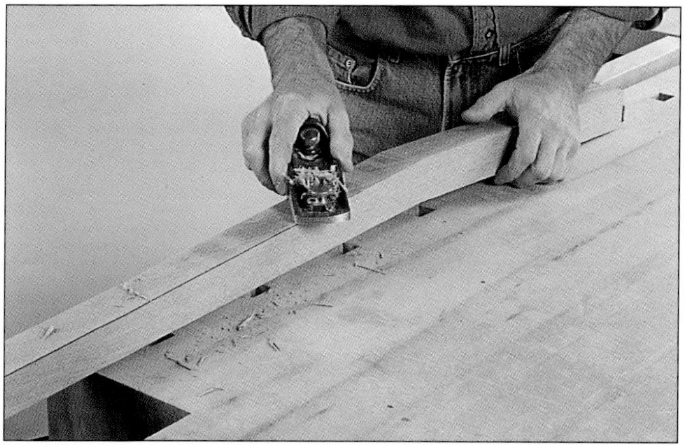

Fig. 1 ***After sawing the rear leg shape, use a sharp plane to remove the saw marks and trim the leg to exact size.***

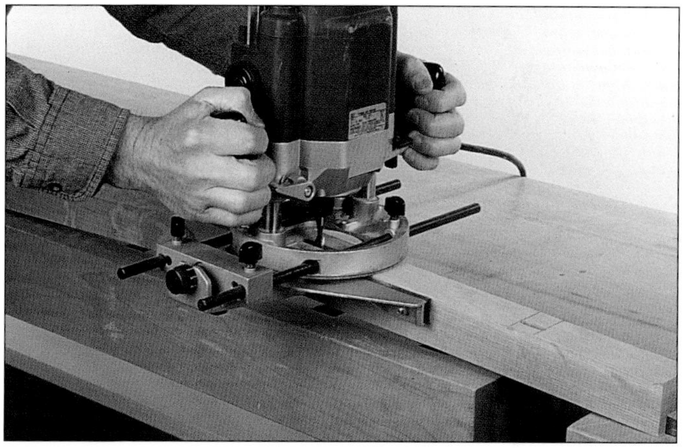

Fig. 2 ***Mark the mortise locations in the chair legs, and use a plunge router with a spiral up-cutting bit and an edge guide to cut the mortises.***

(**Fig. 2**). Square the rounded mortise ends with a sharp chisel.

Cut blanks of 1¾-in.-thick stock for the curved back rails. Before cutting their curved profiles, use a table saw and dado blade to cut the tenons at the ends of the pieces (**Fig. 3**). Note that the tenons are not centered across the thickness of the blanks.

Cut one side of all the tenons first, then readjust the blade height to cut the other side. It's best to cut the tenons about 1⁄32 in. thicker than indicated, and then use a sharp chisel to pare the surfaces smooth and bring the tenons to finished dimension.

Make a cardboard template for the back-rail shape and use it to transfer the shape to each blank. Use a band saw to cut the inside curve of each rail (**Fig. 4**). Then remove the saw marks and smooth the curved shape with a spokeshave (**Fig. 5**). Go back to the band saw to cut the outside curve and smooth that surface with either a block plane or spokeshave.

Fig. 3 *Use a table saw and dado blade to cut the tenons in the blanks for the curved back rails. These tenons are not centered.*

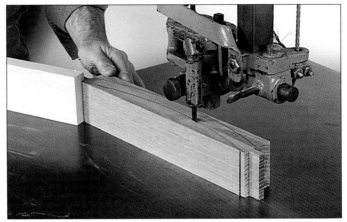

Fig. 4 *Lay out the back-rail curve onto the edge of each rail blank. Then cut the inside curve on the band saw.*

Fig. 7 *When cutting the opposite tenon faces on the rails, reverse the ramp on the jig and readjust the dado blade height.*

Fig. 8 *Finish the rail tenons by cutting the top and bottom shoulders with the miter gauge and dado blade in the table saw.*

Don't cut the arched profile of the top rails at this time, we'll get to that step later.

Cut stock for the lower front and back rails to finished dimension and use a dado blade in the table saw to cut the tenons. Readjust the blade height and hold the rails on edge to cut the top and bottom shoulders at each rail end.

Next, cut stock to size for the side rails. Study the drawing carefully to be sure that you thoroughly understand the angled tenons on these pieces. Distinctly label each rail with its location in the chair to avoid any confusion when it comes time to cut the joints.

We built a jig to cut the angled tenons (see Angled-Tenon Jig on the illustration). To construct the jig, first attach a hardwood fence to a plywood base, and then screw the assembly to your table saw miter gauge. Glue up four pieces of ¾-in.-thick stock and band saw the stack into a ramp with an angle of 4°. Screw the ramp to the plywood base. To use

the jig, hold a rail on the ramp and push the jig past the dado blade. We used a hold-down clamp mounted on a tapered hardwood block to hold the workpiece.

Cut one surface of each tenon with the ramp angled down toward the dado blade (**Fig. 6**). Then secure the ramp in the opposite direction and readjust the blade height for the opposite side of each tenon (**Fig. 7**). If you're using the hold-down clamp as we have described, you'll need to remount it. Then you'll use the miter gauge without the jig to make the angled cuts for the top and bottom shoulders of the side rails (**Fig. 8**).

Cut strips for the side and back slats. Crosscut the slats to finished length and set them aside.

Lay out the slat mortises in the side rails and in the curved back rails. Mark the side-rail mortises by clamping several rails together and marking across the stack with a square. Mark the curved rails individually.

Fig. 5 *Use a spokeshave to smooth the inside curve of the back rail, and then cut and smooth the outer curve.*

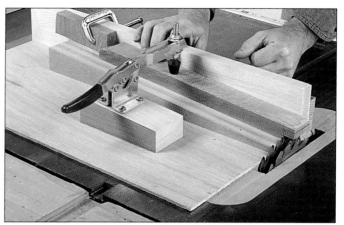

Fig. 6 *To cut the angled tenons on the side rails, support the stock in a table saw jig that holds the work at a 4° angle.*

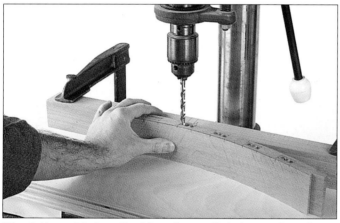

Fig. 9 *Use a ⁵⁄₁₆-in.-dia. bit to bore slightly overlapping holes to remove most of the waste from each slat mortise.*

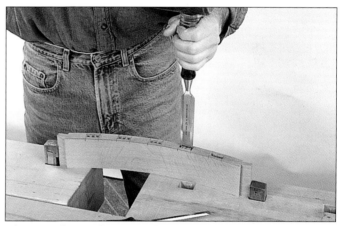

Fig. 10 *Trim and square the slat-mortise walls with a sharp chisel. Then test fit the slats—they should be quite snug.*

Install a ⁵⁄₁₆-in.-dia. bit in the drill press and bore slightly overlapping holes to remove most of the waste from the mortises in both the curved and straight rails (**Fig. 9**). Then use a sharp chisel to pare the walls and square the ends of the mortises (**Fig. 10**).

Test a slat in each mortise—the fit should be snug. Make another template for the arched shape of the top back rail and use the template to trace the shape onto the workpiece. Use a sabre saw to cut the profile (**Fig. 11**).

Now you'll need to mark the shoulders on the top and bottom edges of the curved back rails and use a small backsaw to make the cuts (**Fig. 12**). First, make the cuts into the endgrain of the tenon. Then finish the shoulder by cutting across the grain.

Place guide marks for the ¼-in. chamfer at the top end of each rear leg. Clamp a leg in the bench vise and use a sharp block plane to cut the chamfers.

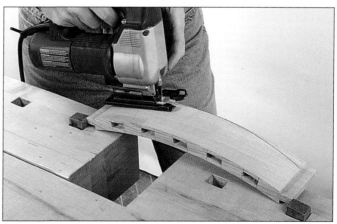

Fig. 11 *Use a template to lay out the arched profile of the upper back rail. Then cut to the line with a sabre saw and then smooth the surface.*

Fig. 12 *Cut the shoulders of the curved back rail tenons with a small backsaw. First cut in from the end, then across the grain.*

Assembly

Sand all parts with 120-, 150-, 180-, and 220-grit sandpaper, dusting thoroughly between grits. Spread glue on the mating surfaces for the front-leg/front-rail joints. Use a small shim to spread glue in the leg mortises and a small brush for the tenons. Spread the glue sparingly on the tenons to avoid excessive squeeze-out at the joints.

Join the rails to the front legs, then clamp the joints and compare opposite diagonal measurements to be sure the assembly is square (**Fig. 13**). Let the glue set for about 20 minutes and pare off any excess. Next, insert the side slats in the mortises of the bottom side rails and position the top side rail over the slat ends. Although you don't need glue in the slat joints, a drop of glue in a loose joint will keep the slat from rattling. Temporarily clamp the rails and slats (**Fig. 14**).

Spread glue in the open mortises of the front-leg assembly and on the front tenons of the side rails, and join the side

Fig. 13 *Join the front rails to the legs and clamp. Compare opposite diagonal measurements to check for square.*

rails to the legs (**Fig. 15**). Join the back slats to the curved rails (**Fig. 16**) and temporarily clamp the assembly. Again, it's not necessary to glue these joints unless a slat is loose. Spread glue on the tenons of the back rails and in the matching mortises in the back legs. Join the rails to the legs, clamp, and compare opposite diagonal measurements (**Fig. 17**).

Once the glue has set on the subassemblies, complete the chair frame by joining the side rails to the back-leg assembly. Spread glue on the mating surfaces and position the joints. Apply clamps to pull the joints tight.Set the chair upright on a flat worktable to be sure that all four legs sit evenly (**Fig. 18**). Adjust the clamps and joints, if necessary, until any rocking is eliminated.

Cut corner blocks to reinforce the joints and provide a means for attaching the seat. Note that the angles for the blocks at the front of the chair are different than those for the rear blocks. Use a miter box to cut the blocks. If your miter

Fig. 16 *Join the back slats to the curved rails. If a slat is too loose in its mortise, add a drop of glue to keep it from rattling.*

Fig. 17 *Join the back rail and slats to the legs. Apply the glue sparingly, clamp, and check that the diagonals are equal.*

Fig. 14 *Join the side slats to the rails. It's not necessary to use glue because the slats are held captive between the rails.*

Fig. 15 *Spread glue on the rail and leg mating surfaces. Join the side rails to the front leg assembly and clamp.*

box won't handle the 41° angle for the rear blocks, make the cuts on a band saw.

Bore and countersink pilot holes through the width of the blocks for attaching the seats. Use a clamp to hold each block in place while you bore and countersink pilot holes for attaching it to the rails (**Fig. 19**). A combination bit and countersink is the most efficient tool for the job. Fasten the blocks to the rails with 1½-in. No. 8 screws.

Finishing

First inspect each chair for scratches, and sand if necessary. We used a water-soluble aniline dye for a beautiful, clear, and lightfast color. To eliminate raised grain problems, completely wipe the chairs with a sponge dampened with clean water. Let the wood dry completely and lightly sand the surface with 220-grit sandpaper.

Follow the manufacturer's directions for mixing and

applying the dye, and be sure to allow sufficient drying time before applying a finish.

For our finish, we used a commonly available sealer/finish. You can brush or wipe on the first coat, which will soak into the wood readily.

Allow the finish to dry overnight. Lightly sand with 320-grit sandpaper and remove all the dust. For the next and subsequent coats, apply the finish and let it sit for about 30 minutes before wiping off any excess. Then let the finish dry overnight.

At this point, you will sand between coats only if the finish is rough. After three or four coats, burnish the surface with 4/0 steel wool to remove any rough spots, and polish with a soft cloth.

Finally, attach the finished slip seats to the frames with screws installed through the corner blocks into the underside of each seat.

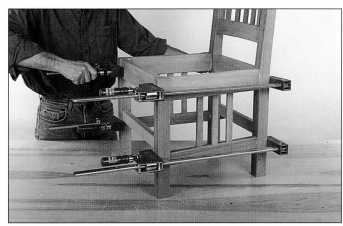

Fig. 18 *Join the back subassembly to the front-leg/side-rail assembly. Work on a flat surface so that the legs remain even.*

Fig. 19 *Use a clamp to hold the corner blocks in position as you bore and countersink pilot holes for fastening to the rails.*

Easy Street

This cozy armchair has soft cushions and an adjustable back that make it perfect for relaxing.

After a hard day in the workshop, there's little that beats settling down into a soft, cushioned armchair. And, if you've made the chair yourself, it's twice the pleasure. Our design is based on Mission-style furniture that was commonly produced in the early 20th century. In contrast to the real thing, we've lightened the proportions to give the chair a more contemporary look and replaced the Mission's typical dark oak with warm, easy-to-work pine. Complete with foam cushions covered in white duck fabric, it's destined to become the favorite chair in any woodworker's household. You may even have to compete with others in the house for time in the chair.

*Key*POINTS

TIME
Prep Time . . . . **10 hours**
Shop Time . . . . **20 hours**
Assembly Time . . . . **18 hours**

EFFORT
Skill Level . . . . **intermediate**

COST / BENEFITS
Expense: **moderate**
• This is an **updated version of a classic** that suits any modern family or living room.
• The design of this chair focuses on strong construction built for **comfort**.

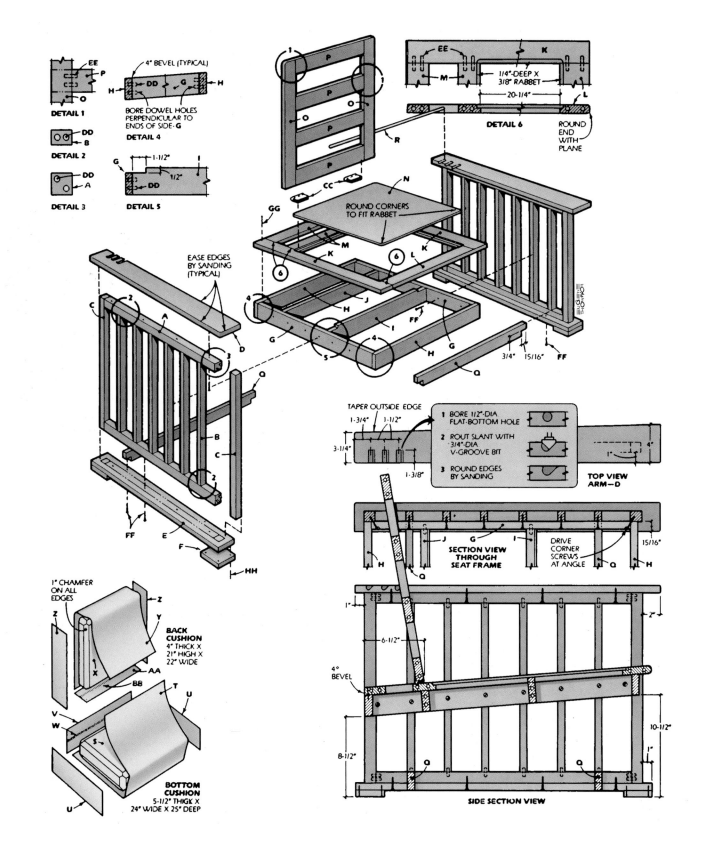

DETAIL 1

EE
P
O

DETAIL 2

DD
B

DETAIL 3

DD
A

DETAIL 4

4" BEVEL (TYPICAL)
DD
H — G — H
BORE DOWEL HOLES
PERPENDICULAR TO
ENDS OF SIDE·G

DETAIL 5

G
1-1/2"
1/2"
DD

4" BEVEL (TYPICAL)

I

P
P
P
P
O
R
CC
GG

DETAIL 6

EE
K
1/4"-DEEP X
3/8" RABBET
M
20-1/4"
L
ROUND
END
WITH
PLANE

N
ROUND CORNERS
TO FIT RABBET
M
K
6
K
L
6
J
H
FF
I
4
H
G
S
G
H
FF
3/4" 15/16" FF
Q

EASE EDGES
BY SANDING
(TYPICAL)

C
2
A
D
3
2
Q
B
C
FF
E
F
HH

TAPER OUTSIDE EDGE
1-3/4"
1-1/2"
3-1/4"
1-3/8"

1 BORE 1/2"-DIA
FLAT-BOTTOM HOLE
2 ROUT SLANT WITH
3/4"-DIA
V-GROOVE BIT
3 ROUND EDGES
BY SANDING

TOP VIEW
ARM—D
4"
1"

1" CHAMFER
ON ALL
EDGES

Z
Z
Y
X
AA
BB

BACK
CUSHION
4" THICK X
21" HIGH X
22" WIDE

T
U
V
W
S
U

BOTTOM
CUSHION
5-1/2" THICK X
24" WIDE X 25" DEEP

J G I
DRIVE
CORNER
SCREWS
AT ANGLE
15/16"
H
Q
Q
H
SECTION VIEW
THROUGH
SEAT FRAME

1"
6-1/2"
4°
BEVEL
8-1/2"
4° BEVEL
Q
Q
2"
10-1/2"
1"
Q
Q

SIDE SECTION VIEW

The chair is made of ¾-in.-thick stock, with the exception of the framing around the spindles. The 1⅛-in.-thick stock that you'll need for these pieces is called 5/4 stock. Aside from pine's good looks and workability, we chose it because it's commonly available and relatively inexpensive. Although our chair may look like it's made from clear stock, we used ordinary No. 2 common pine and simply worked around the knots. If possible, bring your tape measure and materials list along when you buy the wood, and choose boards that will produce the least waste. Then lay out all the chair components on your lumber so that the knots are avoided, and cut each piece oversize.

Start with the Sides

Begin the side frames by ripping the 5/4 frame stock to about $\frac{1}{16}$ in. oversize, planing the sawn edges to exact width, and crosscutting the pieces to length. Then rip and smooth the ¾ x 1⅛-in. spindles the same way.

The frames are assembled with dowel-reinforced butt joints—use a doweling jig to ensure straight, accurately placed holes.

Because there's so little surface area on the ends of the spindles, it makes sense to gang them together in groups of six when boring the dowel holes (**Fig. 1**). Bore the end holes in the 1⅛-in.-square horizontal frame members in exactly the same way.

While the horizontal frame members are clamped together, carefully lay out the spindle positions with a square (**Fig. 2**). Then separate the four pieces and use your doweling jig to bore the holes for joining the spindles to the frame

Fig. 1 ***Use a doweling jig to bore holes in the side pieces. Ganging pieces together helps with the jig alignment and speeds up the work.***

Materials List

Key	No.	Size and description (use)
A	4	1⅛ x 1⅛ x 27¾" pine (side horizontal)
B	12	¾ x 1⅛ x 17¾" pine (spindle)
C	4	1⅛ x 1⅛ x 20" pine (side upright)
D	2	¾ x 4 x 33" pine (arm)
E	2	¾ x 3 x 32" pine (base)
F	4	¾ x 3 x 3" pine (foot)
G*	2	¾ x 2¼ x 28½" pine (frame side)
H*	2	¾ x 2⅜ x 24" pine (frame front)
I	1	¾ x 2¾ x 22½" pine (crossmember)
J	1	¾ x 2¼ x 22½" pine (crossmember)
K	2	¾ x 2¼ x 31" pine (seat frame side)
L	1	¾ x 3 x 19½" pine (seat frame front)
M	2	¾ x 2¼ x 19½" pine (seat frame inner/rear)
N	1	¼ x 20¼ x 21" plywood (seat)
O	2	¾ x 2½ x 22" pine (back frame side)
P	4	¾ x 2½ x 15½" pine (crossmember)
Q	2	¾ x 1⅞ x 24" pine (base cross tie)
R	1	$\frac{7}{16}$"-dia. x 24$\frac{11}{16}$" steel rod
S	1	5½ x 24 x 25" foam (bottom cushion)
T	1	25¼ x 56¾" fabric (top, front, bottom)
U	2	6¾ x 26¼" side boxing
V	2	4⅜ x 25¼" back boxing
W	1	24" zipper
X	1	2 x 21 x 22" foam (back cushion)
Y	1	23¼ x 47¼" fabric (front, top, back)
Z	2	5¼ x 22¼" side boxing
AA	2	3⅝ x 23¼" bottom boxing
BB	1	22" zipper
CC	2	2½ x 1$\frac{9}{16}$" butt hinge
DD‡		¼"-dia. x 1" dowel
EE‡		¼"-dia. x 1½" dowel
FF‡		1½" No. 10 fh screw
GG‡		2" finishing nail
HH‡		1¼" finishing nail

Misc.: Glue; sandpaper; oil finish; satin finish varnish.
*Overall dimension.
‡As required.

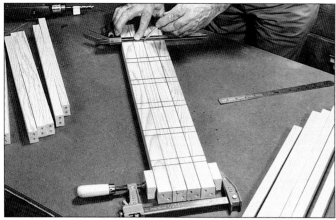

Fig. 2 *To space the spindles accurately, clamp the horizontal frame members squarely together when marking the spindle locations.*

Fig. 3 *Align the doweling jig at each spindle location and bore ¼-in.-dia. x ⁹⁄₁₆-in.-deep holes. The tape on the bit indicates the boring depth.*

Fig. 4 *Place the side frame pieces on a flat board and clamp for gang sanding. The wood strips between the stock and the clamps protect the stock.*

(**Fig. 3**). It's best to sand the frame components before they're assembled. After the dowel holes have been bored in the horizontal frame members and spindles, lay similar pieces together on a flat board and sand them in groups to avoid rounding the corners excessively (**Fig. 4**).

Next, prepare to assemble the side frames by applying glue sparingly to the holes in the horizontal members and then clamp them (**Fig. 5**). Check the assembly for square by measuring the diagonals, and then repeat the procedure for the other side frame.

After the glue has set, use the dowel centers inserted in the ends of horizontal members to mark the hole locations on the vertical frame members (**Fig. 6**). As you did before, apply glue sparingly and join the vertical members to the frame assembly.

While the glue is drying, cut the base pieces and feet to exact size as shown in the drawing, and sand them. Glue and

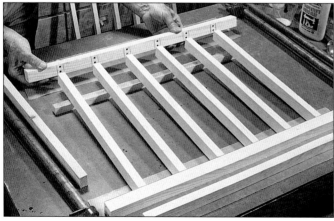

Fig. 5 *Apply glue to the dowel holes, assemble the spindles to the horizontal pieces, and clamp. Check the assembly for square by measuring the diagonals.*

Fig. 6 *Use the dowel centers for locating the dowel holes in the vertical frame pieces. The stock clamped to the frame ensures alignment.*

nail the feet to the bases with 4d finishing nails. Then clamp the bases to the frames and bore and countersink the screw pilot holes (**Fig. 7**). Secure them with 1½-in. No. 10 fh screws.

Making the Arms

Each arm features angled slots that hold the ends of the ⁷⁄₁₆-in.-dia. steel rod. As the rod is moved from one slot to the next, the back angle changes.

First, cut the stock for the arms to 4 in. wide and to exact length. Then lay out the three ½-in.-dia. hole positions on each arm as shown in the drawing. Center the holes just slightly more than ¼ in. from the stock face. Use a brad-point drill with a doweling jig or drill press and bore the holes 1⅜ in. deep (**Fig. 8**).

Then install a V-groove bit in your router. Clamp the stock in your worktable and secure a stop along the edge of the arm to limit router travel. A straight strip clamped squarely across the stock is used to guide the router.

Adjust the guide and bit depth so that the cut will be tangent to the hole and then rout the forward edge of each hole (**Fig. 9**).

Finish by carefully sanding with an emery board and a dowel wrapped with sandpaper (**Fig. 10**).

After the slots are finished, lay out the tape along the outside edge of each arm. Saw the taper leaving approximately ¹⁄₁₆ in. space, and then trim the line with a hand plane.

Temporarily clamp each arm to the top of each frame. Secure with 1½-in. No. 10 screws driven from the underside of the top frame members.

Seat and Back Frame

The seat support structure is composed of a box frame that will be attached to the sides and a top frame that holds a plywood panel.

Fig. 8 *The angled slots are started by boring ¹⁄₂-in.-dia. holes near the face of the arm stock. Use a brad-point drill bit for the best results.*

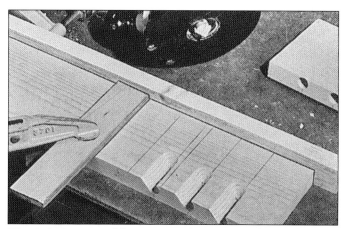

Fig. 9 *A V-groove bit routes a slope on the forward edge of the slots. Clamp the strip securely to the guide router. The strip at the edge limits router travel.*

Fig. 7 *After assembling the base and feet, clamp the base to the frame, and bore and countersink the screw pilot holes. Then secure.*

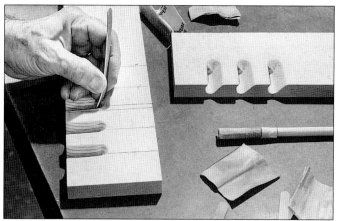

Fig. 10 *Finish the angled slots by hand sanding. An emery board and a dowel wrapped with sandpaper help working in the tight space.*

Fig. 11 *Use a doweling jig at the end of the mitered sides of the box frame. A simple shopmade jig guides the bit for matching the holes in the stock face.*

Fig. 12 *After the seat frame is assembled, use a ³⁄₈-in. rabbeting bit to rout the ¹⁄₄-in.-deep rabbet that holds the plywood seat.*

Fig. 13 *Clamp the seat box frame to the side and bore and countersink pilot holes. Holes at each end are bored at an angle to reach the frame.*

First, rip the box frame side components to the appropriate width. Lay out the 4° miters on the ends and trim the stock to length.

The front and rear box frame components are then ripped to width at a 4° bevel and cut to length. Prepare the crossmembers by cutting to size, notching the ends of crossmember (**Part I**), and boring the dowel holes as shown in the drawing.

Bore dowel holes in the ends of the side pieces. The doweling jig ensures that these holes will be perpendicular to the mitered-end surfaces. Then bore corresponding holes in the front and rear pieces and bore the holes in the sides to receive the crossmembers.

A simple shopmade guide insures straight and accurate holes when boring into the stock face (**Fig. 11**). Make your own by copying the one shown here. Assemble the box frame and clamp until the glue sets.

Construct the seat and back frame by cutting pieces to size and joining with dowels as shown in the drawing. Install a ³⁄₈-in. rabbeting bit in your router and set the depth of a cut to ¼ in. Then rout the recess in the seat frame that holds the plywood panel (**Fig. 12**). Cut the plywood seat to size and round the corners as shown in the drawing.

Lay a chair side on your worktable and place the box frame in position. Bore and countersink screw pilot holes, secure the frame, and then attach the other side (**Fig. 13 and 14**). Note that the front and rear of the frame is secured by screws driven at an angle. Then install the cross ties between bases.

Place the seat frame in position and check for fit. Then attach the hinges to the back of the frame. Insert the steel rod in the slots and position the back so that it leans squarely against the rod. Mark the hinge positions on the seat frame and bore the screw holes (**Fig. 15**). Unscrew the box frame from the sides and secure the seat frame to the box frame with 6d finishing nails. Set the nails and fill.

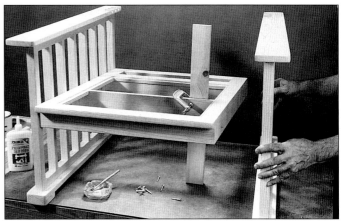

Fig. 14 *Use scrap stock clamped to the box frame for supporting the seat assembly when aligning the other side. Secure it with screws.*

Fig. 15 *Secure the hinges to the back first. Then insert the rod and place the back in position. Carefully mark the hinge screw locations on the seat frame.*

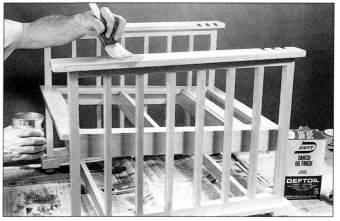

Fig. 16 *Two coats of oil finish are applied for a clear, durable finish. For extra protection, apply a last coat of polyurethane.*

Finish sand the entire chair and gently round all harsh corners.

Cushions and Finish

We finished our chair with clear, oil finish to give the wood a warm glow and enhance the beauty of the grain. This type of penetrating oil soaks deep into the wood and contains urethane resins that harden upon drying to help protect the typically soft surface of the pine. The finish is actually more durable than you might expect, and is completely appropriate for a high-use piece such as this.

The finish is brushed on heavily and the excess is wiped off after about a half hour. A second coat is applied after the first has dried for one hour. This finish is easy to work with because dust and brush marks are eliminated.

Although the penetrating oil finish stands up well on its own, extra protection can be achieved by applying a final top coat of satin or gloss finish polyurethane (**Fig. 16**).

The cushions are made from foam blocks covered with almond-colored duck fabric. Because the foam is generally available in thicknesses of up to 4 in., you'll have to add a 1½-in.-thick piece when making the seat cushion. Use a spray adhesive suitable for use on foam to join the pieces.

You can usually have the foam cut to the required sizes by your supplier. If you're going to cut it yourself, an electric carving knife or serrated bread knife will do the job. For a professional look, don't forget to chamfer the corners of the foam as shown on the drawing.

The fabric sizes in the materials list allow ⅝ in. on each edge for the seams. The sewing is done inside out starting with the installation of the zippers.

Then attach the side boxing strips followed by the large pieces that cover the cushion faces. Pull the covers inside out through the zipper opening and insert the foam.

TECH *Tips*

Milled Joints
Milled joints, such as the tongue-and-groove and shaped glue joint, make stock alignment and assembly easy, while increasing the surface area for a stronger glue joint. These joints can be made on a table saw or shaper.

To make a tongue-and-groove joint on a table saw, first install a dado blade and set the width for the width of the groove—usually one-third the stock thickness. Set the fence for a centered cut, and cut the groove. Making the tongue requires two cuts—one on each side of the edge of the mating piece.

You can also use a molding head with tongue-and-groove cutters. These specially shaped cutters are more efficient because they enable you to complete the joint in two passes.

The shaped glue joint is made with a single glue-joint cutter that produces both mating pieces. To use the cutter, first shape the edge of the first piece. Then shape the edge of the second piece, flip the piece over, and join the two. Because of the reversible profile, the faces will be aligned.

When making any of these milled joints on a table saw, always secure a wooden board to the metal table saw fence so that the fence can be adjusted up to the cutter.

Super Sofa

This turn-of-the-century couch design is still eminently stylish today.

One of the most well-known proponents of the American Arts & Crafts movement in the early 1900s was Gustav Stickley. He designed and manufactured a line known as Craftsman furniture, while his younger brothers, Leopold and J. George Stickley, developed their own line of furniture. The popularity of these styles encouraged other designers to follow suit. Today, the term Mission furniture refers loosely to the work of various builders influenced by the Stickley family. Our sofa project is based on one of Leopold and J. George Stickley's designs. You'll find the style and comfort fit right in whatever your other furnishings.

*Key*POINTS

TIME

Prep Time	8 hours
Shop Time	18 hours
Assembly Time	12 hours

EFFORT

Skill Level	advanced

COST / BENEFITS

Expense: **expensive**

- **Stickley design** is a classic example of Arts & Crafts styling—beautiful enough for the well-appointed living room, rugged enough for a rough-and-tumble den.

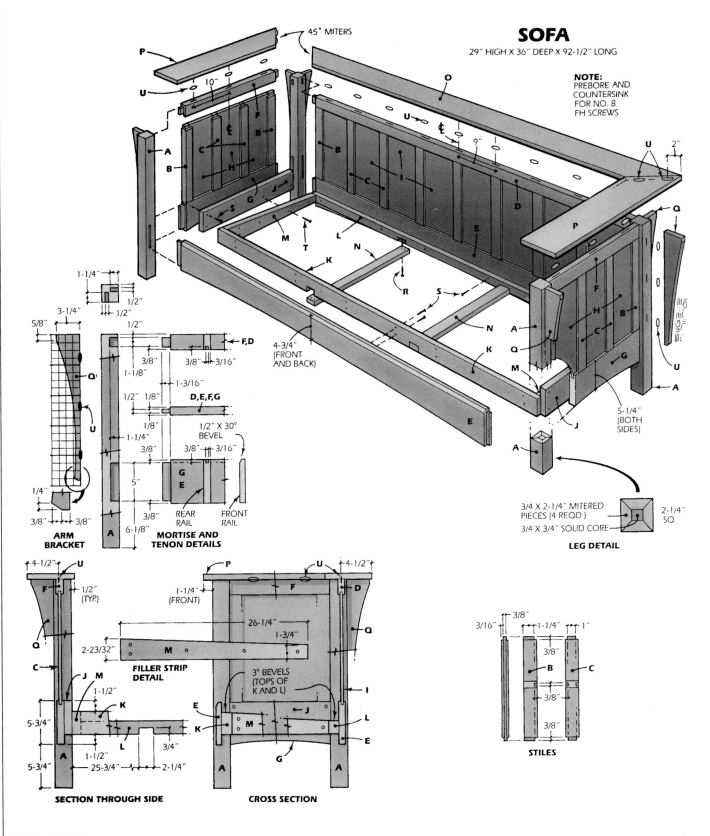

SOFA
29" HIGH X 36" DEEP X 92-1/2" LONG

NOTE:
PREBORE AND
COUNTERSINK
FOR NO. 8
FH SCREWS

45° MITERS

4-3/4"
(FRONT
AND BACK)

5-1/4"
(BOTH
SIDES)

ARM BRACKET

MORTISE AND TENON DETAILS

1/2" X 30° BEVEL

REAR RAIL

FRONT RAIL

D,E,F,G

F,D

LEG DETAIL

3/4 X 2-1/4" MITERED PIECES (4 REQD)
3/4 X 3/4" SOLID CORE

2-1/4" SQ.

SECTION THROUGH SIDE

FILLER STRIP DETAIL

2-23/32"

26-1/4"

1-3/4"

CROSS SECTION

3° BEVELS
(TOPS OF K AND L)

STILES

A lthough you could use most any hardwood for this piece, quarter-sawn white oak is the wood generally associated with the style. After building our sofa, we had an upholsterer make the cushions. Although leather would be the traditional choice, we chose a vinyl material that resembles leather in both appearance and feel. The core of each cushion is Dacron-wrapped foam. To support the cushions, our upholsterer installed a rubber mat to the interior cleats shown in the drawing. Alternatively, you could modify the cleats and install slats to support the seat cushions.

Start with the Legs

Construct the legs by gluing up four strips of stock, with mitered edges, around a ¾-in-square central core. First cut stock to rough size for the leg faces. Then set up the table saw to cut the 45° angles along both edges of each strip. To achieve good results, make sure your table saw is adjusted to exactly 45°, or the corner joints will not come together properly. Clamp a featherboard hold-down to the table saw rip fence (**Fig. 1**). This will keep your fingers away from the blade and help yield a smoother surface on the mitered edges.

After ripping the mitered edges, readjust the saw and cut the four central core pieces for the legs.

Apply glue to all the mitered edges and all sides of the central core strip. Loosely assemble the pieces, then apply clamps (**Fig. 2**). After about 30 minutes, scrape off any excess

Fig. 1 *Rip the mitered leg sides on a table saw. A featherboard clamped to the table fence holds the stock for a smoother, more accurate cut.*

Fig. 2 *After applying glue to the core and the mitered side pieces, clamp the assembly until the glue sets. Alternate the clamps for even pressure.*

Materials List

Key	No.	Size and description (use)
A*	4	2¼ x 2¼ x 28¼" oak** (leg)
B	6	¾ x 1¾ x 15½" oak (end stile)
C	11	¾ x 1¾ x 15½" oak (middle stile)
D	1	¾ x 2 x 82⅞" oak (back top rail)
E	2	¾ x 5¾ x 82⅞" oak (wide rail)
F	2	¾ x 2 x 28⅞" oak (side top rail)
G	2	¾ x 5¾ x 28⅞" oak (side bottom rail)
H	6	⅜ x 7⅛ x 15½" oak (side panel)
I	8	⅜ x 8¹¹⁄₁₆ x 15½" oak (back panel)
J	2	1⅛ x 4¼ x 26½" maple (filler)
K	1	1¼ x 2¾ x 80½" maple (front cleat)
L	1	1¼ x 1¾ x 80½" maple (back cleat)
M	2	1¼ x 2²³⁄₃₂ x 26¼" maple (side cleat)

Key	No.	Size and description (use)
N	2	¾ x 2¼ x 28¾" maple (cross brace)
O	1	¾ x 6½ x 92½" oak (back arm)
P	2	¾ x 6½ x 36" oak (side arm)
Q	7	¾ x 3¼ x 19¼" oak (arm bracket)
R	8	1½" No. 8 fh screw
S	26	1¾" No. 8 fh screw
T	10	2" No. 8 fh screw
U**		No. 20 joining plates (as required)

Misc.: Transparent finish; English brown aniline dye.

*Overall dimension given. Build from four mitered ¾-in.-thick boards with square core as shown.

**Quarter-sawn white oak.

Fig. 3 *Use a plunge router and edge guide to cut the leg mortises. A spare leg clamped to the side of the workpiece helps to support the router.*

Fig. 4 *After the mortises have been routed, use a sharp chisel to square the mortise ends so that the rail tenons will fit snugly.*

TECH *Tips*

Jointer End Grain Planing
Planing end grain with a jointer almost always chips and splinters the wood at the end of the cut. But this won't happen if you first make a short cut with the jointer and then reverse the work to complete the cut. The knives of the cutter head merely pass under the initial cut without cutting, resulting in a good looking, chip-free corner. Remember that the ends of a board should always be planed first, then the sides—with the grain—for the best results.

glue with a spokeshave or plane, and then let the glue thoroughly set.

Crosscut the legs to finished length on the table saw and lay out the mortises. Cut the mortises with a plunge router and edge guide. A spiral-flute, up-cutting bit eases the load on the router and results in a smoother cut with no burning.

Clamp a leg between bench dogs on the workbench and make the mortise cut in several stages, with each cut taking no more than ⅜ in. in depth.

To help support the router base when making the top rail mortise cuts, clamp a spare leg to the side of your workpiece, extending past its top end (**Fig. 3**). Square the ends of each mortise with a sharp chisel (**Fig. 4**).

The Frame Pieces

Choose the stock for the stiles that divide the panels, and rip and crosscut the stiles to finished dimension. Set these aside.

Fig. 5 *Use a dado blade to cut the tenon faces on the rail ends. A stop block clamped to the table ensures consistent tenon length.*

Select the stock for the sofa rails, and cut these pieces to finished dimension. Orient each piece as it will appear on the finished sofa, selecting for best grain figure, and mark the exposed face to indicate the top and bottom edges. Use a dado blade in the table saw to cut the broad tenon faces on the rail ends (**Fig. 5**). Clamp a stop block to the saw table to aid in making the tenons the same length. Readjust the blade height to cut the top and bottom shoulders on each tenon.

It's best to cut the tenons just slightly oversize and then pare to finished dimension with a sharp chisel. This practice eliminates the small ridge marks that most dado blades leave on the surface of the cut (**Fig. 6**). Note that the tenons are ¹⁄₁₆ in. shorter than the mortise depth to allow a place for the excess glue to go.

Use a dado blade to cut the tenons on the ends of the stiles. On these tenons, however, only make the cheek cuts, as the shoulders will be automatically formed when you cut the panel grooves. Readjust the dado blade in the saw to cut the grooves in the top edges of the bottom back and side rails, bottom edges of the top back and side rails, and the edges of the stiles. Use a featherboard clamped to the saw table to hold the pieces tight against the rip fence (**Fig. 7**).

Next, mark the arched profile on each bottom rail. To achieve a smooth curve, spring a ¼-in.-thick strip of pine or poplar between the clamps on each end of the rail and trace along the strip to make the arch (**Fig. 8**). Use a band saw or sabre saw to cut these arches (**Fig. 9**), and use a spokeshave to remove the saw marks (**Fig. 10**).

Use a 30° chamfer bit in the router to cut the chamfer on the top front edge of the front rail. Clamp the rail to the workbench before routing (**Fig. 11**).

Select the stock for the back and side arms of the sofa. If you cannot cut all the arms from one board, try to match the pieces for color and grain pattern so that the arm has unified

Fig. 6 *After cutting the tenons slightly oversize, use a chisel to pare them down for a snug fit. Paring also removes the dado blade marks.*

Fig. 7 *Reset the dado blade, and cut the grooves for the panels and the stiles. Use a featherboard to hold the work against the fence.*

Fig. 8 *Bend a thin strip over the lower rail pieces to lay out a smooth curve. Clamp the strip at the ends and trace the curve with a pencil.*

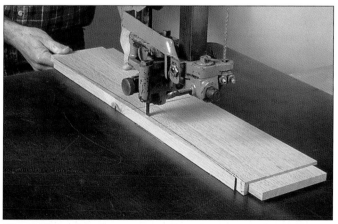

Fig. 9 *Use a band saw or a sabre saw to cut the curve on the lower rails. Stay just to the waste side of the layout line.*

Fig. 10 *Smooth the curves to the layout line with a spokeshave. Cut down the curve from each end to avoid tearing the wood.*

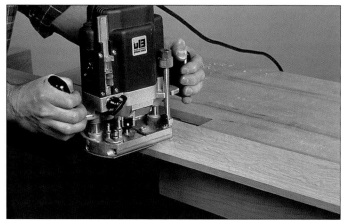

Fig. 11 *Rout a chamfer along the top front edge of the front rail. Use a 30° chamfer bit with a ball-bearing pilot for the job.*

appearance. After ripping the stock to width, use a miter gauge on the table saw to cut the 45° mitered ends on each piece, then cut the square ends on the two side arms.

Make a plywood or cardboard template of the arm bracket shape, using a thin strip to create a smooth curve. Then trace the template onto the appropriate pieces of stock. Use a band saw or sabre saw to cut out the shape, and remove the saw marks with a spokeshave.

Prefinishing the Panels

If possible, make each panel from a single board. Otherwise, glue narrower stock together to achieve the necessary width.

Plane the panel stock to ⅜-in. thickness. If you do not own a thickness planer, you can usually find a lumberyard or professional woodworker who will plane your stock for a modest fee. Rip and crosscut the panels to finished dimension (**Fig. 12**), and sand thoroughly, finishing with 220-grit sandpaper.

Prefinishing the panels ensures a neat job and eliminates the possibility of raw wood appearing if the panels shrink in a dry environment.

To color the wood, we used a water based aniline dye. Before applying the dye, wipe the wood with warm water to raise the grain. When dry, lightly sand the wood with 320-grit

Safety Sense

SAW BLADE SAFETY

Saw blades are most effective—and safest— when they're sharp. Dull blades are dangerous and will not only tear wood, they can grab the workpiece and cause injury to the operator.

Replace a blade once it has become dull, and never use a blade with cracked or chipped teeth. Store blades between pieces of cardboard to protect the teeth from damage. Whenever you're changing blades, be sure that the saw is disconnected from the electrical outlet.

Saw blades often collect sticky wood resin and pitch, which can affect performance and create a

dangerous situation. To remove gummy buildup, soak the blade in turpentine or kerosene. Then remove the softened resin with steel wool. Another way to remove stubborn resin is with spray-on oven cleaner. After cleaning the blade, apply a light coat of machine oil to the blade to resist rust.

All saw blades have a maximum rpm rating. This is not an approximate rating. Never use a blade on a saw that exceeds the blade's rating. Be sure that all blade guards are in place and operating properly before you use any saw. And, of course, always wear eye protection when operating any power tool.

Fig. 12 *After planing the panel stock to ³/₈ in. thick, use a crosscut table mounted on the table saw to make the square panel cuts.*

Fig. 13 *Apply warm water to raise the grain, let the panels dry, and then sand. Then color the panels with aniline dye following the manufacturer's instructions.*

sandpaper before applying the dye. Dust off thoroughly and apply the dye according to the manufacturer's directions, and let it dry before proceeding (**Fig. 13**).

Next, seal the surface of the panels by applying one coat of the finish of your choice (**Fig. 14**). We used a transparent finish. One coat will protect the stained surface and keep any further stain from penetrating the panels when the body of the sofa is finished. Allow the sealer to dry completely before beginning the final assembly.

Assembly and Finishing

First, assemble the side frame rails, stiles, and panels. Mark the stile locations on the rails to ensure proper positioning. Apply glue to the rail grooves where the stile tenons will rest, and apply glue to the tenon ends. Don't glue the panels in the grooves. Position the stiles in the bottom rail groove, slide the panels into place, then install the top rail. Clamp the

Fig. 14 *Apply one coat of the final finish after the dye has dried. This protects the panels when the fully assembled sofa is dyed.*

SHOP*Helper*

LINING UP CUTS
Lining up the cutting mark (on a workpiece) with the blade on your table saw is easy if you use this trick. Stick a piece of white tape on the saw table in front of the blade and make an ink mark on it in line with the inside edge of the blade. Crank the blade up and use a straightedge to ensure that the line is accurate. Now you can line up a workpiece mark with the mark on the tape, grip the work against the miter gauge, and push into the blade. Just like magic, the cut will be on target every time!

Fig. 15 *Apply glue to the stile tenons and to the rail grooves at the stile locations. The panels are held in the grooves without glue.*

Fig. 16 *After mitering the arm pieces, use a plate joiner to cut the slots for joining the components with plates (biscuits).*

Fig. 17 *When the arm has been assembled, flip it over and lay the inverted sofa assembly on top. Then mark the plate joints.*

MATERIAL*Matters*

Good Wood

Unlike a synthetic material whose properties can be tailored to suit a purpose, we take wood as it comes. It isn't designed be made into furniture, it's best suited to be part of a living tree. Some of the properties that make wood work so well in a tree can cause real problems for the woodworker. The cellular structure of wood contributes to its ability to shrink and expand with changes in humidity. To make matters worse, wood is naturally round in cross section. It grows in a series of concentric rings. When it dries, it shrinks to a greater degree concentrically (around the tree) than it does radially (from the center out).

Flatsawn lumber—boards sawn in parallel layers across the width of the log—show a pattern of growth rings running in arcs across the width of the board. A flatsawn board will cup as its moisture content varies due to the different rates of shrinkage parallel to and across the growth rings. In other words, you can expect common flatsawn wood to cup as sure as the seasons change. Knowing how the wood will cup can help you to produce more successful projects. For example, when gluing together several narrow boards to create a wide panel, reversing the direction of the growth-ring arcs will even out the cupping effect. Drawer fronts should have the heart wood (inside of the log) facing out. If the wood dries, the joints at the top and bottom will be forced tightly together.

Quarter-sawn lumber has an end grain pattern called vertical, in which the growth rings run from face to face across the thickness of the board. In this case, the wood will not cup as its moisture content changes, but will instead simply shrink or expand more uniformly. Because quarter-sawing produces less usable lumber per log, boards cut this way are more expensive than flatsawn boards. Although quartersawn lumber in certain species is available from larger furniture-grade wood dealers, most of the lumber you're likely to come across is flatsawn. It's not unusual, however, to find wide common-pine boards that have been sawn right through the center of the log. Effectively, a 2x12 sawn this way will produce two roughly 5-in.-wide vertical-grained boards. Avoid using the center, or pith, of the tree. This wood will move and check more rapidly than the surrounding wood.

Grain is important in selecting lumber. In addition to cupping, stresses imparted as the tree grew—or varying grain densities—can cause the wood to deform either while it's drying or when you're cutting it. Checking the uniformity of the grain on the edges and faces can provide clues as to whether a board is likely to deform. Uniform, straight, parallel lines mean that the board is likely to react uniformly to drying and cutting. Long uniform arches on the board's face are also a good sign, but if there are many circular patterns, quickly changing arches, or rapid changes from dense to less-dense wood, you may be in for trouble. Not only are these boards more likely to deform, they're more difficult to work with.

Fig. 18 *Position the slots in the rail using a fence on the joiner. Clamp a board to the underside of the arm, to position the corresponding slots.*

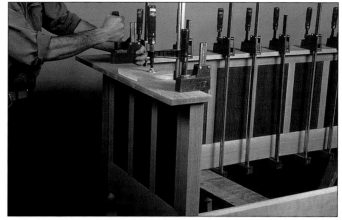

Fig. 19 *Apply glue to the plate joints for the connecting arm subassembly to the frame. Then clamp the arm to the frame and let the glue dry.*

assembly, and compare opposite diagonal measurements to guarantee that the frame is square. Scrape off any glue squeeze-out before it completely hardens. After the side frames are done, assemble the back frame and clamp (**Fig. 15**).

When the glue dries, join the side frames to the legs. Apply glue to the mortise-and-tenon joints and to the edges of the stiles that abut the legs. Next, join the two sides to the front and back rails. Be sure to complete the assembly on a flat surface to avoid imparting a twist to the frame.

Cut and install the filler strips on the inside of each side bottom rail. Use glue and screws to attach these strips. Cut poplar or maple stock to size for the cleats that support the sofa set cushion. Note the beveled top edge on the front and back cleats. Use the table saw and dado blades, or handsaw and chisel, to cut the notches in the bottom edges of the front and back cleats. Bore and countersink pilot holes in the cleats, and attach them to the frame with screws and glue. Cut the crossbraces and install them in the notches in the front and back cleats.

Mark the positions of the two joining plates in each arm miter joint, then cut the slots with the plate joiner (**Fig. 16**). Apply glue and assemble the arm, clamping in two directions to keep the miters aligned. Lay the arm upside down on a padded surface. Position the sofa frame on the arm, also upside down, and align the two for proper overhang on all sides. Mark joining plate positions on the arm and top rail (**Fig. 17**). Cut the slots on the bottom face of the arm, locating the plate joiner by clamping a straightedge guide to the arm to yield the proper setback. Use the plate joiner fence to center the slots in the rail top edge (**Fig. 18**).

Apply glue to the rail edge, joining plate slots and plates, install the plates and assemble the arm to the sofa. Use bar clamps to pull the joints tight, and let the glue dry (**Fig. 19**).

Mark and cut the plate slots in the arm brackets, legs and center back stile. Use the plate joiner fences to position the cuts

Fig. 20 *Use a plate joiner to join the arm brackets to the legs and arm assembly. Hold the brackets in place with tape until the glue dries.*

on the legs (**Fig. 20**), but a straightedge guide must be clamped to the sofa back to position the slots in the center stile.

Use masking tape to hold the arm brackets in place until the glue sets. If the joints won't close, a light blow with a mallet will do the job. Dye the sofa frame as described in the section prefinishing the panels. When working with water-based dyes, it's important to keep a wet edge at the point of application to avoid lap marks. Therefore, start at a corner and work your way around the piece in one continuous application. If dye splashes onto the prefinished panels, simple wipe the panel dry and proceed.

When the dye is dry, use a brush, rag or sponge to apply the finish, then wipe off most of the finish leaving only a thin film. Let the finish dry overnight between coats. Three or four coats of finish, applied in this way, should be sufficient. To smooth the final finish, lightly buff the surface with 4/0 steel wool and polish with a soft cloth.

Table Projects

Table Manners

Solid joinery and simple lines make our oak dining table a classic for all generations.

Although Arts & Crafts design came to prominence in the early 20th century, it's still a very popular choice for modern homes. And it's no surprise why. The straight, square lines and lack of surface decoration are in keeping with today's styles, yet the look is distinctly traditional, providing a sense of heritage and permanence. As it would have been nearly 100 years ago, our table is constructed of solid, quarter-sawn white oak—the wood responsible for the unique grain figure characteristic of the style. As for utility, you'll be able to seat as many as eight people—12 if some of them are small children. It's truly a table for all occasions.

*Key*POINTS

TIME
Prep Time .... **15 hours**
Shop Time .... **19 hours**
Assembly Time .... **10 hours**

EFFORT
Skill Level .... **advanced**

COST / BENEFITS
Expense: **expensive**
- Generational **legacy piece** built to last for an extremely long time.
- A showcase of **Arts & Crafts style**, with fine wood graining.

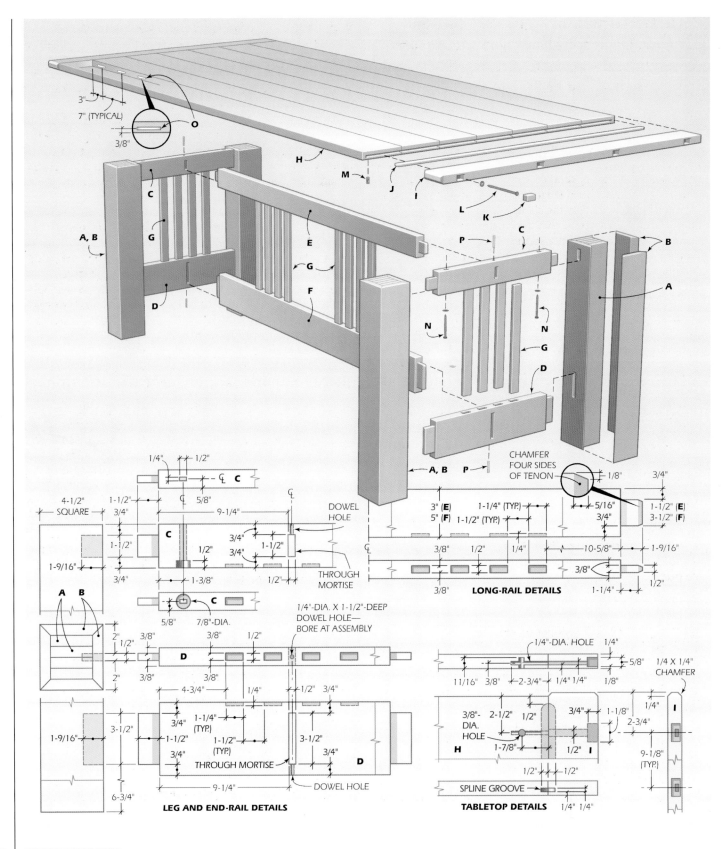

3"

7" (TYPICAL)

3/8"

O

H

M

J

I

L

K

A, B

C

G

D

E

G

F

P

C

N

N

G

D

B

A

A, B

P

CHAMFER
FOUR SIDES
OF TENON

1/8"

3/4"

1/4" 1/2"

C L C

4-1/2"
SQUARE

1-1/2"

3/4"

5/8"

9-1/4"

DOWEL
HOLE

3" (E)
5" (F)

1-1/4" (TYP.)
1-1/2" (TYP.)

5/16"

3/4"

1-1/2" (E)
3-1/2" (F)

1-1/2"

C

3/4"
3/4"

3/4"
1/2"

1-1/2"

1-9/16"

1/2"
1-3/8"

1/2"

THROUGH
MORTISE

3/8"

1/2"

1/4"

10-5/8"

1-9/16"

A B

C

3/8"

5/8"

7/8"-DIA.

1/4"-DIA. X 1-1/2"-DEEP
DOWEL HOLE—
BORE AT ASSEMBLY

3/8"

3/4"

LONG-RAIL DETAILS

1-1/4"

1/2"

2"
1/2"
2"

3/8"

3/8"

3/8"

D

1/2"

1/4"-DIA. HOLE

1/4"

5/8"

1/4 X 1/4"
CHAMFER

1-9/16"

3-1/2"

6-3/4"

4-3/4"

3/4"
1-1/2"
3/4"

1-1/4"
(TYP.)

1-1/2"
(TYP.)

THROUGH MORTISE

1/4"

3/4"
3-1/2"
3/4"

DOWEL HOLE

9-1/4"

D

1/8"

11/16" 3/8" 2-3/4" 1/4" 1/4"

3/8"-
DIA.
HOLE

2-1/2"

1/2"

3/4"

1-1/8"

1/4"

I

2-3/4"

H

1-7/8"

1/2"

I

9-1/8"
(TYP.)

1/2" 1/2"

LEG AND END-RAIL DETAILS

SPLINE GROOVE

TABLETOP DETAILS

1/4" 1/4"

Our table is made of ¾-, 1-, and 1¼-in.-thick stock. If you don't have a jointer and planer, ask your lumber supplier to prepare the boards, but the material must be flat and straight.

Leg Construction

Each leg is formed by surrounding a solid core with mitered face boards. First rip stock for the leg cores, using up any wood that has defects in its appearance. Crosscut these boards a few inches longer than finished length. Spread glue, assemble them in stacks of four, and apply the clamps. After about 20 minutes, scrape off any glue that has oozed from the joints.

Secure a tall auxiliary fence to the table saw rip fence and clamp a hold-down featherboard to the auxiliary fence. Set the table saw blade at 45° and rip bevels along both edges of each face board (**Fig. 1**). Then, crosscut the boards to match the cores. Apply glue to the face-board mating surfaces and to all sides of a core for one of the legs. Assemble the leg, alternating clamp direction so that even pressure is applied on all sides (**Fig. 2**). Construct the remaining legs in the same manner and scrape off all excess glue after about 20 minutes. When the glue is dry, use a band saw and miter gauge to crosscut the legs to finished length.

Lay out the leg mortises as shown in the drawing. Then, use a plunge router with a spiral up-cutting bit and edge guide to cut them (**Fig. 3**). Take two or three passes to reach the full mortise depth so you don't burn the bit or overload the router. Square the ends of the mortises with a sharp chisel.

The Rails and Slats

Use a dado blade in the table saw to cut the rail tenons (**Fig. 4**). Because the blade will leave small ridges, it's best to cut the tenons about 1/32 in. oversize and then pare to the exact size. Clamp a stop block to the saw table to set the tenon length. Hold the rails on edge to cut the shoulders at the top and bottom edges. Use a sharp chisel to pare the small ridges

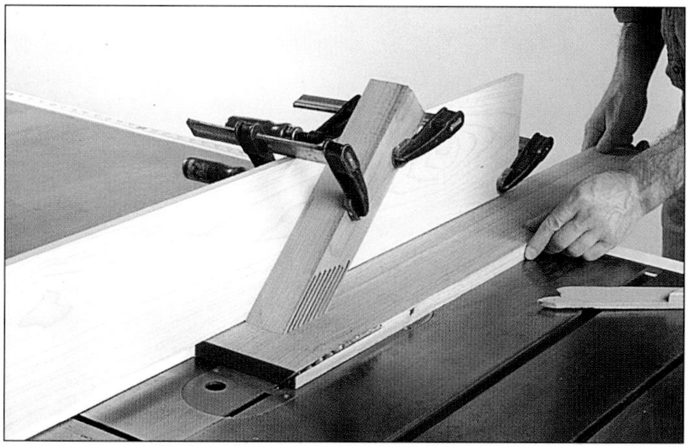

Fig. 1 ***With a featherboard holding the stock against the table, rip a 45° bevel on both edges of each leg face board.***

Fig. 2 ***Spread glue on the joint surfaces and clamp the face boards to the leg core. Alternate clamp directions to pull the joints tight.***

Materials List

Key	No.	Size and description (use)
A	16	3/4 x 3 x 28" oak (leg core)
B	16	3/4 x 4 1/2 x 28" oak (leg face board)
C	2	1 1/4 x 3 x 22" oak (end top rail)
D	2	1 1/4 x 5 x 22" oak (end bottom rail)
E	1	1 1/4 x 3 x 55 7/8" oak (long top rail)
F	1	1 1/4 x 5 x 55 7/8" oak (long bottom rail)
G	16	1/2 x 1 1/4 x 14 1/2" oak (slat)
H*	1	1 x 42 x 83" oak (top panel)
I	2	1 x 3 1/2 x 42 1/2" oak (breadboard end)
J	2	1/4 x 1 x 41" oak (spline)
K**	8	3/8 x 5/8 x 1 1/8" oak (plug)
L	8	1/4"-20 x 5" rh machine screw, washer
M	8	1/4"-20 steel cross dowel
N	4	1/4"-dia. x 3" lagscrew, washer
O	as reqd.	No. 20 joining plate
P**	4	1/4"-dia. x 1 1/2" dowel

Misc.: Medium fumed oak aniline dye.

*Overall size, laminate from available stock.

**Finished dimension. Cut oversize and trim flush.

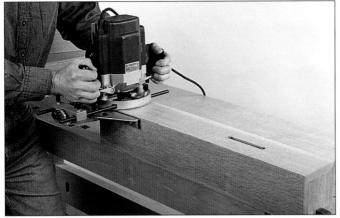

Fig. 3 *Rout the leg mortises with a spiral up-cutting bit. Reach the finished depth in several passes to reduce strain on the router motor.*

Fig. 4 *Use a dado blade in the table saw to cut the rail tenons. A stop block clamped to the table ensures consistent cuts.*

Fig. 7 *Use a sharp chisel or block plane to chamfer the ends of the tenons that extend through the end-rail mortises.*

Fig. 8 *Lay out the slat locations in the rails and rout the mortises. Clamp two rails together to form a base for the router.*

off the faces of each tenon. Lay out the through mortises in the end rails and use a ⁷⁄₁₆-in.-dia. bit in the drill press to bore slightly overlapping holes that remove most of the waste from each mortise (**Fig. 5**). Use a sharp chisel to finish cutting the joints (**Fig. 6**). Work halfway through the joint from one face, then turn the rail over to finish from the other side.

Test fit each through tenon in its mortise. Mark around each tenon end to indicate the outer surface of the rail. Using this line as a guide, chamfer the tenon ends (**Fig. 7**).

Rip and crosscut the base slats to size and lay out the slat locations on the rails. Use the plunge router with an edge guide to make the cuts (**Fig. 8**). Clamp two rails together to provide a wider base for the router. Square the ends of each mortise with a chisel, and test fit the slats. Next, mark the hole locations in the end top rails for fastening the tabletop. Use a Forstner bit to counterbore the recess for each bolt head (**Fig. 9**), and then bore two side-by-side ¼-in.-dia. holes

for each bolt. Use a sharp chisel to remove the waste between the holes, leaving elongated slots. These wide bolt holes will allow the top to move with seasonal changes in humidity.

Base Assembly

Begin assembly of the base by joining the slats to the end rails. It's not necessary to use glue unless the slats are too loose. Use two clamps to hold the assembly together until it's joined to the legs (**Fig. 10**).

Spread glue in the leg mortises and on the rail tenons for one end of the table. Join the end rails to the legs, apply clamps, and compare opposite diagonal measurements to be sure that the assembly is square (**Fig. 11**). Then let the glue cure and repeat the procedure for the other table end.

Join the slats and long rails, install clamps and then compare diagonal measurements. Spread glue on the through-tenon joints and assemble the table base. Use clamps on either

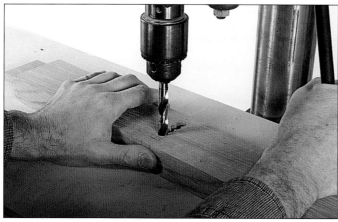

Fig. 5 *Using a ⁷/₁₆-in.-dia. bit, bore slightly overlapping holes to efficiently remove the bulk of the waste from the end-rail mortises.*

Fig. 6 *Finish the through mortises with a sharp chisel. Work halfway through from each face to avoid tearing the wood surfaces.*

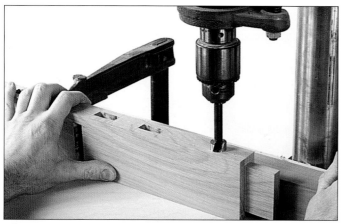

Fig. 9 *Use a Forstner bit and drill press to counterbore recesses for the lagscrews in the bottom edges of the top end rails.*

Fig. 10 *Assemble the end rails and slats. Use two clamps to hold the pieces together until the rails are glued to the legs.*

side of the through tenons to apply even pressure (**Fig. 12**). Bore holes through the top rails and into the through tenons for dowels that will secure the joints. Apply glue and drive each pin into place (**Fig. 13**). Cut off the dowel about ¹/₁₆ in. above the rail surface and use a sharp chisel to pare it flush. Turn the base over and install dowels through the bottom tenons.

The Tabletop

Select the stock for the tabletop, rip the boards to width, and crosscut a few inches longer than finished length. Plane or joint the edges of each board so that they're straight and square, and then lay out joining-plate slots spaced about 7 in. on center. When cutting the slots, hold both the plate joiner and board tightly to your worktable so that the slots will be accurately positioned.

Because the boards are long and heavy, it's best to begin assembly by joining only two. Then, after the glue cures, add

Fig. 11 *Join the end assembly to the legs and clamp. Compare opposite diagonals to be sure that the assembly is square.*

Fig. 12 *Assemble the slats and long rails and glue the long rails to the ends. Use clamps to securely pull the joints tight.*

Fig. 13 *Lock the tenons to the rails by gluing a dowel through the joint. Turn the base over and repeat on the bottom joints.*

Fig. 16 *Cut splines for the breadboard-end joints. A ¹/₂-in. radius on the ends matches the slot profile.*

Fig. 17 *Clamp the breadboard end to the tabletop and use a doweling jig to bore through the strip into the end of the top.*

one board at a time until the panel is complete. Use clamps every 6 to 8 in. along the joint to pull the boards together. After about 20 minutes, scrape off the excess glue, then wait another 30 minutes before adding the next board (**Fig. 14**).

Although the joining plates will ensure a reasonably flat panel, you'll need to plane the top to achieve a truly smooth and even surface. Use a jointer or jack plane to level the top. Make sure that the plane is razor-sharp, and work diagonally across the panel, taking light cuts. Use a cabinet scraper parallel to the grain to remove the plane marks, and then plane the edges parallel and to finished width.

Cut the top ½ in. longer than its final dimension with a circular saw or sabre saw. To make the finished cuts, first mount a ½-in. shank, top-bearing template bit in your router. Clamp a straightedge guide across the top panel, ¼ in. from the end, and double-check that it's square to the panel edge. Then trim the end, allowing the router bearing to follow the

straightedge guide (**Fig. 15**). Use a scrap block clamped to the edge of the panel to prevent tearout at the end of the cut. Trim the opposite end using the same technique.

Rip and crosscut the two breadboard ends to finished size. Next, use a sharp block plane to cut the chamfered profile on the ends of each strip. Use a slotting cutter to rout the ¼-in.-wide x ½-in.-deep spline groove in the ends of the top panel. Note that the groove stops short of the panel edges. Use the same bit to cut a matching groove in one edge of each breadboard end. Cut a spline with a ½-in. radius on the ends for each breadboard-end joint. Fit each spline into its groove in the top panel (**Fig. 16**), install the breadboard ends and temporarily clamp them in place. Using a doweling jig and a long ¼-in.-dia. bit, bore holes for machine screws that will fasten the breadboard ends to the top panel (**Fig. 17**). When that's done, turn the top panel upside down and bore holes for the steel cross dowels using a brad-point bit with depth stop.

Fig. 14 *Begin assembly of the top by joining only two boards. After the glue cures, add one board at a time to reach full width.*

Fig. 15 *To trim the ends of the tabletop, use a template routing bit that follows a straightedge that has been clamped to the workpiece.*

Fig. 18 *Install the steel cross dowels, aligning the holes with the machine screw holes. Then tighten the screws.*

Fig. 19 *Cover the screwheads with small blocks glued into the squared recesses. After the glue cures, trim the blocks flush.*

Remove the end pieces and use a sharp chisel to widen the four holes in each to ½-in. slots. Then use a router with edge guide to cut a mortise centered over each hole. Square the ends of the mortises with a sharp chisel as shown in the drawing.

Assemble the breadboard ends and the top panel, but don't use any glue on the joints. Insert a cross dowel in each tabletop hole, aligning the hole in the dowel with the machine screw hole in the breadboard end (**Fig. 18**). Install the screws and washers to hold the ends in place.

Cut small blocks to plug the mortises over the screwheads, and glue the blocks in place (**Fig. 19**). Let each block protrude from the edge of the strip. When the glue has cured, use a small block plane to trim the blocks flush. Set the tabletop on the base, adjust it for proper overhang on all sides, bore pilot holes and install the 3-in. lagscrews and washers. Then, remove the top and sand all table surfaces working down to 220-grit sandpaper.

Finishing

We stained our table with a water-based aniline dye. To prepare for staining, wipe all surfaces with a damp sponge to raise the grain. When the wood is dry, lightly sand the table with 220-grit sandpaper. Apply the dye solution with a brush or rag, working quickly to avoid lap marks. Let the table dry overnight before applying the first coat of finish. If the wood surface is still rough, lightly wipe with 320-grit sandpaper. Don't sand hard or you'll lighten patches in the dyed surface. Clean with a tack cloth before proceeding.

We finished our table with four coats of sealer/finish. Brush or wipe on the first coat and let it dry overnight. Lightly sand with 320-grit sandpaper and remove all dust. For the next coats, let the finish sit on the wood for about 30 minutes, wipe off excess, and let it dry overnight. When the last coat has fully cured, burnish with 4/0 steel wool and polish with a soft cloth.

Elegant Eating

Masterful accents on this lovely table make for more than memorable meals.

You can't judge a book by its cover, but an incredible surface can certainly affect how a table is perceived. This table features fairly basic styling but is built of mahogany and includes detailing in wenge—a dark, dense African wood. What really sets this table apart, though, are the magnificent surfaces of pomele sapele veneer. This highly figured veneer creates planes of light that appear to have a life of their own. The panels change appearance as you walk around the table to produce a sense of movement and depth that's truly dazzling. It almost seems a shame to cover the top with dishes full of food—no matter how delicious!

*Key*POINTS

TIME
Prep Time	6 hours
Shop Time	11 hours
Assembly Time	9 hours

EFFORT
Skill Level	advanced

COST / BENEFITS
Expense: **expensive**
- **Showstopping surface** will have dinner party guests gasping, and might even spur you to throw out your tablecloths.

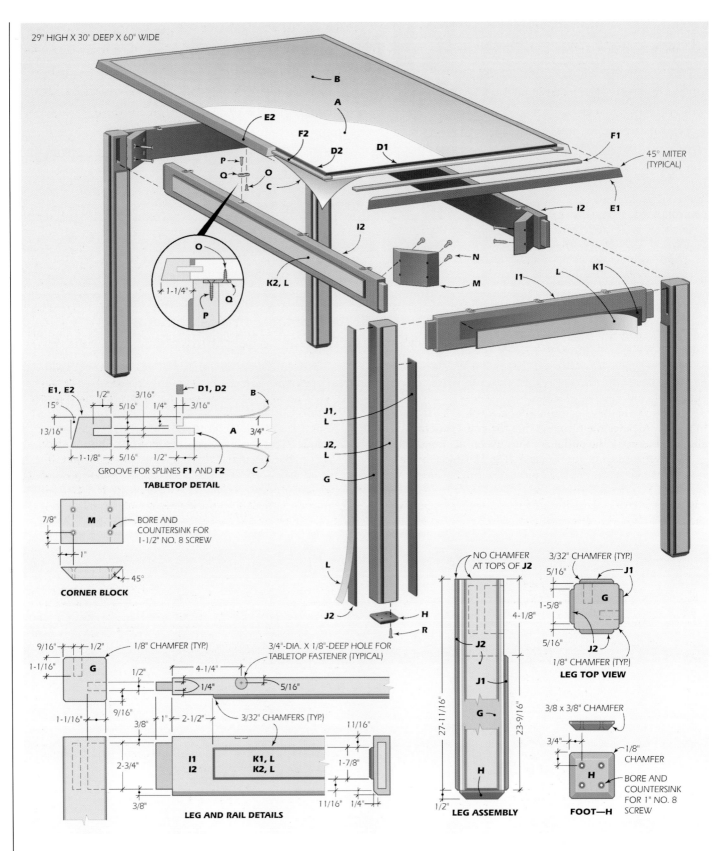

29" HIGH X 30" DEEP X 60" WIDE

B

A

E2

F2

D2

D1

F1

45° MITER (TYPICAL)

P

Q

O

C

I2

E1

O

1-1/4"

Q

P

K2, L

I2

N

M

I1

L

K1

TABLETOP DETAIL

E1, E2

15°

1/2"

3/16"

5/16"

1/4"

3/16"

13/16"

A

3/4"

D1, D2

B

C

1-1/8"

5/16"

1/2"

GROOVE FOR SPLINES **F1** AND **F2**

J1, L

J2, L

G

L

J2

H

R

CORNER BLOCK

7/8"

M

1"

45°

BORE AND COUNTERSINK FOR 1-1/2" NO. 8 SCREW

LEG AND RAIL DETAILS

9/16"

1/2"

1/8" CHAMFER (TYP.)

1-1/16"

G

1/2"

4-1/4"

3/4"-DIA. X 1/8"-DEEP HOLE FOR TABLETOP FASTENER (TYPICAL)

1/4"

5/16"

1-1/16"

9/16"

3/8"

1"

2-1/2"

3/32" CHAMFERS (TYP.)

11/16"

2-3/4"

I1
I2

K1, L
K2, L

1-7/8"

3/8"

11/16"

1/4"

LEG ASSEMBLY

NO CHAMFER AT TOPS OF **J2**

J2

J1

G

H

4-1/8"

27-11/16"

23-9/16"

1/2"

LEG TOP VIEW

3/32" CHAMFER (TYP.)

5/16"

J1

G

1-5/8"

5/16"

J2

1/8" CHAMFER (TYP.)

3/8 x 3/8 CHAMFER

3/4"

H

1/8" CHAMFER

BORE AND COUNTERSINK FOR 1" NO. 8 SCREW

FOOT—H

This spectacular table can serve as the centerpiece of a room or as an accent to an already established decor. If you use it as a dining table, it will comfortably seat four to six adults. But be careful to protect the surface with a table pad and cloth—you don't want burn marks detracting from such a unique appearance. Wenge and pomele sapele veneers are available from various mail-order wood dealers. In addition to the figured veneer, you'll need a small amount of plain mahogany veneer for the bottom face of the table's top panel.

Our figured veneer top is made up of several sheets placed edge to edge. You'll find that the individual pieces are sold in the sequence that they're cut from the log. This gives you control over the repetitive pattern created by the assembled veneer sheets. On our tabletop, we used a book match pattern, in which every other sheet of veneer is flipped over to create a mirror image of the adjacent sheet.

Fig. 1 ***Stack all top veneer pieces and cut them at one time. Align the grain and use a straight board to guide the veneer saw.***

Top Construction

Begin by cutting the ¾-in. MDF (medium-density fiberboard) core stock to size for the top panel. Cut the core a few inches longer and wider than the finished dimensions. We used four sheets of veneer, with the grain running across the tabletop, to cover our panel. Whether you choose to run it across or parallel to the length of the top, position a seam at the center with an equal number of pieces to either side.

Prepare to cut the sheets to uniform size by placing them in a stack. Arrange the pieces so that the grain pattern is aligned, and mark the outline of the cuts on the top sheet.

Use a veneer saw to cut the stack (**Fig. 1**). Guide the flat side of the saw along a straight piece of ¾-in. hardwood or plywood. Make light passes to keep from tearing the delicate edges. Make the cross-grain cuts first, followed by cuts along the grain that will determine the seams. Use the same technique to cut the mahogany veneer for the bottom face.

Lay out the sheets and check that each seam is tight. If necessary, adjust the edges with a block plane. Use perforated paper veneer tape to hold the sheets together. Moisten 6-in. lengths of tape with a damp sponge and place them across the first seam, spaced about 4 to 6 in. apart. Next, place a

Materials List

Key	No.	Size and description (use)
A	1	$\frac{3}{4}$ x 27$\frac{3}{4}$ x 57$\frac{3}{4}$" MDF (top core)
B	as reqd.	pomele sapele (top veneer)
C	as reqd.	mahogany (bottom veneer)
D1	2	$\frac{3}{16}$ x $\frac{9}{32}$ x 27$\frac{7}{8}$" wenge (inlay)
D2	2	$\frac{3}{16}$ x $\frac{9}{32}$ x 57$\frac{3}{4}$" wenge (inlay)
E1	2	$\frac{13}{16}$ x 1$\frac{1}{8}$ x 30" mahogany (edge)
E2	2	$\frac{13}{16}$ x 1$\frac{1}{8}$ x 60" mahogany (edge)
F1	2	$\frac{3}{16}$ x 1 x 26$\frac{3}{4}$" hardwood (spline)
F2	2	$\frac{3}{16}$ x 1 x 58$\frac{3}{4}$" hardwood (spline)
G	4	2$\frac{1}{4}$ x 2$\frac{1}{4}$ x 27$\frac{11}{16}$" mahogany (leg)
H*	4	$\frac{1}{2}$ x 2$\frac{1}{4}$ x 2$\frac{1}{4}$" wenge (foot)
I1	2	1 x 3$\frac{1}{2}$ x 25$\frac{5}{8}$" mahogany (apron)
I2	2	1 x 3$\frac{1}{2}$ x 55$\frac{5}{8}$" mahogany (apron)
J1	8	$\frac{3}{16}$ x 1$\frac{5}{8}$ x 23$\frac{9}{16}$" wenge (decorative panel)
J2	8	$\frac{3}{16}$ x 1$\frac{5}{8}$ x 27$\frac{11}{16}$" wenge (decorative panel)
K1	2	$\frac{3}{16}$ x 1$\frac{7}{8}$ x 18$\frac{5}{8}$" wenge (decorative panel)
K2	2	$\frac{3}{16}$ x 1$\frac{7}{8}$ x 48$\frac{5}{8}$" wenge (decorative panel)
L	as reqd.	pomele sapele (decorative panel veneer)
M	4	1 x 3$\frac{1}{2}$ x 5" maple (corner block)
N	16	1$\frac{1}{2}$" No. 8 fh wood screw
O	14	$\frac{1}{2}$" No. 8 fh wood screw
P	14	$\frac{3}{4}$" No. 8 fh wood screw
Q	14	tabletop fastener
R	16	1" No. 8 fh wood screw

Misc.: Veneer tape; plastic-resin glue; kraft paper; 120-, 220-, and 320-grit sandpaper; 4/0 steel wool; sealer/finish.

*Finished dimension. Cut oversize and trim after assembly.

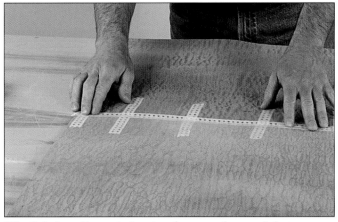

Fig. 2 *Join adjacent sheets of veneer by applying lengths of veneer tape across the seam. Add tape along the length of the seam to hold the joint tight.*

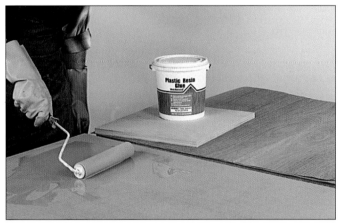

Fig. 3 *Use a foam roller to spread glue on the core. Then carefully invert the core onto the bottom veneer face.*

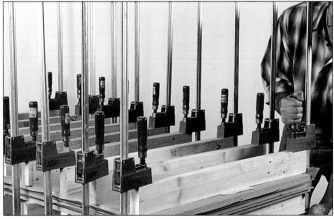

Fig. 4 *Use battens spaced about 6 in. apart to apply pressure across the entire veneer assembly. Clamp from the center out.*

strip of tape along the length of the seam (**Fig. 2**). Now you're ready to tape the remaining seams. If splits occur, use the veneer tape to repair them. Prepare the bottom veneer using the same technique.

To glue the veneer to the core, you will need two cauls of ¾-in. plywood that are the same size as the panel core. You'll also need 22 straight 2x4 battens—one pair every 6 in.—to span across the core on the top and bottom, and some kraft paper or newspaper to place between the cauls and the veneer faces.

Prepare for veneering by placing straight 2x4 support rails between two sawhorses, and laying the bottom row of battens along the rails. Position a 2-in. veneer shim in the center of each batten, and then place the bottom plywood caul over the battens. The veneer shims ensure adequate pressure at the center of the panel. Spread paper over the caul and place the mahogany bottom veneer face, tape side down, over the paper.

We used plastic-resin glue for our panel because it has a long open time. Use a foam roller to evenly spread glue onto one face of the core (**Fig. 3**). Invert the core onto the bottom veneer face and align the edges.

Roll glue onto the top of the core and position the top veneer face, tape side up. Cover the veneer with paper and the top caul, and then add the battens. Place a veneer shim under the center of each batten and, starting at the center of the panel, clamp each pair of battens at both ends (**Fig. 4**). Let the glue set overnight before removing the clamps.

Peel off as much paper as possible and use a cabinet scraper or finish sander to complete the job. Don't use a belt sander—one slip could cause significant damage to the veneer.

Trim the panel to size and use a router and edge guide to cut the rabbet for the wenge inlay that will go around the panel edges (**Fig. 5**). Cut inlay strips ½ in. thicker than the

Fig. 5 *Carefully and precisely trim the top panel to size and use a router to cut the inlay rabbet around the perimeter.*

rabbet depth. Spread some glue in the rabbet on one panel edge and clamp the inlay with strips of masking tape spaced every 2 in. (**Fig. 6**). Repeat this process for each inlay. When the glue has completely set, remove the tape and sand the strips flush. Use a chisel to scrape off any excess glue.

The panel edging is ripped from a single $^{13}/_{16}$-in. mahogany board that is at least 5 in. wide and a few inches longer than the table length. Use a slot cutter and router to cut the spline groove in the panel edge, and then rout the same groove in the edge of the mahogany stock. Rip the first piece of edging off the board, and repeat the slotting and ripping to make the remaining edge pieces. Cut the strips to length with 45° miters at the corners.

Cut hardwood splines and test the fit in the grooves (**Fig. 7**). Then apply glue to the grooves and edges of one strip and panel edge, insert the spline and clamp the edging in place.

Work your way around the panel until all the edging is installed. Mark a line around the top of the panel to indicate the finished edge angle, and use a sharp block plane to trim to the line.

Making the Base

Rip and crosscut the legs to size. Cut blocks of ½-in.-thick wenge for the table feet about ⅟₁₆ in. larger than the leg dimensions. Bore screw holes for securing each foot. Apply glue to the bottom of each table leg, position each foot, and fasten with four 1-in. No. 8 screws (**Fig. 8**). When the glue is dry, sand the foot edges flush with the sides of the legs and add the chamfer with a plane or chisel.

Lay out the locations of the mortises in the table legs and rout them with a spiral up-cutting bit (**Fig. 9**). Finish the mortises by chopping the ends square. Install a chamfer bit in the router table and cut the small bevel along the edges of the table legs (**Fig. 10**).

Fig. 7 *After routing the spline grooves and cutting the mahogany edge strips, test fit the splines. Then glue all the edging, one piece at a time.*

Fig. 8 *Install wenge feet using screws and glue. Cut the feet about* ⅟₁₆ *in. oversize and sand flush after installation.*

Fig. 6 *Apply glue to the rabbet and use masking tape to clamp the inlay to the panel. Sand the inlay flush to the top.*

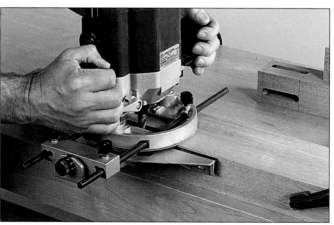

Fig. 9 *Use a spiral up-cutting bit to rout the leg mortises. Make the cut in several passes to ease the load on the router.*

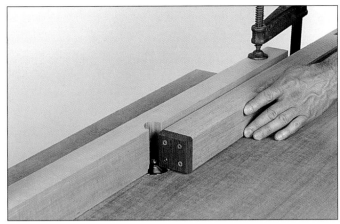

Fig. 10 *After cutting and squaring the mortises, mount a chamfer bit in the router table to cut the bevel along the legs.*

Fig. 11 *Use a dado blade in the table saw to cut the apron tenons. Clamp a stop block to the table to ensure uniform cuts.*

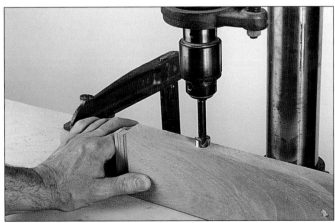

Fig. 12 *Clamp a fence to the drill press table to help position the aprons when cutting the tabletop fastener mortises.*

Rip and crosscut 1-in.-thick stock to size for the table aprons. Use a dado blade in the table saw to cut the tenons. A stop block clamped to the saw table ensures uniform tenon shoulders. Readjust the blade height and hold the aprons on edge to cut the shoulders at the top and bottom edges of each tenon (**Fig. 11**). Then test fit the apron tenons in the leg mortises.

Mark the location of each tabletop fastener on the table aprons. Clamp a fence to the drill press and bore a ¾-in.-dia. recess for each fastener (**Fig. 12**). Use the router table to cut the bevel along the bottom edge of each apron.

The decorative panels for the legs and aprons are made of wenge with pomele sapele veneer faces. Because these panels are very narrow, make blanks wide enough so that you can rip two panels from each piece. To start with, resaw the wenge panels (**Fig. 13**) and plane them to the finished thickness.

Cut the veneer sheets to the same size as the wenge blanks. Because the panels are small, you can apply veneer to more than one piece at a time, then stack and clamp them together. Place the stack between ¾-in.-thick cauls and apply the clamps (**Fig. 14**). Repeat this process for all the decorative panels. When the glue has set, cut the panels to finished dimension and rout the bevels as shown in the drawing.

Hold a panel in place on one of the aprons and lightly mark its outline with a pencil. Spread glue on the back of the panel, place it onto the apron and apply the clamps (**Fig. 15**). Repeat this process with the remaining panels on each apron and leg.

To assemble the base, first spread glue onto the tenons of a long apron (**Fig. 16**). Use a shim to spread glue in the mating mortises, join the parts, clamp, and check that the assembly is square. Repeat for the opposite side. Complete the base by joining the short aprons to the legs.

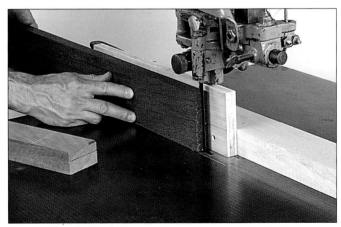

Fig. 13 *Resaw the wenge decorative panel stock on the band saw. Use a tall fence to hold the work parallel to the blade.*

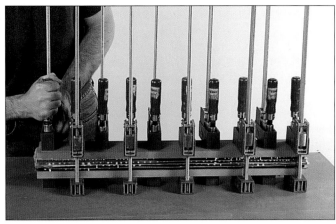

Fig. 14 *Assemble the veneer and wenge in a stack. Separate each panel with kraft paper and use ³/₄-in. plywood cauls.*

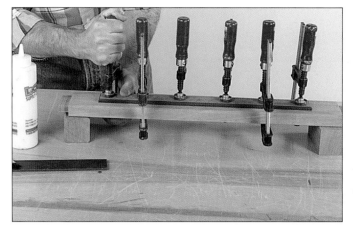

Fig. 15 *After trimming and beveling the panels, lightly spread glue on each, and clamp in place until the glue sets.*

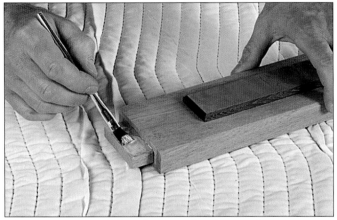

Fig. 16 *Use a small brush to apply glue to the table-apron tenons. Apply glue to the mortises, join the parts, and clamp.*

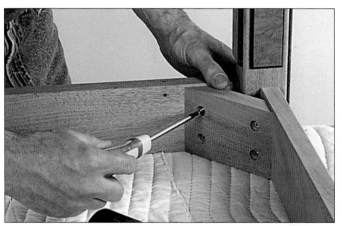

Fig. 17 *Cut the corner blocks to size with 45° angles at each end. Countersink screw holes in the blocks and secure the blocks to the aprons.*

Cut and install the corner blocks as shown in the drawing (**Fig. 17**). Next, bore pilot holes and install the tabletop fasteners (**Fig. 18**).

Finishing

For a simple wipe-on application, we used a sealer/finish. Apply three coats following the manufacturer's instructions, with light sanding between coats. Then, polish with 4/0 steel wool.

To assemble the base and top, invert the top on a padded surface and place the base upside down over it. Adjust the base to provide an even overhang, then bore pilot holes and attach the top with screws. If you are going to use the table as a dining table, consider buying a glass top cut to size, with beveled edges. Before you place the glass on the table, attach several felt circles to the bottom so that no dirt is trapped between the glass and the table.

Fig. 18 *Install tabletop fasteners to the top edges of the table aprons. Use ³/₄-in. No. 8 fh wood screws for the installation.*

Bedside Manner

This nightstand provides storage and a lovely complement to any bed.

Although a bed and dresser are the main components of any bedroom suite, today's well-appointed chamber isn't complete without a pair of night tables to flank the bed. Our design complements the bigger pieces, yet differs enough to create some eye-catching interest. As for utility, there's room for a lamp, clock, and phone on the top, a drawer for pens and paper, plus an ample shelf for books, magazines, or even a laptop computer. As an added bonus of versatility, by lengthening the legs below the bottom shelf, you can use this design to create a handy, handsome end table or lamp table for your living room or family room. Or you can even use the design as is, as an end table in a den.

*Key*POINTS

TIME
Prep Time	4 hours
Shop Time	10 hours
Assembly Time	10 hours

EFFORT
Skill Level	intermediate

COST / BENEFITS
Expense: **moderate**
- Excellent **companion piece**, especially used in pairs.
- **Versatile design** can be adjusted to make lamp or living room end tables.

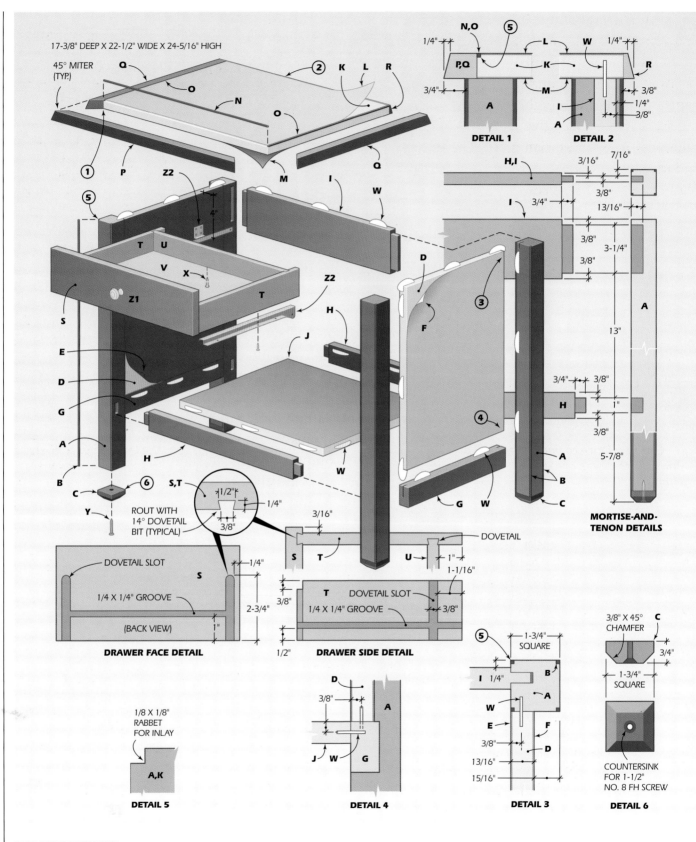

17-3/8" DEEP X 22-1/2" WIDE X 24-5/16" HIGH

45° MITER (TYP.)

N,O ⑤

DETAIL 1

1/4"
P,Q
L
K
M
W
1/4"
R
3/4"
A
I
A
3/8"
1/4"
3/8"

DETAIL 2

H,I
7/16"
3/16"
3/8"
13/16"
I
3/4"
3/8"
3-1/4"
3/8"
③
13"
A
3/4"
3/8"
H
1"
3/8"
A
B
5-7/8"
C

MORTISE-AND-TENON DETAILS

⑥

ROUT WITH 14° DOVETAIL BIT (TYPICAL)

S,T
1/2"
1/4"
3/8"

DOVETAIL SLOT
S
1/4 X 1/4" GROOVE
1/4"
2-3/4"
(BACK VIEW)
1"

DRAWER FACE DETAIL

3/16"
S
T
DOVETAIL
U
1"
1-1/16"
3/8"
T
DOVETAIL SLOT
1/4 X 1/4" GROOVE
3/8"
1/2"

DRAWER SIDE DETAIL

1/8 X 1/8" RABBET FOR INLAY
A,K

DETAIL 5

D
3/8"
A
J W G

DETAIL 4

⑤
1-3/4" SQUARE
I 1/4"
B
A
W
E
F
3/8"
D
13/16"
15/16"

DETAIL 3

3/8" X 45° CHAMFER
C
3/4"
1-3/4" SQUARE
COUNTERSINK FOR 1-1/2" NO. 8 FH SCREW

DETAIL 6

As with several of our other signature pieces, this solid mahogany night table has stunning detailing and inlays of the arresting African wood wenge, and lovely decorative panels veneered with highly figured pomele sapele. These features give vibrant life to an otherwise fairly utilitarian piece. The veneer and lumber are available from a number of mail-order supply houses.

Making the Legs

Rip and crosscut 1¾-in.-thick stock to size for the legs. Then install a straight bit in the router table and use it to cut the ⅛ x ⅛-in. rabbet at the leg corners for the wenge inlay.

To make the inlay, clamp a rip fence to your band saw and cut slightly oversize ⁵⁄₃₂-in.-thick strips of wenge stock (**Fig. 1**). Then rip these pieces into square inlay strips and crosscut them to length.

Apply a small bead of glue to a leg rabbet and position one of the wenge strips. Use masking tape to clamp it in place (**Fig. 2**), and then repeat the process for each inlay. When the glue has set, use sandpaper or a scraper to trim the strips flush.

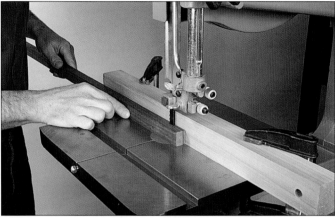

Fig. 1 *Clamp a fence to your band saw and rip ⁵⁄₃₂-in.-square pieces of wenge for the leg-corner and top inlays.*

Fig. 2 *Glue the inlay strips into the leg-corner rabbets. Place masking tape every 2 in. to securely clamp the strip to the leg.*

Materials List

Key	No.	Size and description (use)
A	4	1¾ x 1¾ x 22¾" mahogany (leg)
B*	16	⅛ x ⅛ x 22¾" wenge (inlay)
C	4	¾ x 1¾ x 1¾" wenge (foot)
D	2	¾ x 12¾ x 16¼" MDF (side core)
E	2	12¾ x 16¼" mahogany veneer
F	2	12¾ x 16¼" pomele sapele veneer
G	2	1 x 1¾ x 12¾" mahogany (side rail)
H	2	¾ x 1¾ x 19" mahogany (bottom rail)
I	1	¾ x 4 x 19" mahogany (back rail)
J	1	¾ x 14¼ x 17½" mahogany plywood (shelf)
K	1	¾ x 15⅞ x 20¼" MDF (top core)
L	1	15⅞ x 20¼" pomele sapele veneer
M	1	15⅞ x 20¼" mahogany veneer
N*	1	⅛ x ⅛ x 20¼" wenge (inlay)
O*	2	⅛ x ⅛ x 15¾" wenge (inlay)
P	1	¹³⁄₁₆ x 1⅛ x 22½" mahogany (edge band)
Q	2	¹³⁄₁₆ x 1⅛ x 17⅜" mahogany (edge band)
R	1	⅜ x ¹³⁄₁₆ x 20¼" mahogany (edge band)
S	1	¾ x 3¹⁵⁄₁₆ x 17⅜" mahogany (drawer face)
T	2	½ x 2½ x 13¼" maple (drawer side)
U	1	½ x 1¾ x 16½" maple (drawer back)
V	1	¼ x 12¼ x 16½" plywood (drawer bottom)
W	as reqd.	No. 20 plate
X	3	½" No. 8 rh wood screw
Y	4	1½" No. 8 fh wood screw
Z1	1	Drawer pull
Z2	1	Drawer slide (pair)

Misc.: Glue; 120-, 220-, 320-grit sandpaper; 4/0 steel wool; sealer/finish.

*Finished dimensions, cut oversize and trim flush.

Fig. 3 *Glue and screw ¾-in.-thick wenge foot blocks to the legs. Then use a table saw or sharp plane to chamfer each foot.*

Fig. 4 *Use a straightedge to guide the veneer saw. Make light passes to avoid splitting or tearing the delicate—and expensive—veneer.*

Fig. 5 *Use a foam roller to spread glue onto one face of the cores. Attempt to apply an even coating and do not leave pools of glue.*

Fig. 6 *Arrange the panels in a stack with a layer of kraft or wax paper between each panel. Use as many clamps as possible.*

Next, cut ¾-in.-thick wenge into 1¾-in.-square blocks for the table feet. Bore and countersink a screw hole in the center of each block and secure the blocks with glue and screws (**Fig. 3**). Then use your table saw or a sharp plane to cut the ⅛-in. chamfer around the bottom edges of each foot.

Veneering

Cut the veneer sheets to size for the side and top panels. Because the pomele sapele veneer is quite expensive, use plain sliced mahogany veneer for the inner surfaces. When preparing the veneer, plan to make the panels about 1 in. larger than finished dimension—you'll trim them to exact size when the veneering is done.

Cut the veneer for both the side and top panels, using a straightedge to guide the veneer saw (**Fig. 4**). Make a series of light passes to cut through the sheets. If you press too hard, you run the risk of tearing or splitting the delicate veneer.

Then, cut ¾-in.-thick MDF (medium-density fiberboard) to the same size as the veneer for the panel cores, and prepare two similar-size cauls from ¾-in.-thick MDF, plywood, or other flat stock.

Begin with the side panels. You can easily press two or even four of these small panels at one time. Begin by applying glue to one face of one of the core panels (**Fig. 5**). Invert the core onto one of the veneer sheets and apply glue to the exposed surface. Carefully position the veneer sheet on the second side. Repeat the process for each panel. Stack the panels and place the cauls on the top and bottom of the pile. Use kraft or wax paper sheets between each panel assembly and also between the panels and cauls.

Apply clamps to the stack, beginning in the center and working toward the edges (**Fig. 6**). Use as many clamps as you can fit around the stack to ensure maximum clamping pressure. Then veneer the tabletop. Let the glue set for at least

Fig. 7 *Cut plate slots in the side panels and bottom side rails. Hold the joiner and work against a table to register the cuts.*

Fig. 8 *After you finish gluing the bottom rails to the case sides, use plates to join the sides and the rails to the table legs.*

2 hours, separate the panels and allow them to air-dry overnight. Use a cabinet scraper or sandpaper to remove any paper or glue on the veneered faces, and trim the panels to finished size.

The Sides and Shelf

Cut the side rails to size, mark the joining plate positions, and cut the slots (**Fig. 7**). Apply glue to the slots, plates, and mating edges, join a rail to each panel and clamp until the glue sets. Next, lay out and cut the joining plate slots for the leg/panel joints and assemble the table sides (**Fig. 8**).

Mark the locations of the rail mortises in the side assemblies and use a router with a spiral up-cutting bit and edge guide to cut the joints. Remember to take two or three passes to cut the full mortise depth. With the routing done, finish the joints by squaring the ends of each mortise with a sharp chisel (**Fig. 9**).

Fig. 9 *Use a router to cut the mortises for the front and back rails. Then square the mortise ends with a sharp chisel.*

Cut ¾-in. mahogany stock to size for the front and back rails. Install a dado blade in the table saw to cut the tenons on the rail ends (**Fig. 10**). Readjust the blade height to cut the shoulders of each tenon. Test the fit of the tenons in their joints. If a joint is too tight, you can sand a tenon cheek lightly until it fits. If a joint is too loose, you can glue a veneer shim to the tenon cheek.

Cut the bottom shelf panel to size, then mark and cut the joining plate slots in the panel edges. Cut the mating slots in the bottom rails, then join the rails to the panel (**Fig. 11**).

Cut the plate slots in the table sides for the bottom shelf joint (**Fig. 12**). This job is easy if you clamp a straight board to the side to act as a guide in locating the plate joiner.

Next, lay out and cut the plate slots in the top edges of the side assemblies and back rail. These slots will be used to join the tabletop to the base.

Making the Top

Rout the inlay rabbet along the front and two side edges of the veneered top (**Fig. 13**). Cut the inlay strips to length, and glue them into the panel rabbets using masking tape as a clamp (**Fig. 14**). After waiting at least an hour, remove the tape and sand or scrape the inlay flush.

Rip ¹³⁄₁₆-in. stock to width for the top-panel edge bands. Note that the back strip is ⅜-in. wide and the side and front strips are 1⅛-in. wide. Cut the strips to length.

Glue the back edge band to the panel first and, when the glue has set, begin to apply the side and front edging strips (**Fig. 15**). When the glue has cured, mark guidelines ¼-in. from the edges and use a sharp plane to shape the angled profile to the lines (**Fig. 16**).

Next, lay out the position of the joining plate slots on the bottom side of the tabletop, and cut the slots with the plate joiner. Apply glue to the mortises, tenons, slots, and plates for assembly of the table base. Join the bottom shelf

Fig. 10 *Install a dado blade in the table saw and cut the rail tenons. A board clamped to the rip fence serves as a stop.*

Fig. 13 *With the top panel cut to exact size, use a straight bit and edge guide to rout the inlay rabbet at the front and two sides.*

MATERIAL*Matters*

Although not critical to the function of the piece, surface blemishes not only detract from the appeal of the finished piece, they are also extremely dispiriting. Few things are worse in woodworking than to put a great many hours and untold effort into a high quality project, only to wind up with a dent, ding, or scratch ruining an otherwise perfect chair or table. Fortunately, you don't need to accept those imperfections.

Simple, shallow dents in the wood surface are usually caused by sharp blows that compress the wood fibers. These can be removed fairly simply by steaming. Place a moistened cloth over the spot and apply heat and pressure using a household iron. Keep the iron moving and use medium heat. The steam causes the compressed wood fibers to swell back to original size. Repeat the procedure until the depression is raised even with the wood surface, then sand to finish.

Small holes and blemishes, such as scratches, are easily patched using any of a wide range of wood-filling compounds. These fillers come in various colors to match different woods, such as ash, birch, maple, mahogany, oak, and walnut. Be careful in your choice of compound and test on a hidden section. Avoid overspreading on coarse-grained woods such as oak, and be aware that these fillers become most conspicuous under stains or clear gloss coatings.

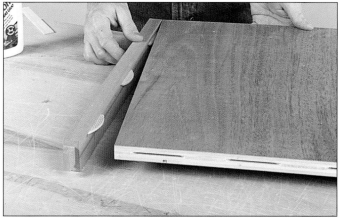

Fig. 11 *Cut plate joint slots in the mahogany-plywood shelf and the front and back lower rails. Then join the rails to the shelf.*

Fig. 12 *Lay out the plate slots in the table sides for attaching the bottom shelf. Use a straight board as a guide for the joiner.*

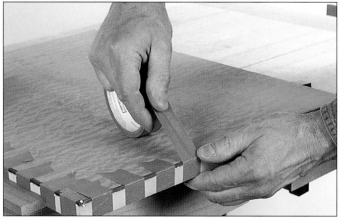

Fig. 14 *Apply glue to the rabbets and install the inlay. Use masking tape to clamp the strips in place, and sand or scrape them flush.*

Fig. 15 *After gluing the back edging strip to the top panel, install the mitered front and side strips and clamp the assembly.*

Fig. 16 *Carefully place guide marks ¼ in. from the edge of the tabletop and use a sharp plane to shape the angled profile.*

Fig. 17 *Spread glue in the side mortises and on the rail tenons. Then join the back top rail and shelf assembly to the sides.*

Fig. 18 *Spread glue in the slots and on the joining plates for joining the top to the sides and the back rail. Securely clamp the assembly.*

Fig. 19 *Use a ½-in. dovetail bit to rout the slots in the drawer face and sides. Guide the cuts with a board clamped to the work.*

assembly and top back rail to one of the table sides, and then add the opposite side (**Fig. 17**). Stand the base on a flat table and apply clamps to pull the joints tight. When the glue has set, add the top to the base assembly (**Fig. 18**).

Drawer Construction

Cut the drawer parts to finished dimension. Use a ½-in. dovetail bit in your router to cut the slots in both the drawer sides and face (**Fig. 19**).

Note that the slots in the face stop short of the top edge, so mark the top limit of the cut and proceed slowly. Clamp a straightedge to the workpiece to act as a guide and run the router base along the edge.

Then, use a ¼-in. straight bit and accessory edge guide to cut the slots for the drawer bottom in the sides and face (**Fig. 20**). Remember that the slot in the drawer face extends only between the dovetail slots.

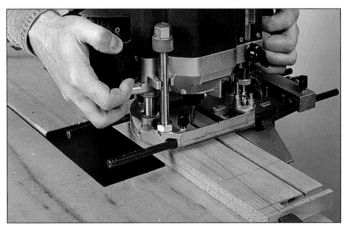

Fig. 20 *Use a ¼-in. straight bit to rout slots for the drawer bottom. The slot in the face runs only between the dovetail slots.*

TECH *Tips*

Glue-line indents are caused when glue is absorbed by the wood, which swells, and the wood is sanded before the water in the glue evaporates and the wood has had a chance to return to its original shape. Indentation lines become extremely apparent under certain finishes, especially those that are reflective. To avoid indentation lines, be sure to allow sufficient drying time after gluing, before you start to sand the piece for finishing. The only fix after the finish has been applied is to sand down the lines and apply the finish all over again.

Install the dovetail bit in a router table and use it to cut the joints on the ends of the drawer sides and back (**Fig. 21**). Clamp a backup board and guide strip to the workpiece when routing to prevent the wood from splitting at the end of the cut. Trim the small notch at the front edge of the drawer sides with a dovetail saw.

Spread glue in the dovetail-joint mating surfaces and assemble the drawer box. If the joints fit properly, you won't need to clamp the joints. Compare opposite diagonal measurements to make sure that the drawer is square and adjust it if necessary. Slide the drawer bottom into position and fasten it to the back with screws.

Screw the drawer slides to the bottom of the drawer (**Fig. 22**) and night table sides (**Fig. 23**), and slide the drawer into position. You should have a 1⁄16-in. margin at the top and sides of the drawer face. If the space is uneven, sand or plane the face until it looks correct. Bore

MATERIAL*Matters*

Wood screws are designated by length in inches, gauge number (shank diameter), and screwhead style. For example: 1¹/₂-in. No. 8 fh (flathead) screw. The higher the gauge number, the larger the screw shank.

However, each gauge number comes in several lengths. Therefore, a 1-in. No. 12 has a thicker shank than a 3-in. No. 8 screw. Wood screws are commonly available with flat, round, and oval heads in slotted, Phillips, and Robertson styles. Also, screw lengths are measured from the screw tip to the part of the head that is flush with the wood. Measure a flathead screw to the top of the head. A roundhead screw is measured to the bottom surface of the head. Whenever possible, screw through the inner piece of wood and into the thicker board.

As a general rule of thumb, ²/₃ of the screw's length should be driven into the thicker board. Here's the proper method of installing a wood screw:

1 Bore a pilot hole to a depth equal to about ³/₄ of the screw length. The pilot hole must be slightly smaller in diameter than the threaded portion of the screw.

2 Bore a screw-shank clearance hole through the first, thinner board only.

3 Countersink the hole.

Fig. 21 *Use the dovetail bit in a router table to cut the angled profile on the ends of the drawer sides and back.*

Fig. 22 *Fasten the drawer slides to the bottom edge of the sides. Note that the slides are held ³/₄ in. back from the face.*

a hole for the knob, but don't install it until the finish has been applied.

Finishing

First remove the drawer and slides. Then sand all the parts starting with 120-grit sandpaper and working through to 220-grit sandpaper, dusting off thoroughly when switching grits and when complete.

We used sealer/finish for our table. You should use a brush or rag to liberally soak all surfaces, and let all the parts sit for about 30 minutes before thoroughly wiping off any excess.

Allow the parts to dry overnight, then sand lightly with 320-grit sandpaper and dust off before applying the next coat. Apply at least three coats in this manner. After the final coat has cured, rub the surface with 4/0 steel wool and polish it with a soft cloth.

Fig. 23 *Screw the drawer slides to the sides of the nightstand. Bore pilot holes to guarantee that they are accurately positioned.*

China Bound

This sideboard is designed as more than an accent—
it will care for precious china, linens, and cutlery.

U sually, a sideboard is considered just a
companion piece to a dining room table. As
such, people frequently purchase the two as an
ensemble, along with chairs and maybe a china cabinet
or hutch. But this doesn't have to be the case. These
days it's not uncommon to see a pine wardrobe housing
stereo equipment in the family room, or a Queen Anne
reproduction end table next to an overstuffed
contemporary sofa. This sideboard is a prime example
of a multi-use piece that will complement a range of
other furniture styles and settings. It serves equally well
in a hall, dining room, or family room.

Key POINTS

TIME
Prep Time	4 hours
Shop Time	10 hours
Assembly Time	8 hours

EFFORT
Skill Level	intermediate

COST / BENEFITS
Expense: moderate

- Multi-use piece that provides a wealth of storage and lovely dining room accent.
- Sideboard style allows for placement in other rooms.

135

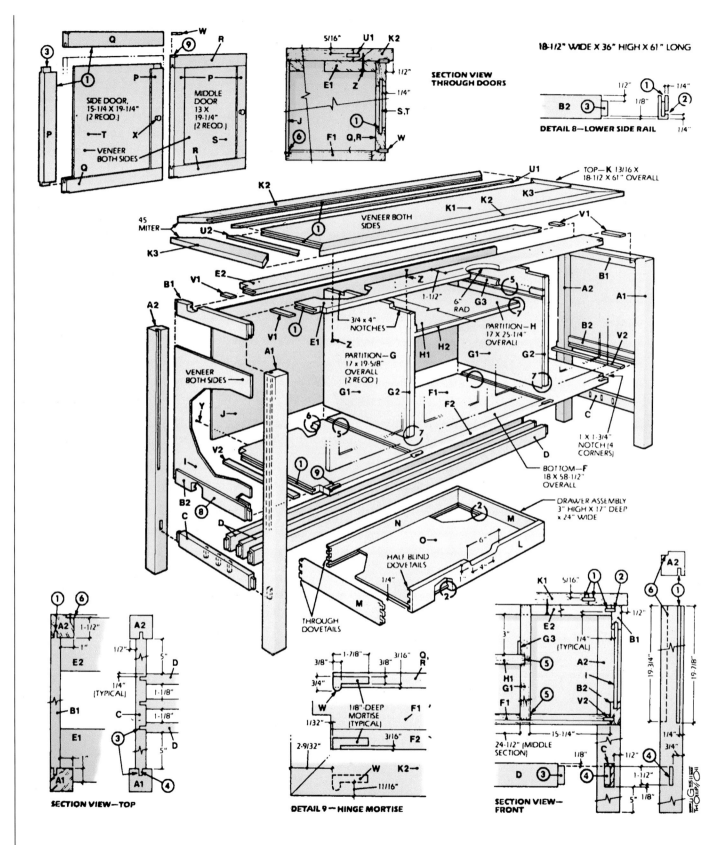

SECTION VIEW
THROUGH DOORS

18-1/2" WIDE X 36" HIGH X 61" LONG

SIDE DOOR,
15-1/4 X 19-1/4"
(2 REQD.)

VENEER
BOTH SIDES

MIDDLE
DOOR
13 X
19-1/4"
(2 REQD.)

DETAIL 8—LOWER SIDE RAIL

45
MITER

VENEER BOTH
SIDES

TOP—K 13/16 X
18-1/2 X 61" OVERALL

VENEER
BOTH SIDES

3/4 x 4"
NOTCHES

6"
RAD

PARTITION—H
17 X 25-1/4"
OVERALL

PARTITION—G
17 x 19-5/8"
OVERALL
(2 REQD.)

1 X 1-3/4"
NOTCH (4
CORNERS)

BOTTOM—F
18 X 58-1/2"
OVERALL

DRAWER ASSEMBLY
3" HIGH X 17" DEEP
x 24" WIDE

HALF BLIND
DOVETAILS

THROUGH
DOVETAILS

SECTION VIEW—TOP

1-1/2"
1"

1/4"
(TYPICAL)

1/8"-DEEP
MORTISE
(TYPICAL)

DETAIL 9 — HINGE MORTISE

SECTION VIEW—
FRONT

1/4"
(TYPICAL)

24-1/2" (MIDDLE
SECTION)

15-1/4"

19-3/4"

19-7/8"

136 | CHINA BOUND

We thought it would be extremely worthwhile to build a sideboard with generous open storage space so that the piece could be used in other rooms just as easily as the dining room. And it certainly doesn't hurt that in the process, we managed to feature some high-class veneer work with some truly spectacular fiddleback mahogany veneer. This kind of surface lends distinction to any style, and is perfect for the period style we chose for the sideboard. As you can see, the basic design roots of this piece come from the Mission furniture style, but we hope our refinements have brought the piece into a more contemporary environment. Regardless of what style your dining room pieces may be, this sideboard should provide an excellent complement.

Stock Preparation

Begin by preparing the solid stock. Cut pieces to rough size, and joint and thickness plane to specified dimension. Then cut legs, stiles, rails, and stretchers to finished size. Rip the top frame pieces and edge banding to width, leaving them to be cut to length later.

Cut the plywood pieces to rough size for the case bottom and partitions (**Fig. 1**). When the glue has dried, use a sharp plane to trim the edge banding flush to the surface of the panels. Then cut all plywood parts to finished size.

Using a router with a ¾-in. straight bit, cut the stopped dadoes in the bottom for case partitions. Use a sharp chisel to square the end of each dado. Next, use a band saw or sabre saw to cut the notch in the partition tops for the front and rear stretchers. Then cut the notches in the bottom front corner of the partitions so that they will fit into their stopped dadoes (**Fig. 2**). Complete the partitions by cutting the

Fig. 1 Cut the mahogany plywood to size for the bottom and interior case partitions. Glue and clamp the edge banding in place.

Materials List

Key	No.	Size and description (use)
A1	2	1¾ x 1¾ x 35¼" mahogany (leg)
A2	2	1¾ x 1¾ x 35¼" mahogany (leg)
B1	2	¾ x 1¾ x 15½" mahogany (side rail)
B2	2	¾ x 1¾ x 15½" mahogany (side rail)
C	2	¾ x 1¾ x 15½" mahogany (side stretcher)
D	3	¾ x 1¾ x 58½" mahogany (bottom stretcher)
E1	1	¾ x 4 x 58½" mahogany (top stretcher)
E2	1	¾ x 4 x 58½" mahogany (top stretcher)
F1	1	¾ x 17 x 58½" mahogany plywood (bottom)
F2	1	¾ x 1 x 58½" mahogany (edge band)
G1	2	¾ x 16½ x 19⅝" mahogany plywood (partition)
G2	2	½ x ¾ x 19⅝" mahogany (edge band)
G3	2	¼ x 1 x 17" mahogany (drawer spacer)
H1	1	¾ x 16½ x 25¼" mahogany plywood (partition)
H2	1	½ x ¾ x 25¼" mahogany (edge band)
I	2	¼ x 15½ x 17½" veneered plywood (side)
J	1	¼ x 19¾ x 57½" mahogany plywood (back)
K1	1	¾ x 12½ x 55" veneered MDF (top)

Key	No.	Size and description (use)
K2	2	¹³⁄₁₆ x 3 x 61" mahogany (side frame)
K3	2	¹³⁄₁₆ x 3 x 18½" mahogany (end frame)
L	1	1 x 3 x 24" mahogany (drawer front)
M	2	½ x 3 x 16½" mahogany (drawer side)
N	1	½ x 3 x 24" mahogany (drawer back)
O	1	¼ x 16 x 23½" mahogany plywood (drawer bottom)
P	8	¾ x 1¾ x 16¾" mahogany (door stile)
Q	4	¾ x 1¾ x 15¼" mahogany (side door rail)
R	4	¾ x 1¾ x 13" mahogany (middle door rail)
S	2	¼ x 10½ x 16¾" veneered plywood (middle door panel)
T	2	¼ x 12¾ x 16¾" veneered plywood (side door panel)
U1	2	¼ x 1 x 57" hardwood (spline)
U2	2	¼ x 1 x 14½" hardwood (spline)
V1	4	¼ x ¾ x 3" hardwood (spline)
V2	2	¼ x ¾ x 14½" hardwood (spline)
W	8	⅜ x 1⅞" knife hinge
X	4	bronze door pull
Y	as reqd.	⅝" No. 5 rh screws
Z	16	1¼" No. 8 fh screws

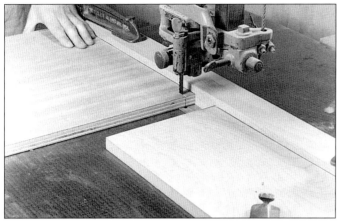

Fig. 2 *Cut the appropriate notches in the bottom and partitions by hand or with a table saw. For the latter, use a stop block clamped to the table.*

Fig. 3 *Using a router and edge guide, cut a ¼ x ½-in. rabbet—for the case back—along the back edge of the bottom panel.*

Fig. 4 *Using a router and straight bit, with an edge guide, cut stopped dadoes in the bottom and partitions. Square the dado ends with a chisel.*

Fig. 5 *Cut the legs to size, then using a router and guide, cut a stopped groove in each leg. The groove accepts the side rails and panels.*

stopped dadoes for the horizontal drawer partition.

Next, cut the notches in the bottom panel and top stretchers to accommodate the legs, and carefully cut the arc in the front edge of the top stretcher that serves as clearance for drawer access. To complete, rout a rabbet in the case bottom to receive the back.

Clamp each rear leg between bench dogs and rout a stopped rabbet to receive the case back (**Fig. 3**). Then readjust the router, and use a ¼-in. straight bit and edge guide to cut the stopped dado in each leg (**Fig. 4 and 5**). This groove will accommodate both the rails and the side panels. Also, cut the mortise in the legs for side stretchers by boring overlapping holes and squaring them with a chisel.

Install dado blades in a table saw and make these cuts: the panel grooves in the door rails and stiles; the panel grooves in the side rails; the spline grooves in the top frame member; and the spline grooves in the side rails.

Adjust the dado blades and cut the tenons on the ends of the side rails, side stretchers, bottom stretchers, and door stiles (**Fig. 6**). Complete the tenons by cutting the proper shoulders with a sharp backsaw. Then, use a router with a slotting bit to cut the spline grooves in the top panel, the bottom panel, and the ends of the top stretchers. Sand all parts smooth with 120-grit sandpaper, then begin assembly.

The first stage of assembly entails gluing and clamping the case partitions to the horizontal drawer partition. When dry, glue and clamp the case bottom to the partitions and glue and screw the top stretchers in place. Check the assembly for square before you set it aside.

Now you can begin veneering. As previously stated, we chose a fiddleback mahogany veneer for our project. Generally, veneers are sold in sheets from 1 ft. to 16 ft. long with the width changing depending on the species. The amount of veneer necessary for a given project will vary according to the lengths and widths available and the pattern you want to achieve. Probably the most common pattern is bookmatching, in which consecutive sheets of veneer are joined together side-by-side to form a mirror image of the grain pattern. This is the method used on this piece. Keep in mind that you must veneer both sides of the panel; therefore, we used a less expensive backing veneer that matched the density of the face veneer.

Begin by cutting the sheets to rough length using a utility knife and straightedge guide (**Fig. 8**). Score the veneer twice and lift it to separate the pieces. Arrange a straightening jig by placing a flat panel with a straightedge at least as long as the veneer on the worktable. Place the two sheets of veneer you want to match on the panel, overhanging the straightedge by about ⅛ in. Clamp a board over the veneers with its edge held back from the panel's straightedge. Use a router with a flush trimming bit to trim the edges.

Safety Sense

Right Routing
A good rule of thumb for routing is that if the router base can cover the entire piece you're working on at any time, then the router should be mounted on a table and the wood should be run using a fence and pushstick. When in doubt, always use more precaution. When you are using a router that is not table mounted, always be sure to keep both your hands on the router.

Fig. 6 *Cut all the necessary tenons on the side rails, case stretchers and door stiles, using a dado blade in a radial-arm or table saw.*

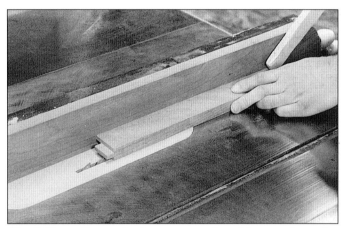

Fig. 7 *The rails need edge grooves for side panels, and face grooves for bottom and stretcher splines. Cut the grooves with a dado blade.*

Fig. 8 *To cut the veneer to length, score the sheet with a sharp utility knife using a straightedge guide. Lift the sheet to separate.*

Fig. 9 *To bookmatch two pieces of veneer, apply small pieces of veneer tape across the seam and a full piece of tape along the seam.*

Fig. 10 *When the veneer is ready, cut the core panel to size. Then roll glue over the surface of panel. Do not apply glue to the veneer.*

Fig. 11 *Place the veneer on top of the core panel, then clamp in place. Use cauls and battens to ensure even clamping pressure.*

Fig. 12 *Once the glue is dry, remove the panel from the clamps and scrape the veneer tape off the surface using a sharp cabinet scraper.*

The veneer is temporarily joined together using preglued veneer tape, available at veneer suppliers. Wet the tape with a damp sponge. Hold the pieces in proper alignment and apply the tape as shown (**Fig. 9**).

Cut the plywood for the veneer panel slightly oversize to allow for trimming after the veneer is applied (**Fig. 10**). Keep in mind that these days most ¼-in.-thick plywood actually measures somewhere between ³⁄₁₆ and ⁷⁄₃₂ in. thick. Because of this, once our panels are veneered on both sides, they will fit in the ¼-in.-wide grooves that we specify. If you use full ¼-in.-thick plywood, increase the width of all case grooves and tenons. Also, be sure to orient the panels so that the grain on the plywood runs at 90° to the face veneer grain.

To apply the veneer, an adequate press must be constructed. Make top and bottom cauls of ¾-in. flakeboard slightly larger than the panel size. Then cut some slightly crowned battens (**Fig. 11**); they will bear on the cauls and distribute the clamping pressure evenly.

Begin by covering the bottom caul with waxed paper and laying down the sheet of backer veneer over the paper. Using a small roller, spread glue over the entire surface of the plywood panel.

Then place the glued surface onto the veneer. Apply glue to the top side of the panel, and place the face veneer, taped side up, onto the plywood. Cover the veneer with waxed paper, followed by the upper caul. Place the battens under and over the assembly, then position the clamps. Start at the center of the panel and tighten the clamps, working toward the outside edges. Let the panel sit in the clamps for at least four hours. Then trim all panels to finished size.

Final Assembly

Use the router and slot cutter to cut the spline groove around the top panel and along the inside edges of the top frame pieces (**Fig. 13**). Cut the mitered ends on the top frame

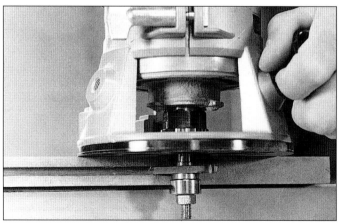

Fig. 13 *Top frame members are joined to the top panel with splines. Cut grooves in the mating edges with a router and slotting cutter.*

members (**Fig. 14**). Then join them to the top panel with glue and splines. Use bar clamps to hold the joints tight.

Assemble each case side, applying glue only to the places where the rails and stretchers join the legs. Do not glue the side panels in place. They should simply float.

Next, join the case side assemblies to the interior case assembly with glue, splines, and clamps. At this point, attach the back to hold the case square. Attach the top by driving screws up through the top stretchers. Assemble the doors, again gluing only the mortise-and-tenon joints and leaving the panels loose. Construct the drawer, following the dimensions provided in the plans. Attach the mahogany drawer spacer to the partitions with glue and brads. Set and fill the brad heads.

Lay out the hinge location on the case bottom and top,

then cut the mortises for each hinge and trim the doors to allow a uniform 1/16-in. space around the perimeter. Next, lay out and cut the hinge mortises on the top and bottom edges of each door. Attach one leaf of each top hinge to the door (**Fig. 15**). Install its mating leaf on the underside of the case top. Then attach both leaves of each lower hinge to the case bottom. Lift each door into place and slide the post on the top hinge into its mating socket, then attach the bottom hinge to the bottom edge of the door.

Remove the doors and case back, then sand the entire case thoroughly with 220-grit sandpaper. We stained the case using antique cherry tungseal wood stain, available at lumber yards and most large home centers. Allow the piece to dry overnight. To finish the sideboard, apply two coats of high-quality, high-gloss varnish.

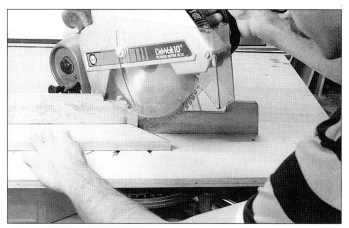

Fig. 14 *Cut miters on the ends of the top frame members using a miter box or table saw. Make precise cuts to create tight joints.*

Fig. 15 *Clamp each door in a vise, then cut the hinge mortises. Slide the hinge in place, bore clearance holes, and drive the screws.*

TECH *Tips*

Final finishing is the icing on the cake where woodworking is concerned. The last thing you want is a poor finish that detracts from your workmanship. When it comes to varnishing, use this 4-step process to ensure drips and bare spots don't mar the beauty of your newly finished piece.

1 CORRECT GRIP. Hold the brush in much the same way you would hold a pencil, with your thumb draped over the brush handle, and your fingers completely supporting the body of the brush. A correct grip will provide you the most control over finish application.

2 START BY LOADING. Dip the brush and brush liberal amounts of varnish over the wood surface, ensuring that the surface grain is completely coated. Use bright lights from different angles to check that you've left no bare spots.

3 LEVEL THE VARNISH. Draw the brush across the grain, and clear it each time against the rim of the can or a drip wire. Be sure to remove all excess varnish from the surface and constantly check for drips.

4 TIP OFF. Level the final coat and remove all extra varnish by drawing an almost-dry brush across the surface with the bristles held at a 30° angle. Make a complete pass across the surface, end to end, and then wipe the bristles on a clean, lint-free cloth or paper towel. Each stroke should overlap the preceding one.

Write On

This elegant two-tone ebonized writing table is surprisingly simple to build.

T his writing table is constructed with two of the most elegant hardwoods available, cherry and mahogany. Both have been prized by generations of woodworkers for their beauty and dimensional stability. The top panel is mahogany plywood edge banded with solid mahogany strips that are mitered at their corners and secured to the panels with splines. Using plywood, as opposed to solid wood, makes the top relatively simple to make. The base is ebonized cherry, which lends the distinctive styling to the piece. An ebonized finish is one in which the wood is considerably darkened, to look like ebony, while still allowing its grain and character to be evident.

Key POINTS

TIME
Prep Time . . . . 6 hours
Shop Time . . . . 12 hours
Assembly Time . . . . 8 hours

EFFORT
Skill Level . . . . basic

COST / BENEFITS
Expense: moderate
• Durable work surface and **unique, formal style** combine to make this desk an extremely useful showpiece.

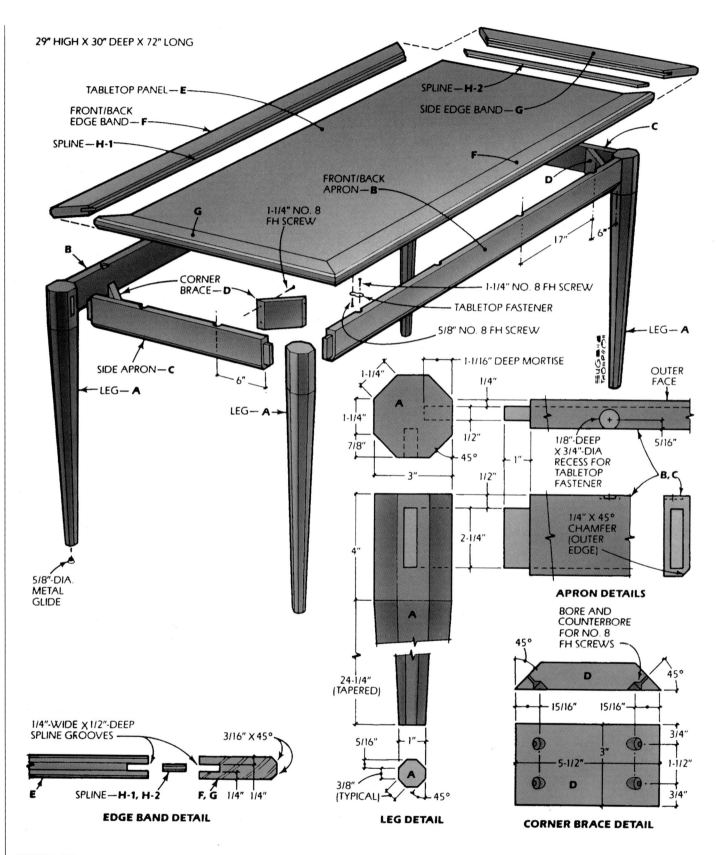

29" HIGH X 30" DEEP X 72" LONG

TABLETOP PANEL—**E**

FRONT/BACK EDGE BAND—**F**

SPLINE—**H-1**

SPLINE—**H-2**

SIDE EDGE BAND—**G**

C

F

D

FRONT/BACK APRON—**B**

1-1/4" NO. 8 FH SCREW

G

17"

6"

B

CORNER BRACE—**D**

1-1/4" NO. 8 FH SCREW

TABLETOP FASTENER

SIDE APRON—**C**

5/8" NO. 8 FH SCREW

LEG—**A**

6"

LEG—**A**

LEG—**A**

5/8"-DIA. METAL GLIDE

LEG—**A**

1-1/16" DEEP MORTISE

OUTER FACE

1-1/4"

1/4"

A

1-1/4"

1/2"

7/8"

45°

3"

1/2"

1"

5/16"

1/8"-DEEP X 3/4"-DIA RECESS FOR TABLETOP FASTENER

B, C

1/2"

2-1/4"

4"

1/4" X 45° CHAMFER (OUTER EDGE)

A

APRON DETAILS

BORE AND COUNTERBORE FOR NO. 8 FH SCREWS

45°

45°

D

24-1/4" (TAPERED)

5/16"

1"

15/16"

15/16"

3/4"

3"

3/4"

1/4"-WIDE X 1/2"-DEEP SPLINE GROOVES

3/16" X 45°

3/8" (TYPICAL)

45°

5-1/2"

1-1/2"

D

E

SPLINE—**H-1, H-2**

F, G 1/4" 1/4"

A

EDGE BAND DETAIL

LEG DETAIL

CORNER BRACE DETAIL

The top of this unusual and head-turning table is stained with an aniline dye to bring out the mahogany's warm red tones and provide a great base for the finish. It's finished with a traditional brushed varnish finish. This creates a fine sheen and protects against abrasion from objects and, of course, writing. The result of our combining contrasting, sophisticated tones and textures is a quiet elegance that belies the table's simple, but sturdy, construction.

Legs

For the table legs, use either 3-in.-thick cherry, or glue up thinner stock. If you opt to glue up the legs, start with slightly oversize stock and cut the workpieces to dimension after the glue has set.

Use a radial-arm saw or table saw to crosscut the leg blanks. Clamp a stop to the radial-arm saw fence, or an extension to the miter gauge, to ensure the legs are crosscut to the same length.

Lay out the octagon shape of the legs on top and bottom ends of each leg blank. Note that the legs begin to taper 4 in. down from the top, and measure 1 in. across at the bottom.

Mark a line around each leg about 4 in. down from the top to indicate the start of the taper (**Fig. 1**). Extend the octagon corner marks down the face of the legs. Then mark the position of the apron mortises on the leg faces.

Next, clamp a fence on the drill press table to help position the work, and use a ½-in.-dia. drill bit to bore overlapping holes. Remove most of the waste from each mortise (**Fig. 2**).

Fig. 1 *Draw a line around the leg to mark where it starts to taper, and extend taper lines down the leg. Mark the leg for the apron mortises.*

Fig. 2 *To clear the mortises, butt the leg against a fence clamped to the drill press table and bore overlapping holes with a ½-in-dia. bit.*

Fig. 3 *With the leg secured between bench dogs, use a sharp chisel and mallet to square the ends and smooth the walls of the mortise.*

Materials List

Key	No.	Size and description (use)
A	4	3 x 3 x 28 ¼" cherry (leg)
B	2	1 x 3 x 66" cherry (apron)
C	2	1 x 3 x 24" cherry (apron)
D	4	1 x 3 x 5 ½" cherry (corner brace)
E	1	¾ x 24 x 66" mahogany plywood (top)
F	2	¾ x 3 x 72" mahogany (edge band)
G	2	¾ x 3 x 30" mahogany (edge band)
H1	2	¼ x 1 x 67" plywood (spline)
H2	2	¼ x 1 x 25" plywood (spline)

Misc.: 12 top fasteners; 28-1¼" No. 8 fh screws; 12-⅝" No. 8 fh screws; 4-⅝"-dia. glides; medium brown mahogany stain; retarder; jet black stain; medium brown walnut stain.

Fig. 4 *Cut the leg tapers on a band saw. Feed the leg smoothly into the blade, and cut just to the waste side of the taper line.*

Fig. 5 *Use a belt sander to remove the saw marks and refine the leg taper. Be sure that the workpiece is firmly held to the bench.*

Fig. 6 *After the leg has been smoothed, connect the marks at the top of the leg to those on the bottom to draw remaining facets.*

Fig. 7 *Use a chamfer bit in a router to rough out the remaining leg facets. Each chamfer should be about ³⁄₈ in. wide.*

Fig. 8 *Finish shaping the legs with a hand plane. Work in the direction of the grain. If it's used against the grain, the plane will tear out wood.*

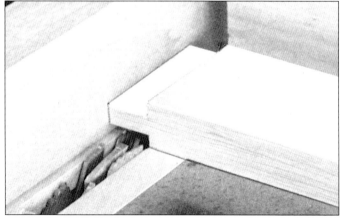

Fig. 9 *Cut the tenon cheeks on the aprons using a dado blade in the table saw. Butt the apron against the fence, and use a miter gauge to guide the cut.*

Then use a sharp chisel and mallet to square the ends and smooth the walls of the mortise (**Fig. 3**).

Next, use a band saw or sabre saw to make the taper cuts (**Fig. 4**). Cut on the waste side of the line. Then clamp the leg to the workbench, and use a belt sander to remove saw marks and bring the taper right to the line (**Fig. 5**). Mark the taper for the remaining sides on the newly cut surface, and saw the next tapers. Again, smooth the tapers with the belt sander working down to the layout line.

Mark the lines for the remaining leg facets (**Fig. 6**) and rough out the facets with a ⅜-in. chamfer bit (**Fig. 7**). Clamp the leg to the workbench, and carefully finish shaping the leg with a hand plane (**Fig. 8**).

Aprons/Base Assembly

Rip and crosscut the 1-in.-thick stock for table aprons. Use a stop block while crosscutting to ensure the aprons are the same length. Lay out the apron tenons. Using the dado blades in the table saw, make the cheek cut for the tenons (**Fig. 9**). You can leave the blade height in the same position to cut the shoulder at the apron's bottom edge (**Fig. 10**), but then raise the blade to cut the shoulder at the apron's top edge. Cut the tenons a hair large. Hold the apron in a bench hook and pare away the ridges left by the dado blades using a sharp chisel.

Test fit each mortise-and-tenon joint. The joints should be snug, but should not require great force to bring together. Finish shaping the aprons by using the chamfer bit in the router to cut the chamfer on the bottom edge apron members.

Mark the locations of the tabletop fasteners along the aprons' top edges, and use a ¾-in.-dia. multispur or Forstner bit in the drill press to cut each fastener's recess (**Fig. 11**).

Clamp a fence to the drill press table to keep the apron aligned under the bit. Begin the base assembly by joining two legs to each long apron. Apply glue to both mortise walls and the tenons, and use long bar clamps to bring the joints

Fig. 10 *Tip the apron on its side to cut the bottom tenon shoulder. Lower the blade height to cut the top tenon shoulder.*

Fig. 11 *Butt the apron to a fence clamped to the drill press table. Use a multispur or Forstner bit to bore the recess for the tabletop fasteners.*

MATERIAL*Matters*

Although most woodworkers have an idea of the difference between hardwoods and softwoods, the true difference is their source. Hardwoods come from deciduous trees (trees that shed their leaves in winter— with the exception of the bald cypress and larch). Softwoods come from conifers (needle-bearing trees). Hardwoods are generally more expensive than softwoods (with a few notable exceptions, such as furniture grade clear white pine) because they need more space and take more time to grow.

Hardwoods and softwoods have different lumber grading systems. The best cutting grade of hardwoods is called "Firsts." Then, in descending quality, come Seconds, Select, No. 1 Common, No. 2, No. 3A, and No. 3B Common. The gradings set standards for maximum allowance of waste material, minimum size of boards, minimum amount of surface area, and clarity of surface.

Softwoods are graded into two basic categories: Select and Common. Select grades are B and better, C, and D. The best grade of softwood is used for trim, moldings, and finish woodwork, where appearance is a primary consideration. Grade C has minor defects, and grade D has minor defects on one side, but larger defects on the other. Common grades descend in quality from No. 1 through No. 5.

Fig. 12 *Glue and clamp a pair of legs with an apron. Clamp a temporary support at the foot of the legs to maintain proper spacing.*

Fig. 13 *Glue and clamp together the subassemblies with the short aprons. Cut corner braces to span long and short aprons, and install.*

Fig. 14 *Cut a plywood panel for the tabletop. Here, a sliding table jig is used on the table saw, but a handheld circular saw works too.*

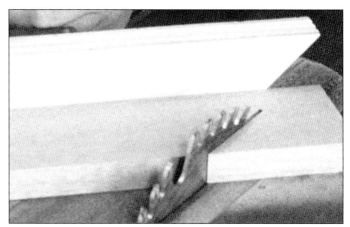

Fig. 15 *Cut the mitered edge band on the table saw. The edge band is cut to length, and the inside edge of the saw blade bisects the corner.*

Fig. 16 *Use a slot cutter in the router to make a spline groove in the panel and in the edge band. Cut the spline so that it fits snugly in the groove.*

Fig. 17 *Clamp the end edge bands in place first. Prevent the clamps from coming in contact with the glue by supporting them on strips.*

tight. To maintain equal spacing at the top and bottom of the leg, clamp a scrap board reaching from the foot of one leg to the other (**Fig. 12**). Cross measure the diagonals to check for square, adjust the clamps if necessary, and let the assembly dry.

Complete the base assembly by joining the short aprons to each side (**Fig. 13**). Carry out this assembly on a flat surface to avoid imparting any twist to the base. Again, cross measure to check for squareness, adjust if necessary, and let set.

Next, cut the corner braces for the base as shown in the plan. Use a table saw, radial-arm saw, or a miter box to cut the 45° angles at their ends (**Fig. 15**). Next, use a slotting cutter and router to cut the spline grooves in the panel and edge bands (**Fig. 16**). Cut the splines from ¼-in.-thick plywood or solid wood. Check that the plywood fits snugly in the groove, as the plywood is often less than ¼ in. thick. If the spline is loose, the panel and edge band won't accurately align.

Glue and clamp the end edge bands to the panel (**Fig. 17**). Spread glue on the panel and edge band and in the spline grooves. Clamp until the glue sets. Apply glue to the mitered surfaces, and apply the remaining two edge bands.

Use the chamfer bit in the router to cut the edge profile along the top and bottom edges of the tabletop.

Finishing

Sand the base and top with 120- and 220-grit sandpaper. Be careful throughout the sanding process not to sand through the panel's face veneer.

Sand the underside of the tabletop first, to get the feel of sanding mahogany veneer, which is relatively soft and easily removed by sanding. Vacuum off the dust and wipe clean with a tack cloth before proceeding.

The top was stained with medium brown mahogany aniline dye. We added retarder to this to prevent it from drying too rapidly and leaving lap marks. Let the stain dry for two hours before applying the top coat.

We used several heavy applications of aniline dye to ebonize the base (**Fig. 18**). The proportions we used were two parts jet black, four parts medium brown walnut, and two parts medium brown mahogany.

Mix the stains and apply the mixture with a cloth, brush, or spray. If you apply the stain with a cloth or a brush, add retarder to prevent lap marks. Let the stain dry for one hour, and apply a second coat. Let that coat dry, and apply a third coat, if you want the darkest color possible. When aniline stains dry, they appear considerably lighter than they will under the top coat. The color of the wet stain is closest to the finished color.

Next, we brushed on two coats of satin varnish to all parts, front and back. Let it dry overnight, and sand between coats with 600-grit, wet-or-dry paper. As with all varnish finishes, you can apply more coats for greater protection and a "deeper" looking finish. Because this is a satin finish,

Fig. 18 *Apply the ebonizing stain with a rag, brush, or by spraying. Wear gloves and use organic filter cartridges in your respirator.*

however, adding more coats will not increase its glossiness. If you desire a high-gloss finish, then apply a gloss varnish. A high-gloss varnish requires more work to rub out dust specks and other imperfections, such as lap marks.

With a high-gloss finish, follow the finish manufacturer's directions, as explained on the can label. With the 20-coat finish, use the tack cloth to wipe up the varnish dust. Use 4/0 steel wool to remove dust marks from the second coat and apply a light coat of wax.

When the finish is dry, attach the tabletop fasteners to the aprons with 1½-in.-long No. 8 fh screws. Invert the tabletop on a padded surface, and invert the base over it. Check for uniform overhang on all sides.

Then attach the top to the base using ⅝-in. No. 8 fh screws. When preboring the top for these screws, use a stop collar on the bit or mark the bit with a piece of masking tape. This should prevent you from boring through the top.

SHOP*Helper*

One of the most common problems around a woodshop is dropped nails, screws, and other fine pieces of metal. Instead of sweeping away money, or crawling around with a magnet, use this handy magnetic sweeper. Mount a strong magnet on a rectangular block of wood. Drill a hole on the opposite side for a broom handle, and secure in the hole. Now screw simple wheels onto the ends of the block and you have a rolling metal catcher, great for picking up screws and nails from the workshop, garage, or driveway.

Side Order

Now you can store CDs, DVDs, videos, and cassettes in high style with this useful classic side table.

This traditional-looking storage table keeps your CDs and tapes out of sight, but at the same time makes them easily accessible. Electronic entertainment media are everywhere these days. Cassette recorders, VCRs, and DVD and CD players have changed the way we enjoy our leisure time. These devices provide an almost unlimited selection of enriching and entertaining pursuits. Unfortunately, the more we use them, the more storage space we need. Most entertainment-center cabinets provide for some storage, but often this space is insufficient. To address this need, we designed a small side table with three drawers sized specifically for these items. Of course, it can also serve for other items such as papers and pens.

*Key*POINTS

TIME
Prep Time .... 4 hours
Shop Time .... 8 hours
Assembly Time .... 6 hours

EFFORT
Skill Level .... intermediate

COST / BENEFITS
Expense: moderate
- A one-of-a-kind piece that combines usefulness and classic styling.
- Attractive piece for many rooms in the house.

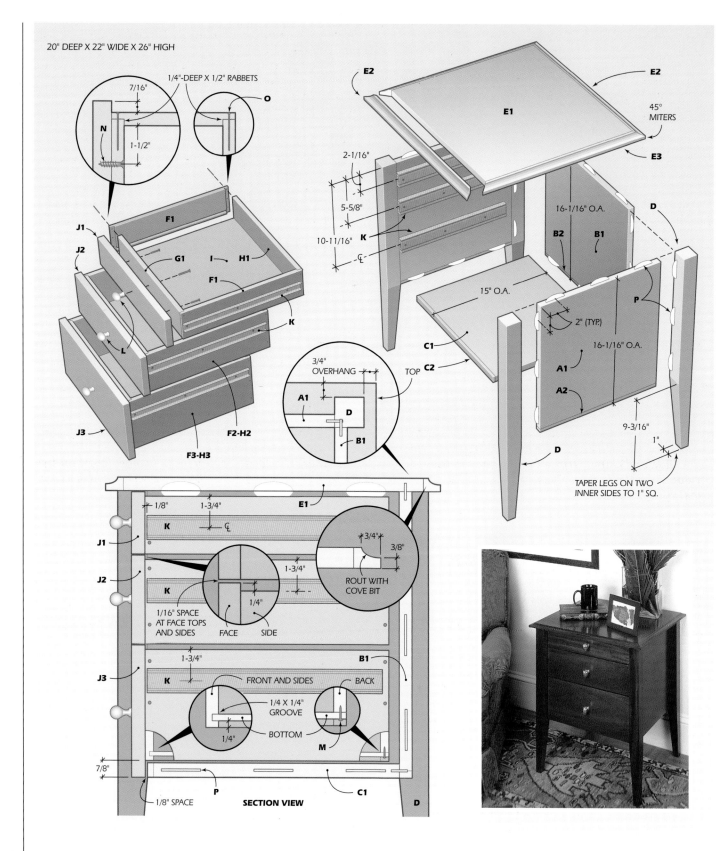

20" DEEP X 22" WIDE X 26" HIGH

1/4"-DEEP X 1/2" RABBETS

7/16"

O

N

1-1/2"

F1

J1

J2

G1   I   H1

F1

K

L

F2-H2

J3

F3-H3

E2

E2

E1

45° MITERS

E3

2-1/16"

5-5/8"

10-11/16"   K

C

16-1/16" O.A.

B2   B1

D

15" O.A.

2" (TYP.)

P

A1

16-1/16" O.A.

A2

C1

C2

9-3/16"

1"

D

3/4" OVERHANG

TOP

A1

D

B1

TAPER LEGS ON TWO INNER SIDES TO 1" SQ.

1/8"   1-3/4"

E1

K   C

3/4"

3/8"

ROUT WITH COVE BIT

J1

1-3/4"

J2

K

1/4"

1/16" SPACE AT FACE TOPS AND SIDES   FACE   SIDE

B1

1-3/4"

J3

K

FRONT AND SIDES   BACK

1/4 X 1/4" GROOVE

1/4"

BOTTOM

M

7/8"

P

1/8" SPACE   **SECTION VIEW**   C1   D

We built our table from solid mahogany and mahogany plywood, but it would look equally attractive in cherry or walnut. It has drawer boxes built of solid maple with slide-in plywood bottoms.

Building the Base and Top

Begin construction on your side table by cutting slightly oversize blanks for the table sides, back, and bottom from mahogany plywood. Rip and crosscut mahogany edge-banding strips.

Glue and clamp the strips. After 20 minutes, scrape off excess glue, then let the glue cure. Use a plane to trim the edge banding flush to the panel (**Fig. 1**). Next, trim the panels to finished dimension. Rip and crosscut the table legs, and mark their tapered profiles. Use a band saw to cut the legs to shape (**Fig. 2**). Clamp each leg to the workbench, then use a block plane to remove saw marks (**Fig. 3**).

Lay out the locations of the joining-plate slots on the sides, back, bottom, and legs. Use the plate joiner to cut all the slots except those in the rear legs that receive the case back. These are cut later. Hold a leg firmly to the workbench, and cut the joining-plate slot (**Fig. 4**). Cut the joining-plate slots in the panel edges and along the bottom edge of the

Fig. 1 *Glue and clamp strips of mahogany to the plywood panel edges, and then trim them flush to the panel with a block plane.*

Fig. 2 *Mark the taper on two faces of each leg, then cut the tapers on a band saw. Stay on the waste side of the pencil line.*

Materials List

Key	No.	Size and description (use)
A1	2	$^3/_4$ x 15 x 15$^{11}/_{16}$" plywood (side)
A2	2	$^3/_8$ x $^3/_4$ x 15" mahogany (edge banding)
B1	1	$^3/_4$ x 15$^{11}/_{16}$ x 17" plywood (back)
B2	1	$^3/_8$ x $^3/_4$ x 17" mahogany (edge banding)
C1	1	$^3/_4$ x 14$^5/_8$ x 17" plywood (bottom)
C2	1	$^3/_8$ x $^3/_4$ x 17" mahogany (edge banding)
D	4	1$^3/_4$ x 1$^3/_4$ x 25$^1/_4$" mahogany (leg)
E1	1	$^3/_4$ x 18 x 20" plywood (top)
E2	2	$^3/_4$ x 1 x 22" mahogany (molding)
E3	2	$^3/_4$ x 1 x 20" mahogany (molding)
F1	2	$^1/_2$ x 3$^1/_4$ x 14$^1/_2$" maple (drawer side)
F2	2	$^1/_2$ x 4$^3/_4$ x 14$^1/_2$" maple (drawer side)
F3	2	$^1/_2$ x 6$^1/_4$ x 14$^1/_2$" maple (drawer side)
G1	1	$^1/_2$ x 3$^1/_4$ x 15$^1/_2$" maple (drawer front)
G2	1	$^1/_2$ x 4$^3/_4$ x 15$^1/_2$" maple (drawer front)
G3	1	$^1/_2$ x 6$^1/_4$ x 15$^1/_2$" maple (drawer front)
H1	1	$^1/_2$ x 2$^3/_4$ x 15$^1/_2$" maple (drawer back)
H2	1	$^1/_2$ x 4$^1/_4$ x 15$^1/_2$" maple (drawer back)
H3	1	$^1/_2$ x 5$^3/_4$ x 15$^1/_2$" maple (drawer back)
I	3	$^1/_4$ x 14$^1/_4$ x 15$^1/_2$" plywood (drawer bottom)
J1	1	$^3/_4$ x 3$^1/_2$ x 16$^7/_8$" mahogany (drawer face)
J2	1	$^3/_4$ x 5 x 16$^7/_8$" mahogany (drawer face)
J3	1	$^3/_4$ x 7$^7/_8$ x 16$^7/_8$" mahogany (drawer face)
K	3	pair 14" drawer slides
L	3	knob
M	3	$^1/_2$" No. 6 rh screw
N	9	1" No. 6 fh screw
O	36	1$^1/_2$" 4d finishing nail
P	30	No. 20 plate

Note: All plywood to be veneer- or MDF-core with mahogany face veneers.

Fig. 3 *Clamp each leg to the top of the workbench. Then use a block plane to completely remove saw marks and refine the leg taper.*

Fig. 4 *Mark joining-plate centers on each leg, then cut the plate slots. Hold the leg firmly to the work surface while doing this.*

Fig. 6 *Assemble two legs and one table side with glue and joining plates. Apply pressure with a clamp at each plate location.*

back panel (**Fig. 5**). Apply glue to the joining-plate slots in the legs, the slots in the side panels, and the joining plates. Then clamp together the two subassemblies, each consisting of two legs and a side panel (**Fig. 6**).

When the glue has fully cured on the subassemblies, use the plate joiner to cut the slots in the rear legs for the joints with the back panel.

Clamp a straightedge to the assembly to help position the plate joiner when cutting the slots. Note that these plate slots will slightly intersect with the plates that form the side-panel joints.

Next, join the back and bottom panels with joining plates, glue, and clamps (**Fig. 7**). Complete the base by joining this subassembly with the side panels and legs (**Fig. 8**).

Cut the plywood panel for the table's top, and prepare the edge banding. Cut miters on the ends of two pieces of edge banding so they correspond to the dimensions of the top, and

Fig. 5 *Clamp a tall backstop to the workbench, and hold a panel firmly against it. Cut joining-plate slots in the panel edge.*

Fig. 7 *Glue and clamp together the table back and bottom. Take this subassembly and join it to the leg-side subassemblies.*

Fig. 8 *Use bar clamps at the location of each joining plate to evenly distribute pressure when assembling the table case.*

Fig.9 *Glue and clamp two mitered edge-banding strips to the top. Then, cut the mitered banding strips that fit between them.*

then glue and clamp these to the top. Cut mitered ends on the remaining edge banding, then glue and clamp these to the top (**Fig. 9**).

Gently plane the edge banding flush to the top after the glue has cured, and cut the molding on the edge banding with a router and cove bit. We used a shallow-cutting cove bit. Cut joining-plate slots in the bottom of the tabletop, and then glue and clamp the top to the table base using standard plate-joining procedure.

Drawer Making

Rip and crosscut the drawer box pieces and the bottoms, then cut the rabbets and grooves in them using a dado blade in a table saw. Drill ¹⁄₁₆-in.-dia. pilot holes in the drawers (**Fig. 10**). Slide each bottom into its groove and install the drawer slides on the table's sides and on the drawer boxes according to the manufacturer's instructions. Cut drawer faces to size and install them (**Fig. 11**). Install a knob on each drawer face.

Install the drawers, and adjust the slides so the drawers have a uniform ¹⁄₁₆-in. margin on all sides. Remove the drawers from the table and remove the knobs and slides before finishing. Sand all surfaces with 120-, 150-, 180-, and 220-grit sandpaper. Dust off the surfaces between grits.

Because mahogany is an open-grained wood, the first finishing step is to apply a grain filler. To apply the filler, thin it with naphtha to a creamy consistency, then spread it over the surface with a paintbrush. When the filler appears dull, scrub it off with a burlap rag. Let the filler dry overnight, then sand the surface with 320-grit sandpaper.

We stained our table with a non-grain-raising, dye-based medium brown mahogany stain. Although this stain is meant to be applied with a spray gun, it can be brushed on if you add a retarder to it. Let the stain dry overnight before applying the first coat of transparent finish. Apply this according to the directions on the container.

Fig. 10 *The drawer box is built with rabbeted and grooved pieces. Assemble the box with glue and finishing nails.*

Fig.11 *Clamp the drawer front to the drawer box, bore pilot holes, and attach the front with flathead screws.*

Shaker Style

This understated, timeless end table comes
in handy in any room of the house.

The simple lines and crisp details of this small table were inspired by the Shaker furniture tradition. The Shakers were known for their lean, well-balanced designs, many of which—not surprisingly—fit into home decors just as well today as they did when they were built. We think this table is a perfect example of the style's adaptability. Whether you want to use it as a living room side table or need a bedroom nightstand, it will prove a tasteful addition anywhere it's placed. And it goes with most furniture styles to be found in different rooms of the house. We've finished this one in natural tones that are typical of most Shaker furniture, but you might choose a subtle stain to make it fit with other pieces.

*Key*POINTS

TIME

Prep Time	4 hours
Shop Time	7 hours
Assembly Time	9 hours

EFFORT

Skill Level	basic

COST / BENEFITS

Expense: **low**

- A subtle **period companion piece** brings delicate detailing that delightfully complements most other furnishings.

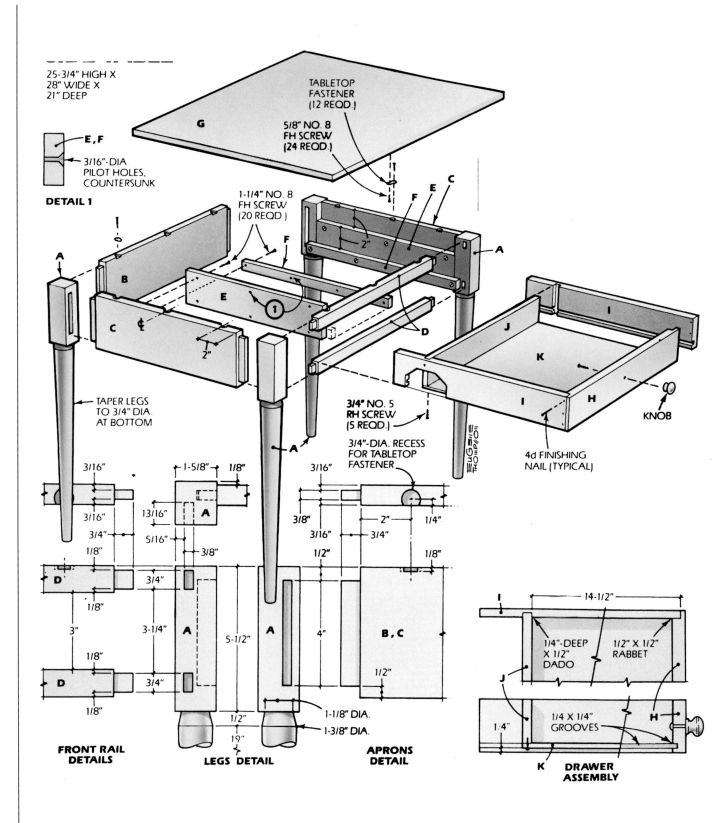

25-3/4" HIGH X
28" WIDE X
21" DEEP

E,F

3/16"-DIA.
PILOT HOLES,
COUNTERSUNK

DETAIL 1

TABLETOP
FASTENER
(12 REQD.)

5/8" NO. 8
FH SCREW
(24 REQD.)

G

1-1/4" NO. 8
FH SCREW
(20 REQD.)

F

C

E

F

A

2"

A

B

E

¢

C

D

2"

J

I

K

H

I

TAPER LEGS
TO 3/4" DIA.
AT BOTTOM

A

3/4" NO. 5
RH SCREW
(5 REQD.)

3/4"-DIA. RECESS
FOR TABLETOP
FASTENER

KNOB

4d FINISHING
NAIL (TYPICAL)

3/16"

1-5/8"

1/8"

3/16"

3/16"

13/16"

A

3/16"

2"

1/4"

3/4"

3/16"

3/4"

5/16"

3/8"

1/2"

1/8"

D

3/4"

A

A

4"

B,C

3"

3-1/4"

5-1/2"

1/8"

1/2"

D

3/4"

1/8"

1-1/8" DIA.

1-3/8" DIA.

1/2"

19"

**FRONT RAIL
DETAILS**

LEGS DETAIL

**APRONS
DETAIL**

I

14-1/2"

1/4"-DEEP
X 1/2"
DADO

1/2" X 1/2"
RABBET

J

J

1/4"

1/4 X 1/4"
GROOVES

H

K

**DRAWER
ASSEMBLY**

Our side table is built of solid maple and uses traditional joinery. Like any Shaker table, it will provide many years of service.

Construction

Begin by ripping and crosscutting ¾-in.-thick boards, slightly oversize for the tabletop. Square the edges of the stock on a jointer or with a hand plane. Spread glue on the boards' edges and clamp them together. Alternate the clamps above and below the panel to apply pressure evenly (**Fig. 1**).

Wait until the glue is rubbery, not hard, to scrape it off. When the glue has dried, clamp the top down and, with a hand plane, smooth and flatten the top. Rip and crosscut the top to the finished dimensions.

Rip and crosscut stock for the legs. If you cannot get stock thick enough for the 1⅝-in.-sq. legs, glue and clamp together two boards. Lay out the mortise positions as shown on the drawing. Use a sharp pencil, knife or, better yet, a mortise marking gauge to mark the layout lines.

Clamp a fence to the drill press table to position the legs for boring. Bore a series of overlapping ⅜-in.-dia. holes, ¹³⁄₁₆ in. deep for the mortise (**Fig. 2**). The mortise is ¹⁄₁₆ in. deeper than the tenon to allow for glue squeeze-out. Clamp the legs to the bench and, using a chisel, pare the walls of the mortise flat and square to one another (**Fig. 3**). If the tenon fits the mortise too tightly, it's easier to adjust the tenon, rather than the mortise.

Next, measure 5½ in. down from the top of each leg and

Materials List

Key	No.	Size and description (use)
A	4	1⅝ x 1⅝ x 25" maple (leg)
B	1	¾ x 5 x 21½" maple (back apron)
C	2	¾ x 5 x 17¾" maple (side apron)
D	2	¾ x 1 x 21½" maple (front rails)
E	2	¾ x 3 x 16¼" maple (side runner)
F	2	¾ x 1 x 17¾" maple (bottom runner)
G	1	¾ x 21 x 28" maple (tabletop)
H	1	¾ x 3 x 20" maple (drawer face)
I	2	½ x 3 x 18¼" pine (drawer side)
J	1	½ x 2½ x 19½" pine (drawer back)
K	1	¼ x 14¾ x 19½" birch plywood (drawer bottom)

Misc.: 1 drawer pull; 12 tabletop fasteners; 24-⅝" No. 8 fh screws; 20-1¼" No. 8 fh screws; 5-¾" No. 5 rh screws; 4d finish nails; glue; 120-, 220-, 320-grit sandpaper; 4/0 steel wool; wax; transparent polyurethane.

Fig. 1 *Glue and clamp the panel alternating clamps above and below to apply pressure evenly. The panel should be slightly oversize.*

Fig. 2 *With a scrap wood fence clamped to the drill press table, use a ⅜-in. drill bit to bore overlapping mortise holes.*

Fig. 3 *Pare the walls of the mortise flat with a chisel, working carefully to the mortise lines. If the tenon is too tight, pare it, not the mortise.*

Fig. 4 *Cut a ³/₁₆-in.-deep kerf around the leg blanks to prevent chip-out when turning. Extend the miter gauge with a scrap piece.*

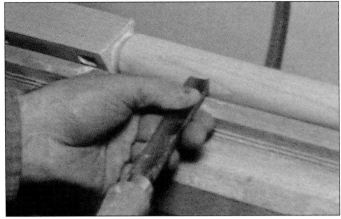

Fig. 5 *Use a ³/₄-in. or 1-in. gouge to turn the tapered portion of the legs. Use a ³/₈-in. gouge to shape the small cove at the top of the leg.*

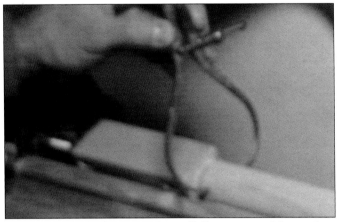

Fig. 6 *Check the large and small diameters with a pair of calipers. Smooth the leg progressively with 100-, 120-, and 220-grit sandpaper.*

Fig. 7 *Cut the tenon on a table saw using dado blades and a miter gauge. A parallel jaw clamp acts as stop for positioning the workpiece.*

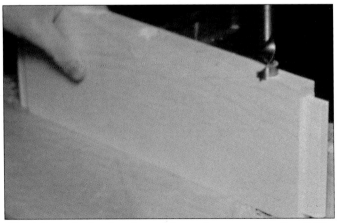

Fig. 8 *Bore holes for the tabletop fasteners on the drill press. Hold the workpiece against a fence clamped across the drill press table.*

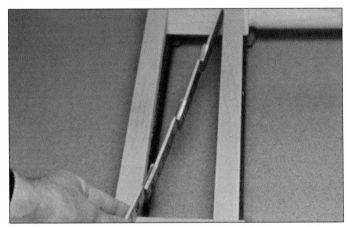

Fig. 9 *Glue and clamp the front rail and leg assembly. Check that the drawer opening is square by comparing diagonal lengths.*

cut a ³⁄₁₆-in.-deep kerf around the leg's perimeter on the table saw (**Fig. 4**). The kerf prevents tear-out during turning.

Mount the legs on the lathe and turn them to shape using a ¾-in. or 1-in. gouge (**Fig. 5**). Shape the small cove at the leg's top with a ⅜-in. gouge. Check the diameter of the legs as you turn them using calipers (**Fig. 6**). Sand the legs with 100-, 120-, and 220-grit sandpaper.

Rip and crosscut the ¾-in.-thick stock for the drawer rails and aprons. Using dado blades and a miter gauge, cut the aprons' tenons on the table saw. A parallel jaw clamp fastened to the miter gauge acts as a stop to position the rails and aprons during the cut (**Fig. 7**). Pare down the ridges left from the dado blades using a sharp chisel.

Switch back to the drill press and bore the holes in the aprons and front drawer rail for the tabletop fasteners. Again, use a fence to position the workpiece (**Fig. 8**).

Apply glue to the front rail tenons and the mortises on the front legs and clamp them together. Measure diagonally across the drawer opening to check that the assembly is square (**Fig. 9**).

Glue and clamp together the rear legs and apron. Complete the leg-apron assembly by gluing and clamping the side aprons to the front and back legs (**Fig. 10**). Work on a flat surface to avoid putting a twist into the assembly during clamping. Measure diagonally across the assembly's top to check for square, and adjust the clamps as necessary.

Cut the pieces for the side and bottom drawer runners to dimension. Bore and countersink the holes for No. 8 flathead screws that hold them in place. Fasten the runners to the leg-apron assembly with the 1¼-in.-long screws (**Fig. 11**). The runners will have to be removed, so don't glue them in place.

Now, cut the drawer parts to dimension. Use a dado blade in the table saw to cut the rabbets on the drawer front and the dadoes in the drawer sides that hold them back. Use a thinner dado blade set up to cut the groove in the drawer front and sides.

Bore pilot holes through the sides into the drawer front for the nails that attach the sides to it. Nail and glue together the drawer parts. Use screws to hold the bottom to the drawer back. Check that the drawer is square and let the glue dry. Test fit the drawer. Sand or plane its sides if it fits to tightly. Attach the tabletop fasteners (**Fig. 12**).

Sand the table with 120- and 220-grit sandpaper. Dust it off and wipe it with a tack cloth. We finished the table inside and out with three coats of transparent polyurethane. Sand lightly between the outside coats (don't bother sanding inside) with 320-grit sandpaper. Rub down the last coat with 4/0 steel wool.

The first step in attaching the top is to remove the drawer runners. Cover the workbench top with a blanket to protect the top. Lay down the top, and invert the table over it. Screw the top in place with the correct overhang around the perimeter. Finish the job by reattaching the drawer runners.

Fig. 10 *Complete the leg-apron assembly by gluing and clamping the side rails to the legs. Measure opposite diagonals for square.*

Fig. 11 *Bore and countersink holes for the screws in the drawer runners. Lubricate the screws with wax. Hold the runners in place with clamps.*

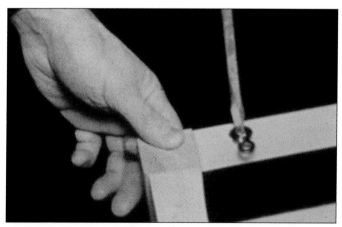

Fig. 12 *Install the tabletop fasteners. Apply finish outside and inside the table. Invert the table on a padded workbench and fasten the top.*

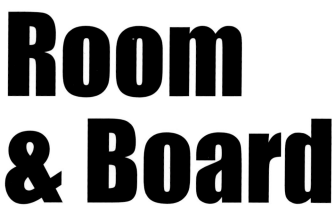

Room & Board

Craftsman style and ample storage make this sideboard a great dining room accessory.

This Arts & Crafts sideboard is a stunning period piece that not only provides an eye-catching addition to the dining room, it also offers a wealth of storage space for everything from plates and silverware to fine linens. This handsome piece is built of quarter-sawn white oak and follows the lines and details you would expect in an original Greene & Greene or Stickley sideboard. The piece features two spacious compartments for storing dishes, serving pieces, and glassware. The design also includes three drawers for silverware, table linens, and miscellaneous items. And, of course, there's plenty of surface area on top.

*Key*POINTS

TIME
Prep Time . . . . 4 hours
Shop Time . . . . 12 hours
Assembly Time . . . . 8 hours

EFFORT
Skill Level . . . . advanced

COST / BENEFITS
Expense: expensive
• **Excellent period piece** that works well with a variety of other styles, and in a wide range of home decors.

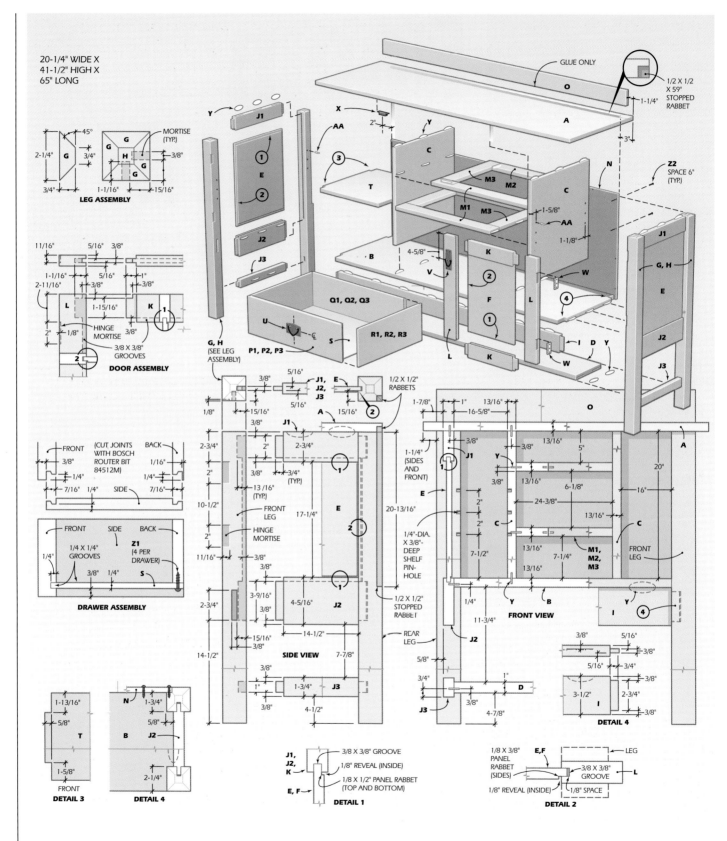

20-1/4" WIDE X
41-1/2" HIGH X
65" LONG

LEG ASSEMBLY

DOOR ASSEMBLY

(CUT JOINTS WITH BOSCH ROUTER BIT 84512M)

DRAWER ASSEMBLY

DETAIL 3

DETAIL 4

SIDE VIEW

DETAIL 1

DETAIL 2

FRONT VIEW

DETAIL 4

The construction techniques for this sideboard are a combination of traditional mortise-and-tenon joinery and modern joining-plate methods. Although the individual skills required are not particularly difficult, the overall complexity of the piece makes this a project more suitable for experienced woodworkers. If you are a less-experienced craftsman, allow extra time and make sure you have the materials necessary. Review the plans carefully before beginning.

Making Components

Begin by selecting stock for each of the case parts. Note that the case is built from a combination of 4/4 and 5/4 stock, while ½-in.-thick material is used for the panels and drawers. Pay careful attention to the size requirements of each piece when selecting material. Try to match the stock that will be used in individual parts for similar grain pattern. Because the cabinet will be stained, it is not as important that you match for color. Rip and crosscut stock to rough size for each part, and label the parts to avoid confusion later.

Joint or plane the edges of each board that will be used to glue up the panels for the case top, bottom, and partitions. If you do not have stock wide enough to form the bottom shelf of the case, you should select stock to glue up for that shelf. Each edge must be straight and square to the face. Lay out joining-plate locations along the mating edges of each board spaced 6 to 8 in. on center, and then use a plate joiner to cut the slots.

Fig. 1 *Panels are edge-glued together so that there is a pleasing mix of grain patterns produced on the panel's final face.*

Materials List

Key	No.	Size and description (use)
A	1	$^{13}/_{16}$ x 20$^1/_4$ x 65" oak (top)
B	1	$^{13}/_{16}$ x 18$^1/_2$ x 59$^1/_4$" oak (bottom)
C	2	$^{13}/_{16}$ x 18$^1/_2$ x 20" oak (partition)
D	1	1 x 8$^1/_4$ x 59$^1/_4$" oak (shelf)
E	2	½ x 15 x 18" oak (side)
F	2	½ x 12 x 15$^1/_4$" oak (door panel)
G	16	¾ x 2$^1/_4$ x 38$^7/_{16}$" oak (leg face)
H	4	¾ x ¾ x 38$^7/_{16}$" oak (leg core)
I	1	1 x 3$^1/_2$ x 59$^1/_2$" oak (rail)
J1	2	1 x 2$^3/_4$ x 16" oak (rail)
J2	2	1 x 4$^5/_{16}$ x 16" oak (rail)
J3	2	1 x 1$^3/_4$ x 16" oak (rail)
K	4	1 x 2$^{11}/_{16}$ x 12$^1/_2$" oak (rail)
L	4	1 x 2$^{11}/_{16}$ x 19$^7/_8$" oak (stile)
M1	2	$^{13}/_{16}$ x 3 x 24$^3/_8$" oak (drawer frame)
M2	2	$^{13}/_{16}$ x 3 x 18$^3/_8$" oak (drawer frame)
M3	4	$^{13}/_{16}$ x 3 x 15$^1/_2$" oak (drawer frame)
N	1	½ x 21$^5/_{16}$ x 59" oak plywood (back)
O	1	$^{13}/_{16}$ x 3 x 62$^1/_2$" oak (rail)
P1	1	$^{13}/_{16}$ x 4$^{15}/_{16}$ x 24$^5/_{16}$" oak (drawer front)
P2	1	$^{13}/_{16}$ x 6$^1/_{16}$ x 24$^5/_{16}$" oak (drawer front)
P3	1	$^{13}/_{16}$ x 7$^3/_{16}$ x 24$^5/_{16}$" oak (drawer front)
Q1	1	½ x 4$^5/_{16}$ x 24$^5/_{16}$" oak (drawer back)
Q2	1	½ x 5$^7/_{16}$ x 24$^5/_{16}$" oak (drawer back)
Q3	1	½ x 6$^9/_{16}$ x 24$^5/_{16}$" oak (drawer back)
R1	2	½ x 4$^5/_{16}$ x 18$^1/_{16}$" oak (drawer side)
R2	2	½ x 6$^1/_{16}$ x 18$^1/_{16}$" oak (drawer side)
R3	2	½ x 7$^3/_{16}$ x 18$^1/_{16}$" oak (drawer side)
S	3	¼ x 17$^{15}/_{16}$ x 23$^{13}/_{16}$" oak (drawer side)
T	2	$^{13}/_{16}$ x 16$^9/_{16}$ x 17$^7/_{16}$" oak (shelf)
U	3	drawer pull
V	2	door pull
W	4	1$^1/_2$ x 2" hinge
X	2	door catch
Y	as reqd.	No. 20 joining plate
Z1	as reqd.	¾" No. 8 rh wood screw
Z2	as reqd.	1" No. 8 rh wood screw
AA	8	¼"-dia. shelf pin

Note: All plywood to be veneer or MDF-core with oak face veneers.

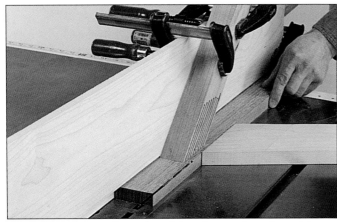

Fig. 2 *Bevel the edge of each leg face using the table saw. Use a featherboard and a holddown to steady the workpiece.*

Fig. 3 *Glue and clamp four beveled face pieces around a leg core. Numerous clamps are needed for this to provide adequate pressure.*

Apply glue to the slots and edges of the stock for one of the panels, then spread a bit of glue on each of the joining plates before placing them in their slots. Assemble the panel and use clamps to pull the joints tight (**Fig. 1**). Let the glue set for about 20 minutes, then use a putty knife to scrape off any excess that has squeezed from between the joints. Allow the panel to sit for at least an hour before removing the clamps. Assemble each panel in this way.

Next, prepare the ½-in.-thick stock for the side and door panels. It's really not a good idea to use joining plates on these thin panels because the outline of the joining plates can sometimes be seen after the finish is applied. Instead, use a clamp at each end of the panel during glue-up to keep the stock aligned.

When the glue has cured on all the panels, rip and crosscut them to the finished dimension.

Study the plans to be sure you understand the construction details of the case legs. Each leg is formed by joining four mitered strips around a solid core. This produces legs that have quarter-sawn figure on all sides instead of just two faces.

Rip the stock for the leg faces to 2¼ in., leaving each strip a few inches longer than the finished leg dimension. Adjust the table saw to cut a 45° bevel, and, using an auxiliary rip fence and featherboard, cut the two beveled edges on each workpiece (**Fig. 2**). Be sure to use a pushstick at the end of the cut to keep your hand far from the blade. Readjust the saw, and rip the core strips to a dimension of ¾ in. square.

Using a foam roller, apply a light coating of glue to all joint surfaces for a case leg. Assemble the leg and apply alternating clamps along its length, so that the joints come together tightly and the leg stays square (**Fig. 3**). Once all the legs are glued up, use the miter gauge on the table saw to crosscut them to finished length.

Clamp the legs together with their ends flush, and mark

the top and bottom lines that designate the mortises for the front- and side-rail tenons. Next, use a mortise marking gauge to scribe the mortise width on each leg. Use a plunge router with a spiral up-cutting bit and edge guide to cut the mortises in the legs (**Fig. 4**). Do not try to cut the full depth of the mortises in one pass. Instead, make two or three passes to prevent burning the bit or overloading the router motor. Cut the mortise ends square using a sharp chisel.

Next, rip and crosscut the stock for the case and door rails and the door stiles. Because the setup is essentially the same for both the case and door tenons, it makes sense to cut them all at the same time. Install dado blades in the table saw, and clamp a wood auxiliary fence to the rip fence to act as a stop for cutting the tenons (**Fig. 5**). As is normal when using dado blades to cut tenons, you should cut the joints about ½₂ in. oversize, and pare the surfaces of

Fig. 4 *Cut the leg mortises with a plunge router and a spiral up-cutting bit. Make two to three passes per mortise to avoid overheating the router motor.*

the tenons to a final fit. First make the cheek cuts for each tenon, then readjust the blade height and hold the rails on edge to cut the shoulders at the top and bottom edges of the rails.

Because the door rails have longer tenons, you will have to make two passes for each tenon. Also note that the door rails have haunched tenons. This means that the shoulder on the outside of each rail is stepped to fill the end of the panel groove on the mating stile. Be sure to properly adjust the rip fence stop when making these cuts.

Readjust the dado blades to cut the panel grooves in the case sides, door rails, and door stiles. Securely clamp a featherboard to the saw table to help hold the stock against the rip fence (**Fig. 6**).

Use the router and edge guide to cut the panel grooves in the legs. Note that these grooves extend between the top and middle rail mortises. Lay out the notches in the case bottom panel to accommodate the legs, then use a jigsaw to make the cuts so that the notches fit tightly to the legs when assembled.

Mark the joining-plate positions in the case top and bottom panels and in the top and bottom ends of the partitions. Use the fence on the joiner to locate the slots in the ends of the bottom panel. Note that these slots must be centered ¼ in. from the bottom face of the panel (**Fig. 7**).

Clamp a straightedge guide across a panel to locate the joiner when cutting the slots in the panel face. To locate the slots for the joint with the front rail, you can clamp the rail to the case bottom to act as a guide (**Fig. 8**). Use the flat worktable top as a registration surface for cutting the slots in the partition ends.

Next, lay out the stopped rabbets at the back edge of the case top and rear legs. These rabbets house the back panel. Use the router and edge guide to cut the rabbets (**Fig. 9**), and then square the ends of the rabbets with a sharp chisel.

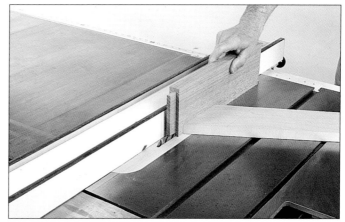

Fig. 6 *Cut the panel grooves using a dado blade in the table saw. Use a featherboard to keep the workpiece firmly against the fence.*

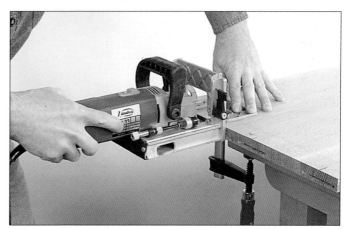

Fig. 7 *Cut each joining-plate slot in the case bottom panel so that its center is ¼ in. above the panel's bottom edge.*

Fig. 5 *Install a dado blade in the table saw and an auxiliary fence on the table. Cut the tenon cheeks by pushing them over the blade.*

Fig. 8 *Cut joining-plate slots in the top of the front rail, and then use the rail as a guide to cut the slots in the case bottom.*

Fig. 9 *Install a fence on a router, and with a straight bit in its chuck, cut the stopped rabbet in each case side.*

Fig. 10 *Begin the case assembly by joining the drawer frames to the case partitions. Test fit the parts before gluing.*

Fig. 11 *Use cauls to distribute pressure around the frame-partition assembly. Shims ensure equal pressure all around.*

Assembly

Spread glue in the slots and on the mating surfaces for the bottom/front rail joints. Then assemble all the parts and securely clamp them.

Next, cut the stock to finished size for the drawer frames, and use the plate joiner to cut the slots. Apply glue to the joints and plates, then clamp the frames. When the glue has set on the frames, mark the plate slot locations for the partitions. Cut the slots, apply glue to the joints, and then assemble the frames and partitions (**Fig. 10**). Clamp the assembly, and use cauls with a veneer shim under their center to equally distribute clamping pressure (**Fig. 11**).

Use the router and edge guide to cut the rabbets on the case sides and door panels. Carefully sand the panels with 220-grit sandpaper.

Next, use the plate joiner to cut the slots in the middle rails for the case bottom joints. Also cut the plate slots on the inside surfaces of the bottom rails and the ends of the bottom shelf. Finally, cut the slots in the top edges of the top rails.

Glue together three side rails and one leg, then slide the panel into position (**Fig. 12**). Add the second leg, then clamp the assembly. Repeat this procedure on the other side.

Use a sharp knife and mortise marking gauge to mark hinge locations on the legs, then use a sharp chisel to cut the hinge mortise. When the hinge is set into the mortise, its surface should be flush with the surrounding wood. Bore the shelf pinholes in the case sides and partitions. Sand the case's inside surfaces with 220-grit sandpaper.

Glue and clamp the case bottom and bottom shelf to the side assemblies. When the glue has set, glue and clamp the partition assembly to the bottom shelf (**Fig. 13**). When the glue has set on those joints, glue and clamp the case top to the assembly (**Fig. 14**).

Cut a piece of ½-in.-thick oak plywood for the case back. Sand it with 220-grit sandpaper, then use screws to fasten it

Fig. 12 *Begin assembling a case side by joining the rails to the legs. Slide the side panel into position, then clamp the assembly.*

Fig. 13 *Join the sides and case bottom assembly. Next, glue and clamp the drawer frames and partitions to the case bottom.*

Fig. 14 *Use cauls and long bar clamps to join the top to the case body. Note that the clamps are aligned with the case partitions.*

to the legs, top, bottom, partitions, and drawer frames. Cut the back rail to the finished dimension, and sand it and the case top with 220-grit sandpaper. Glue and securely clamp the rail to the top.

Glue and clamp together the door stiles, rails, and door panel. Be careful not to get any glue in the panel grooves. When both doors are complete, hold them in their respective openings, with ¹⁄₁₆-in.-thick shims on all edges, to check for proper fit. Plane or sand the doors until you have a uniform ¹⁄₁₆-in. margin around each door, then mark the position of the hinge mortises and cut them using the same techniques previously employed.

Using only the center screw hole in each hinge leaf, mount the hinges to the case and the doors to the hinges for a test fit (**Fig. 15**). Use steel screws to test mount the hinge.

Drill pilot holes for the door pulls, and install them. Mount the door catches under the case top, then mount the door strikes on the doors.

There are many types of drawer joints, but we used a drawer lock joint cut with a Bosch router bit mounted in a router table. To cut the profile on a drawer side, clamp a guide strip to the side and run it upright over the bit (**Fig. 16**). Cut the profile on the face and back, moving each horizontally.

Cut the groove in the drawer face and sides using a dado blade in the table saw. Now glue and clamp together the drawer boxes, and check that each is square. Slide the bottom into the box after the glue has set. Test fit the drawers and sand them if necessary to achieve a smooth fit. Finally, cut the adjustable shelves to size and test fit them.

To prepare for finishing, remove all hardware from the doors and drawers. Go over the entire piece with 220-grit sandpaper. Then wipe all surfaces with a damp sponge and let dry. Lightly sand the roughened surface with 220-grit sandpaper, and apply the dye. When the stain is dry, apply transparent finish. Replace the case back and reassemble.

Fig. 15 *Use one steel screw installed in the center of each hinge leaf when test fitting the doors to the case.*

Fig. 16 *Cut the joints in the drawer sides by holding them vertically with clamps, and support them with a guide strip.*

Cool Console

Basic woodworking skills will be put to good use in building this solid cherry console table.

This simple console table is a great beginner's project. Its straightforward lines are reminiscent of Shaker pieces built over 100 years ago. But simple doesn't have to mean unsophisticated. This solid cherry piece is well-tailored, crisply built and can fit just about anywhere: your front hall, behind a living room sofa, in an upstairs bedroom, or even in your bathroom if you're blessed with enough extra space. But good design isn't the whole story. This piece is also easy for a beginner to build. It has only nine parts: four legs, four rails and a top. And we show you how to build it with nothing more than hand tools and a few portable power tools. Sometimes the simple things are the most pleasing.

*Key*POINTS

TIME

Prep Time	8 hours
Shop Time	10 hours
Assembly Time	10 hours

EFFORT

Skill Level	basic

COST / BENEFITS

Expense: **moderate**
- **Great beginner project** that is easy and gratifying to build.
- This design uses **classic lines** to create an elegant look out of sheer simplicity.

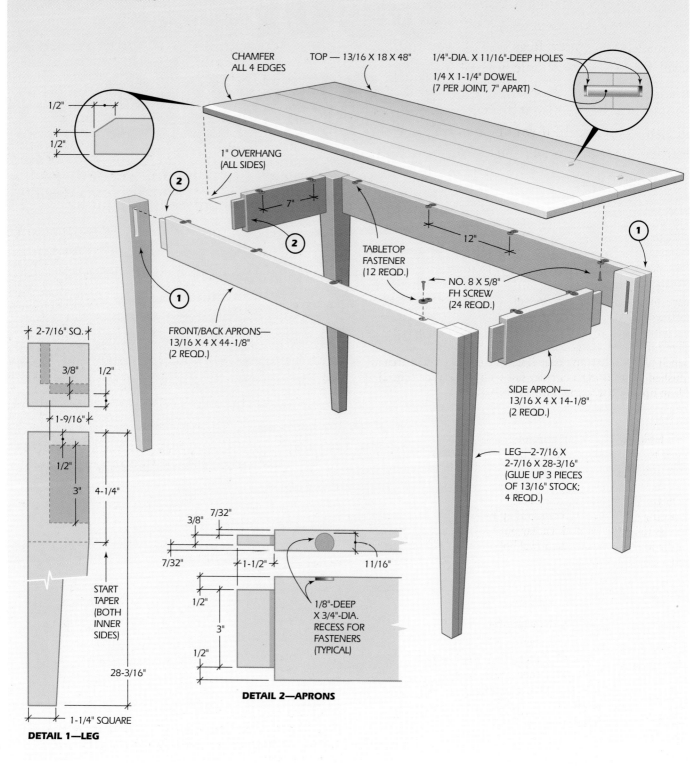

18" DEEP X 29" HIGH X 48" LONG

CHAMFER ALL 4 EDGES

TOP — 13/16 X 18 X 48"

1/4"-DIA. X 11/16"-DEEP HOLES

1/4 X 1-1/4 DOWEL
(7 PER JOINT, 7" APART)

1/2"

1/2"

1" OVERHANG
(ALL SIDES)

2

2

7"

12"

TABLETOP
FASTENER
(12 REQD.)

NO. 8 X 5/8"
FH SCREW
(24 REQD.)

1

1

FRONT/BACK APRONS—
13/16 X 4 X 44-1/8"
(2 REQD.)

SIDE APRON—
13/16 X 4 X 14-1/8"
(2 REQD.)

LEG—2-7/16 X
2-7/16 X 28-3/16"
(GLUE UP 3 PIECES
OF 13/16" STOCK;
4 REQD.)

2-7/16" SQ.

3/8"

1/2"

1-9/16"

1/2"

3"

4-1/4"

START
TAPER
(BOTH
INNER
SIDES)

28-3/16"

1-1/4" SQUARE

DETAIL 1—LEG

7/32"

3/8"

7/32"

1-1/2"

11/16"

1/2"

3"

1/2"

1/8"-DEEP
X 3/4"-DIA.
RECESS FOR
FASTENERS
(TYPICAL)

DETAIL 2—APRONS

Perhaps the best part of this design is that it gives the beginner a chance to really hone his skills, while still offering the intermediate and accomplished woodworker a quick-build, sophisticated project. Regardless of your skill level, if you start this table now, your gratification won't be delayed much longer. You should be able to finish it up in a decent amount of spare time—even if you if you have only just learned how to sharpen a chisel or cut a mortise-and-tenon joint.

Cherry Stock

The material we used for this piece is solid cherry stock that we bought flattened on both sides and jointed on one edge. You'll have to pay more for this service, but it's worth the cost. The standard thickness for this type of hardwood is $^{13}/_{16}$ in.

The first step in preparing the lumber is to crosscut all parts to rough length, a couple of inches longer than their finished lengths. Then check the jointed edge of each piece for flatness and square. If some refinements are required, clamp the board to the side of your worktable and use a bench plane to true the edge (**Fig. 1**). Next, cut the boards to finished width using a circular saw with a rip guide (**Fig. 2**). Clean up any saw marks with a bench plane.

Tabletop

This tabletop was made from four smaller boards that were glued together. Using multiple boards helps keep the top flat over time. If your stock is wide enough to use only three boards, that's fine.

Begin work by laying the boards on a flat surface and choosing the most attractive grain pattern by arranging the boards in several ways. Then lay out the dowel locations on all the joints and bore the dowel holes using a doweling jig and a drill (**Fig. 3**).

Materials List

Key	No.	Size and description (use)
A	1	$^{13}/_{16}$ x 18 x 48" cherry (top)
B	2	$^{13}/_{16}$ x 4 x 44$^{1}/_{8}$" cherry (front/back aprons)
C	2	$^{13}/_{16}$ x 4 x 14$^{1}/_{8}$" cherry (side aprons)
D	4	2$^{7}/_{16}$ x 2$^{7}/_{16}$ x 28$^{3}/_{16}$" cherry (legs)

Misc.: 12 tabletop fasteners; 28-$^{5}/_{8}$" No. 8 fh screws; 21-$^{1}/_{4}$ x 1$^{1}/_{4}$" dowel pins; finishing oil.

Fig. 1 *Begin the top by flattening one edge of each board as necessary, using a bench plane. Make sure the edge is planed square to the face.*

Fig. 2 *Cut each top board to width using a circular saw and rip guide. Make sure that the rip guide follows the planed edge.*

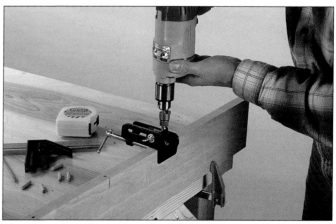

Fig. 3 *Lay out the location of the alignment dowels on the board edges. Then use a doweling jig and drill to bore the holes.*

Fig. 4 *Cover the edges and dowel holes with glue, insert the dowels, and bring the boards together with pipe clamps evenly spaced.*

Fig. 5 *When the glue is dry, remove any squeeze-out, then let the assembly cure completely. Flatten joints if necessary with a plane.*

Fig. 7 *Mark the chamfer around the top, and plane the edges to this line. A scrap block keeps the side edge from splitting.*

Fig. 8 *Cut the leg stock to size, then apply glue to the mating surfaces. Keep the board edges flush when clamping.*

SKILL*Builder*

GLUE BASICS
Using glue might not seem like a skill, but it does take knowledge and a sense of what you're doing to select the right glue for your project, for your stage of construction, the wood, and other conditions. It's not a matter of just apply and go.

Besides strength, there are other characteristics to consider when choosing an adhesive. A fast-setting glue, like hot-melt , lets you assemble small parts very quickly without fussing with clamps. A slow-setting glue, such as hide glue, allows you to work at a leisurely pace, which is necessary when building

large, complex projects. A disadvantage of slow-setting glues is that the assembly must remain clamped for several hours. This can be a nuisance if you don't own a lot of extra clamps.

Other features to consider include heat and moisture resistance, color when dry, and shrinkage. Most glues are relatively inexpensive and, like many items, more economical if bought in large-size containers. Two-part glues, like epoxies and resorcinol, are on the high end of the price scale.

Your best insurance for a successful, long-lasting glue joint is printed right on the container. Glue manufacturers provide

Fig. 6 *Clearly mark the finished length on both ends of the top panel. Then make the cuts with a saw and straightedge guide.*

Fig. 9 *Lay out the tenons on the ends of the table rails with a marking gauge. Keep the gauge base flat on the board surface.*

valuable information, directions, and safety precautions on each label. Be sure to read them carefully. Also, additional specifications are available from the manufacturer in the form of required Manufacturer's Safety and Data Sheets (MSDS). These sheets have to list precautions to use with the chemicals and safety suggestions, such as appropriate venting and dangers of skin contact. In addition, many manufacturers voluntarily include a wealth of information on request, such as the ideal setting and curing environment for their products, recommended applications, and interactions with different woods and veneers. Check websites printed on containers for more information.

SKILL*Builder*

QUICK-MADE CLAMPS
Finding you don't have all the clamps you need to properly clamp up glued pieces is not only frustrating, it can mean that the joints in your piece will not be secure. You could drop everything and sprint out to the local home center, but there's an easier solution to this situation.

Occasionally, after starting a major glue-up operation, you find that you don't have enough clamps for the job. Because the glue is already on the workpiece, you need more clamps in a hurry.

Next time this happens, make emergency clamps out of flat scraps of plywood that are wider than the combined thicknesses of the pieces you are gluing up. Cut a U-shaped recess from the middle of one edge into the plywood (creating a U-shaped piece). The cut should be slightly wider than the thickness of the workpieces.

Once they are cut, you just slide the "clamps" over the pieces where you need pressure. If the fit is loose, use a wedge to tighten it up.

Next, place a drop of glue in each dowel hole and gently tap the dowel in place. Then spread the glue evenly on all the mating edges and push the boards together. Tighten the joints, using pipe clamps (**Fig. 4**), making sure that the pressure is even all over, and check that the panel is flat before letting the glue set. If it's not, readjust the clamps until the surface is flat. After allowing 20 minutes for the glue to harden, scrape off any excess glue from the joints and let the panel dry overnight.

When you remove the clamps, check the panel surface carefully. If the joints are flush, set the panel aside. If they aren't, use a bench plane to smooth the surface (**Fig. 5**). Hold the plane at a 30° angle to the wood grain and make shearing cuts.

Next, cut the panel to finished length, using a circular saw and a straightedge guide (**Fig. 6**). Make sure that both ends are square to the sides before making the cuts.

Then mark guidelines for the edge chamfer around the perimeter of the top and use a block plane to create these bevels (**Fig. 7**). Be sure to clamp a scrap block to each long edge to keep them from splitting when you're working on the end grain.

Complete the tabletop by sanding smooth both sides and all the edges. Begin with 120-grit sandpaper and move through a sequence of 150-, 180-, and 220-grits.

Fig. 10 *Make the cheek cuts on the tenons using a backsaw. Keep the blade kerf just to the waste side of the layout lines.*

Fig. 11 *Make the tenon shoulder cuts with a backsaw. Clamp a scrap block to the board you're sawing to help guide the saw blade.*

Legs and Rails

Crosscut the leg stock to finished length. Note that each leg is formed from three pieces of stock that are glued together. Apply glue to the three boards that make up each leg and clamp them together (**Fig. 8**). Scrape off the excess glue after 20 minutes, and leave each leg assembly clamped for at least an hour. Don't do any further work on these pieces until the glue has cured for 24 hours.

Now crosscut the rail stock to finished length and lay out a tenon on each end, using a marking gauge (**Fig. 9**). Make the tenon cheek cuts with a backsaw (**Fig. 10**). Then make the top

and bottom shoulder cuts (**Fig. 11**) and use a sharp chisel to refine the cuts and remove any saw marks.

Lay out the mortises on the corresponding legs with a marking gauge. Then use a doweling jig and a portable drill to remove most of the waste (**Fig. 12**). Finish up the mortise by squaring the ends and sides with a sharp chisel.

Once the joinery is done, cut the tapers on both inside edges of each leg, as shown in the drawing. Use a circular saw and be sure to cut on the waste side of the layout lines. Finish these tapers with a bench plane (**Fig. 13**), making sure to check for square as you work. Before the legs and rails are

MATERIAL*Matters*

Tool Marks
Wood that has been surfaced on a planer usually comes away with small parallel ripples that run from edge to edge across the board. The spacing of the ripples indicates the feed rate and rotational speed of the planer cutting head. If you use a jointer in your shop, one way to reduce planing marks is to slow the feed rate. Home workshop thickness planers generally have fixed feed rates. But there are other ways to deal with marks.

It is possible to sand away planer marks with an orbital sander. However, the flexible pad of the sander may conform to the imperfections and simply follow their contour rather than remove them. The finish-sanded surface may look fine to the casual examination, but the ripples could very well show up when a clear finish is applied. This makes the orbital sander a bit of an unreliable solution.

A better method for removing marks is to use a cabinet scraper. When it is properly sharpened, this tool will cut the tops of the ripples and leave a silky smooth surface that requires little follow-up sanding.

Severe marks from coarsely planed stock can first be handled with a sharp, finely set hand plane. A plane has the advantage of leveling and flattening the stock without creating hollows. Any marks left from the hand planing operation are removed with the cabinet scraper.

Of course, a belt sander will also remove planer marks. For most projects, however, this tool cuts too fast and will remove more stock than necessary. Unless you're very careful, you'll end up with a smooth surface that is no longer flat. Some belt sanders can be fitted with fence attachments for handling edge sanding.

Fig. 12 *Remove the waste from the mortise using a drill and doweling jig. Square the mortise ends and walls with a sharp chisel.*

Fig. 13 *Rough cut the leg tapers with a circular saw. Then reduce the edges to finished thickness with a bench plane.*

assembled, it's a good idea to finish and sand all the parts with the same progression of grits that was discussed earlier.

Assembly

Begin by joining a long rail to a pair of legs. Spread the glue evenly on the tenons and mortises, and then clamp the pieces together. Do the same with the other legs and long rail. When the glue has cured on these two assemblies, join them together with the short rails. Assemble the parts on a flat surface. Once the clamps are in place, compare opposite diagonal measurements to check for square (**Fig. 14**). If the assembly isn't square, readjust the clamps until it is.

When the base joints have cured, lay out and bore the holes in the rails for the tabletop fasteners. Then turn the top upside down on a padded table and place the inverted base assembly on the underside of the top. Adjust the base so it's centered on the top. Then mark the location of the fastener holes. Bore pilot holes and screw the base to the top (**Fig. 15**).

Examine the parts for scratches that occurred during assembly and sand these with 220-grit paper. Remove all dust and, if you plan to apply an oil finish like we did, finish sand with 320-grit paper. Then remove the dust again and wipe the entire piece with a tack cloth. Apply an oil finish.

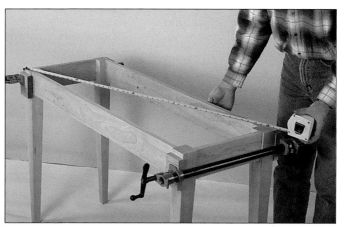

Fig. 14 *Glue and clamp the legs to the rails. Then check for a square assembly by comparing the diagonal measurements.*

SHOP*Helper*

When trimming wood at different angles with your band saw, small wedge-shaped scraps are likely to get stuck in the table's blade slot. Solve this problem by applying a short strip of masking tape over the slot.

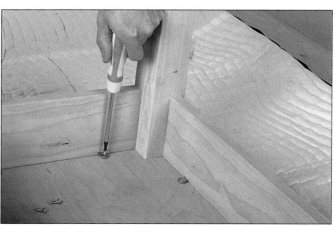

Fig. 15 *Attach the tabletop fasteners to the rails. Then turn the table parts over and screw the fasteners to the underside of the top.*

Fair Game

Enjoy a sporting match on this finely detailed, elegant, yet practical, mahogany game table.

Our fold-over game table is a well-bred piece of furniture with a history going back to 18th-century England. Tables of that period had a fold-over top that was supported by a swing-out leg. But our version follows the novel game-table design that evolved in the 19th century. It features an offset top that rotates a quarter turn so that both leaves are supported evenly on the fixed rectangular base. The table is both functional and decorative, usually being displayed against the wall. It has a storage area beneath the top for game pieces or playing cards and, in keeping with tradition, the table is built from solid mahogany and has a lustrous hand-rubbed finish. With this beautiful piece, you're always a winner.

*Key*POINTS

TIME

Prep Time	6 hours
Shop Time	12 hours
Assembly Time	10 hours

EFFORT

Skill Level	intermediate

COST / BENEFITS

Expense: moderate

- **Elegant detailing** and a fine finish make this a showcase piece.
- **Unique swivel top** creates a utilitarian aspect to the table.

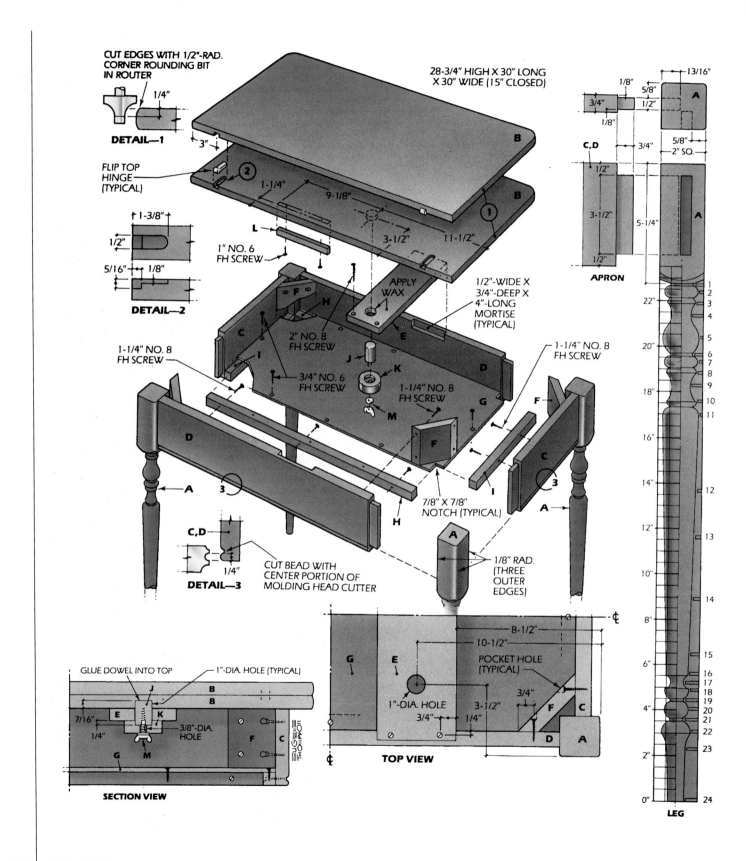

CUT EDGES WITH 1/2"-RAD.
CORNER ROUNDING BIT
IN ROUTER

1/4"

DETAIL—1

3"

FLIP TOP
HINGE
(TYPICAL)

28-3/4" HIGH X 30" LONG
X 30" WIDE (15" CLOSED)

1/8"
5/8"
3/4"
1/2"
1/8"

C,D

3/4"

5/8"
2" SQ.

A

13/16"

1-3/8"

1/2"

5/16"   1/8"

DETAIL—2

1" NO. 6
FH SCREW

L

1-1/4"

9-1/8"

3-1/2"

11-1/2"

B

B

①

②

APPLY
WAX

1/2"-WIDE X
3/4"-DEEP X
4"-LONG
MORTISE
(TYPICAL)

E

1/2"

3-1/2"

1/2"

5-1/4"

APRON

A

3/4"

1-1/4" NO. 8
FH SCREW

C

I

F

H

2" NO. 8
FH SCREW

J

K

3/4" NO. 6
FH SCREW

M

1-1/4" NO. 8
FH SCREW

D

G

F

F

C

I

1-1/4" NO. 8
FH SCREW

A

③

D

A

③

C,D

1/4"

DETAIL—3

CUT BEAD WITH
CENTER PORTION OF
MOLDING HEAD CUTTER

H

7/8" X 7/8"
NOTCH (TYPICAL)

A

1/8" RAD.
(THREE
OUTER
EDGES)

GLUE DOWEL INTO TOP

1"-DIA. HOLE (TYPICAL)

J

B

B

7/16"

E   K

1/4"

3/8"-DIA.
HOLE

F

M

G

SECTION VIEW

G

E

1"-DIA. HOLE

3/4"

8-1/2"

10-1/2"

POCKET HOLE
(TYPICAL)

3/4"

F

C

3-1/2"

1/4"

D

A

TOP VIEW

22"
20"
18"
16"
14"
12"
10"
8"
6"
4"
2"
0"

1
2
3
4
5
6
7
8
9
10
11
12
13
14
15
16
17
18
19
20
21
22
23
24

LEG

The table is a good project for reasonably experienced hobbyists, in that it requires lathe work. Lacking a lathe, you can build it with gracefully tapered legs, rather than turned ones.

The Legs

Glue and clamp together a slab wide enough to make four legs. Rip leg blanks from the slab on the table saw.

Next, mark out the leg mortises. Then bore a series of overlapping holes to remove the bulk of the mortise. Pare the mortise to dimension using a chisel (**Figs. 1 and 2**). Then draw a full-size paper pattern of the leg. Include the diameter sizing grooves at key locations, and hang the drawing behind the lathe.

Carefully center the turning blank on the lathe—any error here will result in a lopsided shoulder where the square meets the round. To turn the shoulder from square to round, draw two guidelines around the square at 4¾ in. and 5¼ in. from the top. Hold the skew chisel vertically, toe down and heel up, and make a nicking cut at the upper mark (**Fig. 3**). This prevents splintering. Next, run in a parting tool to cut the finished diameter of the flat band along the lower guideline.

Now, use the gouge to rough form the cylinder. Starting about 3 in. from the groove, feed the gouge toward the groove to form the round. Then reverse the feed direction from left to right, toward the tailstock to complete the rounding. Pass a wide skew chisel over the cylinder to smooth it.

Make pencil marks on the cylinder at the locations of the depth gauging grooves (**Fig. 4**). These can be set off with a

Materials List

Key	No.	Size and description (use)
A	4	2 x 2 x 28" mahogany (leg)
B	2	¾ x 15 x 30" mahogany (top)
C	2	¾ x 4½ x 11½" mahogany (apron)
D	2	¾ x 4½ x 25½" mahogany (apron)
E	1	¾ x 4 x 12½" mahogany (brace)
F	4	¾ x 3½ x 4" mahogany (brace)
G	1	¼ x 11½ x 25½" mahogany (panel)
H	2	¾ x ¾ x 24" mahogany (cleat)
I	2	¾ x ¾ x 10" mahogany (cleat)
J	1	1"-dia. x 1⁷⁄₁₆" mahogany (pivot)
K	1	¾ x 2¼"-dia. mahogany (cap)
L	1	⁵⁄₁₆ x ½ x 7" mahogany (stop)
M	1	⁵⁄₁₆ x 2" (bolt, washer, nut)

Misc.: No. 20 biscuits; sandpaper; yellow or hide glue; medium red mahogany stain; retarder; shellac; alcohol; paste wood filler; sanding sealer; clear wood finish.

Fig. 1 *Lay out the mortises in the legs. Remove the bulk of the mortise waste by boring a series of holes with a drill press.*

Fig. 2 *Clamp the legs to the bench. Using a razor-sharp chisel, pare the sides of the mortise parallel and the ends square.*

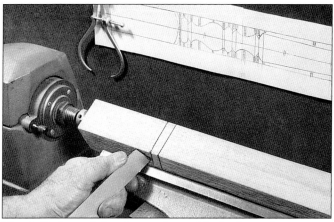

Fig. 3 *Make a nick using a skew chisel where the square leg turns round. Note the leg pattern taped to the wall.*

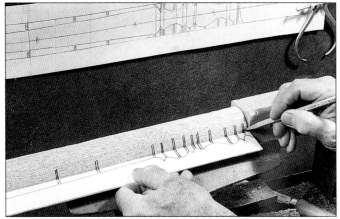

Fig. 4 *For precision, use the half pattern of the leg to mark out in pencil the depth cuts that establish the diameters at key points.*

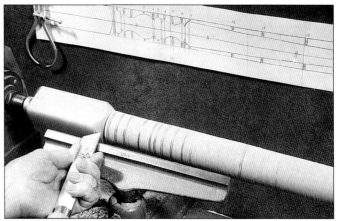

Fig. 5 *Use the skew or the spear-point chisel to turn the round shoulder on the leg. The nick cut made earlier prevents splintering.*

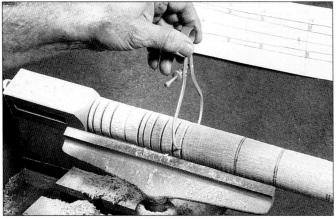

Fig. 8 *Measure the diameter of the leg at the corresponding depth groove. Cut the depth groove until the caliper fits.*

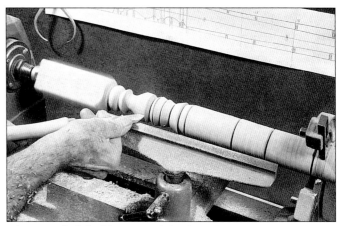

Fig. 9 *To finish this part of the leg, shape the remaining parts of the turned section using the gouge, skew, and spear-point chisels.*

rule using the drawing for reference or, better yet, with a half-section pattern of the leg drawn on cardboard. This is held to the cylinder to transfer the marks.

Shape the curved shoulder with either the skew or spear-point chisels (**Fig. 5**). The diameter gauging grooves are next. Use a caliper for checking the grooves, and run in the parting tool to within 1/16 in. of the finished diameters at the designated locations (**Fig. 6**). Adjust the caliper to the required setting directly on the drawing (**Figs. 7 and 8**). Use the roundnose, spear-point skew chisels and gouge to form the contours (**Fig. 9**). As the leg becomes thinner, it may chatter. To prevent this, use a steady rest (**Fig. 10**).

When the shaping is completed, remove the toolrest and turn up the lathe's speed to 1000 rpm for sanding. Start with 120-grit sandpaper and work through 150-, 180-, and 220-grit. Use sandpaper strips to smooth contoured areas, but use a felt-backed sanding block when sanding the taper (**Fig. 11**).

The Top

Rip and crosscut the boards for the top slightly oversize, and joint their edges. Then group them for the most desirable appearance while arranging their annular rings alternately facing up and down.

We used joining plates to join the boards together, but dowels can be used as well. To cut the plate slots, place the boards on a flat surface in the order in which they will be glued together. Mark the biscuit locations and cut the slots, holding the biscuit joiner and the board flat to the bench (**Fig. 12**).

Glue and clamp the boards together (**Fig. 13**). Prevent the panel from bowing under clamping pressure by using cauls. Wax the cauls' edges where they come in contact with the glue. This prevents the glue from sticking to the caul. After the glue has set, remove the dried glue and small differences in height between the boards using a cabinet scraper (**Fig. 14**).

Cut the mortise for the flip-top hinge with a router and a

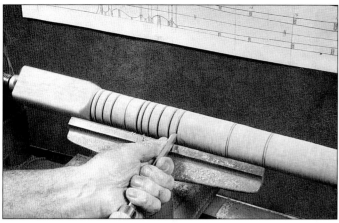

Fig. 6 *Using the parting tool with steady, even pressure, make each of the depth cuts. Back off from the parting tool occasionally to let it cool.*

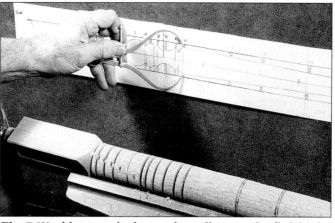

Fig. 7 *Working precisely, set the caliper to the finished diameter of the leg at a given depth groove. Note the groove number.*

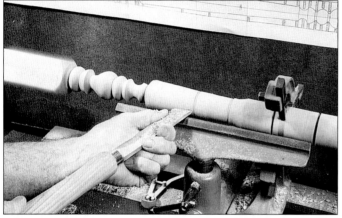

Fig. 10 *The leg becomes increasingly thinner, and not as stiff, as it is turned down. Use a steady rest to prevent chattering.*

Fig. 11 *Use a felt-pad sanding block and 220-grit sandpaper to evenly smooth the long, tapered portion of the turning.*

Fig. 12 *Use a plate joiner to join the boards for the top. Hold the workpiece and the joiner on a flat, clean surface.*

Fig. 13 *Glue and clamp the top panels. Use cauls to keep the assembly from bowing. Waxed cauls will repel glue.*

Fig. 14 *Firmly push a cabinet scraper over the table top panels to remove the dried glue at the joints and to level the panels.*

Fig. 15 *While cutting the hinge mortises, guide the router with a simple frame. Clamp and tack nail the frame in place.*

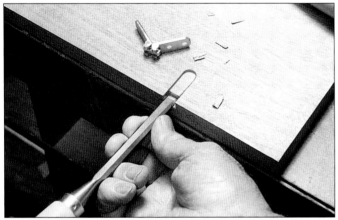

Fig. 16 *Cut a notch for the hinge knuckle at the rear of the mortise. Each half of the mortise is notched to receive a knuckle.*

Fig. 17 *Cut the ellipse on the edge of the top panels by raising the router bit up about halfway, so that it won't cut to full depth.*

½-in.-dia. straight bit. Make a guide frame, and cut the mortises in both leaves at the same time (**Fig. 15**). The frame is made with four strips of plywood ¼ in. x 1½ in. wide. The size of the frame opening is dictated by the size of your router base. After cutting the mortise, chisel out the notch for the hinge knuckle (**Fig. 16**).

TOOL*Care*

Remember that the base dimensions of routers and circular saws vary from one make to the next, so you'll have to determine the exact placement of the fences and stops on each jig to suit your tool.

Cut the radii on the outside corners of the leaves using a sabre saw, then set up the router with a ball-bearing ½-in.-rad. corner-rounding bit. In order to achieve the elliptical edge, adjust the bit so about half its cutting edge projects beyond the base. Shape the edge by making a pass from both sides (**Fig. 17**). Finally, use a 1-in.-dia. Forstner or spur bit to bore the flat-bottomed hole that seats the pivot dowel.

Aprons, Assembly and Finish

Rip and crosscut the apron stock. Use the miter gauge and an auxiliary fence with a stop block to guide the aprons as you push them over the dado head in the table saw (**Fig. 18**). To cut the decorative apron bead, use a molding head in the table saw (**Fig. 19**).

Next, use a chisel to cut the pivot brace mortises on the inside of the aprons. Dry fit the legs and aprons, and bore pilot screw holes in the pivot brace and aprons. Glue and clamp the legs and aprons (**Fig. 20**), then glue and clamp the pivot brace.

Cut the cleats and the bin's bottom panel to size. Temporarily attach the cleats with screws, then remove them. Cut the pivot dowel to size, then bore the pilot hole and install the hanger bolt in it. Cut a 2¼-in.-dia. disc for the pivot cap, then bore and counterbore the hole for the dowel and bolt. Temporarily install the pivot and the top (**Fig. 21**). Check the hinge operation, and pivot the top around. Mark the position of the stop. Disassemble the pivot, stop, and hinges to allow for finishing.

To obtain the deep, rich mahogany color, we applied medium red mahogany stain mixed at a ratio of 6 parts stain to 1 part retarder. The retarder helps you apply this fast-drying stain without leaving brush marks.

Apply the stain to one section at a time, then wipe off any excess with a soft cloth. Allow the stain to dry overnight, then seal it with a wash coat of shellac (6 parts alcohol to 1 part 3-pound cut shellac). Allow the sealer to dry at least 4 hours, and apply a mahogany-colored paste wood filler. If you can't get mahogany-colored filler, use natural-colored filler and add burnt-umber Japan color to suit (available at art supply stores).

Apply the filler in the direction of the grain using a stiff brush. When the coating loses its wet look, wipe off the excess with a coarse cloth such as burlap. Wipe across the grain to remove the excess, then wipe with the grain using a soft cloth. Allow the filler to dry 24 hours, sand it lightly with 220-grit paper to remove filler residue, then wipe off dust.

Apply a coat of sanding sealer, and again sand lightly. Wipe off the dust with a tack cloth, then apply three coats of clear gloss wood finish. Allow 4 hours of drying between coats. Apply the sealer to the underside of the lower tabletop and the apron backs. Install the corner braces, and the project is complete.

Fig. 18 *Cut the apron tenons on the table saw using a dado head. Butt the apron against the stop block to make the cut.*

Fig. 19 *After the tenons are all cut, shape the decorative bead on the aprons with a molding head installed in the table saw.*

Fig. 20 *Glue and clamp together the aprons and legs in one step. Use blocks under the clamp jaws to prevent marring the surfaces of the wood.*

Fig. 21 *Dry assemble the pivot, then position the top on the base to check for movement. Mark the pivot stop position.*

Fine Dining

This simple mahogany dining table makes any meal more than a culinary pleasure.

Few activities better illustrate our need to socialize than our established dining rituals. Not only are these events the time when families get together to discuss the day's news, but they are also the way we choose to make friends and relatives welcome in our homes. That makes the dining room of central importance to both domestic and social life. And, perhaps because of this, it's the one room where most homeowners make a definite effort to assemble coordinated pieces of furniture. The subtle styling on this piece makes it an ideal companion with other styles. Of course, whether Queen Anne or contemporary, the overwhelming choice is wood.

*Key*POINTS

TIME

Prep Time	5 hours
Shop Time	12 hours
Assembly Time	7 hours

EFFORT

Skill Level	intermediate

COST / BENEFITS

Expense: **moderate**

- **Simple design and construction** makes this table a pleasure for craftsman and homeowner alike.

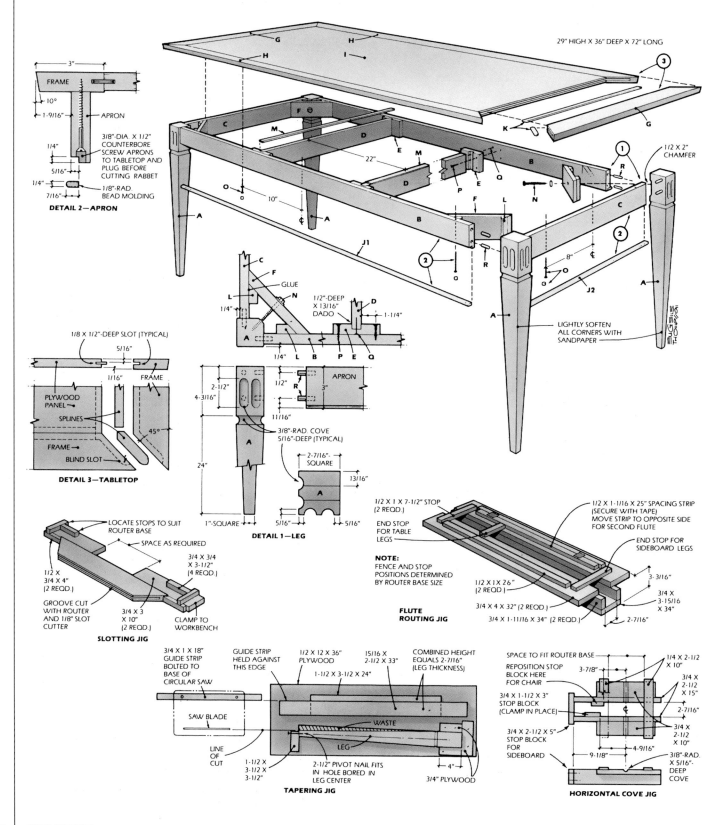

DETAIL 2—APRON

3"

FRAME

10°

1-9/16"

APRON

3/8"-DIA. X 1/2"
COUNTERBORE
SCREW APRONS
TO TABLETOP AND
PLUG BEFORE
CUTTING RABBET

1/4"

5/16"

1/4"

7/16"

1/8"-RAD.
BEAD MOLDING

29" HIGH X 36" DEEP X 72" LONG

1/2 X 2"
CHAMFER

LIGHTLY SOFTEN
ALL CORNERS WITH
SANDPAPER

22"

10"

8"

G   H   I

F

C   M   D   E

B

R

D   M

E   Q

P

O

F   L

B

N

R

J1

C

J2

A

K

1/8 X 1/2"-DEEP SLOT (TYPICAL)

5/16"

1/16"

FRAME

PLYWOOD
PANEL

SPLINES

FRAME

BLIND SLOT

45°

DETAIL 3—TABLETOP

C

F

GLUE

L

N

1/2"-DEEP
X 13/16"
DADO

D

1-1/4"

1/4"

A

1/4"   L   B   P   E   Q

2-1/2"

4-3/16"

1/2"

R

APRON

3"

11/16"

3/8"-RAD. COVE
5/16"-DEEP (TYPICAL)

24"

A

2-7/16"-
SQUARE

A

13/16"

1"-SQUARE

5/16"   5/16"

DETAIL 1—LEG

LOCATE STOPS TO SUIT
ROUTER BASE

SPACE AS REQUIRED

3/4 X 3/4
X 3-1/2"
(4 REQD.)

1/2 X
3/4 X 4"
(2 REQD.)

GROOVE CUT
WITH ROUTER
AND 1/8" SLOT
CUTTER

3/4 X 3
X 10"
(2 REQD.)

CLAMP TO
WORKBENCH

SLOTTING JIG

1/2 X 1 X 7-1/2" STOP
(2 REQD.)

END STOP
FOR TABLE
LEGS

NOTE:
FENCE AND STOP
POSITIONS DETERMINED
BY ROUTER BASE SIZE

1/2 X 1-1/16 X 25" SPACING STRIP
(SECURE WITH TAPE)
MOVE STRIP TO OPPOSITE SIDE
FOR SECOND FLUTE

END STOP FOR
SIDEBOARD LEGS

3-3/16"

1/2 X 1 X 26"
(2 REQD.)

3/4 X
3-15/16
X 34"

3/4 X 4 X 32" (2 REQD.)

3/4 X 1-11/16 X 34" (2 REQD.)

2-7/16"

FLUTE
ROUTING JIG

3/4 X 1 X 18"
GUIDE STRIP
BOLTED TO
BASE OF
CIRCULAR SAW

GUIDE STRIP
HELD AGAINST
THIS EDGE

1/2 X 12 X 36"
PLYWOOD

1-1/2 X 3-1/2 X 24"

15/16 X
2-1/2 X 33"

COMBINED HEIGHT
EQUALS 2-7/16"
(LEG THICKNESS)

SAW BLADE

WASTE

LEG

LINE
OF
CUT

1-1/2 X
3-1/2 X
3-1/2"

2-1/2" PIVOT NAIL FITS
IN HOLE BORED IN
LEG CENTER

4"

3/4" PLYWOOD

TAPERING JIG

SPACE TO FIT ROUTER BASE

REPOSITION STOP
BLOCK HERE
FOR CHAIR

3/4 X 1-1/2 X 3"
STOP BLOCK
(CLAMP IN PLACE)

3/4 X 2-1/2 X 5"
STOP BLOCK
FOR
SIDEBOARD

1/4 X 2-1/2
X 10"

3-7/8"

3/4 X
2-1/2
X 15"

2-7/16"

3/4 X
2-1/2
X 10"

9-1/8"

4-9/16"

3/8"-RAD.
X 5/16"-
DEEP
COVE

HORIZONTAL COVE JIG

This is a fine example of a signature piece in rich mahogany. We'll not only show you how to build it, but even how to complete the job with ordinary portable power tools. You don't need any expensive stationary shop equipment. The detailing, which may look complicated at first glance, was all designed to be executed with the aid of several specialized jigs that we'll show you how to build.

You'll need a sabre saw, router, finishing sander, drill and a circular saw with a cutting depth of at least 2½ in. For accurate boring, have a drill guide and doweling jig on hand.

Starting the Table

The 2⁷⁄₁₆-in.-sq. stock for the table legs is made by gluing up three layers of commonly available ¹³⁄₁₆-in. lumber. If possible, use boards wide enough to get more than one leg from each lamination. Because you'll be hand planing the surfaces smooth, try to keep the grain orientation of each board the same before gluing. If you find it hard to judge the grain direction, make a trial pass with your plane. Keep in mind that mahogany can vary in color when selecting boards for each leg. Mark all pieces as to grain direction and stacking order so that you won't mix them up during assembly.

Ordinary white or yellow carpenter's glue is fine for making the leg laminations. Use a roller or a squeegee to apply it fast and evenly. To keep the boards aligned during assembly, insert a pair of headless nails in the top and bottom boards of each lamination in an area that will become waste (**Fig. 1**). Special double-pointed brads are available for this purpose, or you can snip off the ends of small brads and insert them with pliers. Clamp the boards and let dry.

After the glue has set overnight, clamp the laminated stock to the worktable with a straightedge guide positioned on top for guiding the circular saw (**Fig. 2**). Keep a scrap plywood panel underneath so that you won't cut into your bench. Use a sharp blade for this cut—preferably one that's designed for ripping.

To cut the horizontal cove on the legs you'll need a ⅜-in.-rad. corebox bit mounted in the router. Build a jig to guide the router squarely across the leg faces at the appropriate distances from the end. Then cut the ⁵⁄₁₆-in.-deep cove on each face of every leg (**Fig. 3**).

Next, construct the leg-tapering jig and secure a rip fence to the base of the circular saw with two bolts as shown in the illustration. The saw base rides on a rail that's the same height as the leg thickness. You can plane a piece of 1-in. stock to ¹⁵⁄₁₆ in. and nail it to a 2x4 (1½ x 3½ in.) to get the correct height. Note the nail in the end stop block of the tapering jig. A corresponding hole centered in the bottom of each leg allows you to pivot the leg so that it's positioned correctly for cutting each face. When the leg tapers are completed, use a sharp smoothing plane to dress all the rough-sawn surfaces (**Fig. 4**).

The vertical fluting that appears on the two outward

Materials List

Key	No.	Size and description (use)
A	4	2⁷⁄₁₆ x 2⁷⁄₁₆ x 28³⁄₁₆" mahogany (leg)
B	2	¹³⁄₁₆ x 3 x 64½" mahogany (long apron)
C	2	¹³⁄₁₆ x 3 x 28½" mahogany (short apron)
D	2	¹³⁄₁₆ x 3 x 30⅜" mahogany (cross rail)
E	4	¹³⁄₁₆ x 3 x 4" mahogany (cleat)
F	4	¹³⁄₁₆ x 3 x 7¾" mahogany (brace)
G	2	¹³⁄₁₆ x 3 x 36" mahogany (end frame)
H	2	¹³⁄₁₆ x 3 x 72" mahogany (side frame)
I	1	¾ x 30 x 66" mahogany (top panel)
J1*	2	¼ x ⁷⁄₁₆ x 64½" mahogany (beading)
J2*	2	¼ x ⁷⁄₁₆ x 28½" mahogany (beading)
K**		⅛ x ⅞" plywood (spline)
L	8	¹³⁄₁₆ x 1¾ x 3" mahogany (glue block)
M	2	¹⁄₁₆ x ¹³⁄₁₆ x 30" mahogany (shim)
N	4	⁵⁄₁₆ x 3½" lagscrew and washer
O	18	3" No. 10 fh screw
P	16	1¼" No. 10 fh screw
Q	4	4d common nail
R	16	⅜"-dia. x 1½" dowel

Misc.: Glue; 120- and 220-grit sandpaper; ½" wire brads; red mahogany stain; satin polyurethane varnish.

*⅛" half-round bit and ⅛ x 1½"-dia. slotting bit.

**18 linear ft. required.

Fig. 1 *Select leg stock for color and grain orientation and insert headless brads in a waste area to keep the boards aligned during assembly.*

Fig. 2 *To rip the legs, clamp the laminated leg stock to the worktable with straightedge guide on top and scrap plywood underneath.*

Fig. 3 *A horizontal coving jig guides the router squarely across each face of the leg. For this step, use a ³/₈-in.-dia. corebox bit.*

Fig. 4 *Construct a tapering jig to cut uniform tapers on all the leg sides. Then dress all the rough-sawn surfaces with a hand plane.*

Fig. 5 *Twin flutes cut with a router and ³/₈-in.-rad. corebox bit are positioned accurately with this guiding jig and spacer.*

surfaces of each leg is also cut with the corebox bit. Build the flute routing jig and use a spacer that can be shifted from one side to the other to ensure uniform flute spacing (**Fig. 5**). Set the fences so that the flutes are ⁵/₁₆ in. in from the leg corner. A plunger router is ideal for this stopped fluting. If yours is regular fixed type, build your jig with higher sides and carefully lean the router into the wood at the start of each cut. Complete the legs by cutting a stopped chamfer on the inside corner of each leg with a router and chamfering bit. This simplifies boring the lagscrew hole for the corner block.

Making the Apron

Rip each apron piece to width, dress the sawn edges and cut to exact length. The joints that connect the rails to the legs are doweled. A completely adjustable doweling jig is better than the self-centering type because many of the joints

require off-center holes. Use dowel centers to transfer the hole locations to the legs. The tabletop is fastened to the skirt by 3-in. No. 10 fh screws. Counter bore ⅜-in.-dia. holes in the bottom edge of each rail for recessing the heads. Then bore ³/₁₆-in.-dia. pilot holes through the rails for the screws. The rails are highlighted with ¼-in. beads set into a rabbet. Cut the rabbets with a straight bit mounted in the router and using an edge guide. Don't be tempted to use a piloted bit in lieu of the edge guide because the pilot will fall into the counterbores and ruin the cut.

You can make the bead molding with your router and two special cutters. An ⅛-in.-rad. half-round cutter produces the profile, and a slotting cutter with a pilot rips the trim to thickness. To make this molding, install the half-round bit in the router so its cutting arc is flush with the router base. Then, working with the router base first against one face, and then the opposite face, cut twin half-rounds on one edge of the ¹³/₁₆-in.-thick stock. Then, install the slotting cutter in the router. Adjust it so that it's tangent to the bottom of the half-rounds already cut, and rip slots along the bottom of each bead. Finally, use your circular saw guided by a straightedge to rip the two lengths of beading away from the stock. Use a wide board for making this trim. After each pair of beads is cut off, plane the rough-sawn edge true, and make another set.

Constructing the Top

The table features a top assembled from a mahogany plywood panel and surrounded by a solid wood frame. Begin by cutting the plywood for the tabletop panel square and to exact size. Use your circular saw with a sharp, fine cutting blade guided by a straightedge. Because the circular saw tends to tear the top surface of the wood, select the best side and flip the panel over to make the cut.

Next, rip the tabletop frame pieces to width and plane the sawn edges smooth. Crosscut them slightly oversize in length and hold each piece up to the plywood panel to mark for the miters. The frame miter joints and the frame-to-panel joints are splined.

Use your router with a slot cutter to make the ⅛-in.-wide grooves. The spline joint at the miters doesn't extend through the corner. So, set up a stopping jig to cut these blind slots as shown in the drawing. When cutting the grooves, keep the base of the router on the top face of the frame pieces and panel for accurate registration.

We used ⅛-in.-thick plywood for the splines but similar size hardboard could be used. The splines shouldn't fit too tightly, or when the glue is applied they'll swell, making assembly difficult. If necessary, plane the spline surfaces for a slip fit.

Before the gluing, dry assemble the top to ensure that all the pieces have been cut properly. Draw the long side pieces against the panel with bar clamps and position the ends. If you don't have bar clamps long enough to span the length of the top, use two C-clamps and wedges (**Fig. 6**). Clamp the assembly tight and let the glue set overnight. After the glue has dried, plane the 10° bevel around the perimeter as shown in the drawing.

Assembling the Frame

Cut enough ⅜-in. dowels 1½ in. long to assemble the entire skirt. Chamfer the ends with a file or sandpaper and groove each pin to allow excess glue to escape. Or buy pregrooved dowel pins cut to length.

Begin assembly by applying hide glue sparingly to the holes and dowel pins for the short end rails and legs. After they've set, join them to the two long rails. Make sure the floor you're working on is flat. If necessary, place shims under the legs to keep the frame true.

After the glue has dried thoroughly, lay the tabletop upside down and position the leg and skirt assembly on it. Mark the hole positions for the top fastening screws and lightly mark with pencil the leg corner positions. Then shift the frame aside to bore the screw pilot holes. Use a drill stop or masking tape wrapped around the bit to act as a depth guide.

Slide the frame back in place, align it with the pencil marks and secure the base to the top with 3-in. No. 10 fh wood screws. To ensure extra rigidity to the tabletop panel, add two interior cross rails.

Cut four cross-rail cleats each with a centered ¹³/₁₆-in.-wide x ½-in.-deep dado as shown in the illustration. Then rip the rails to width, crosscut them exactly to length and attach each cleat to a rail end with one 4d nail and glue. Screw the rail assemblies in place with 1¼-in. No. 10 fh screws. Because the plywood panel is ¹/₁₆ in. thinner than the solid frame, you'll have to shim the cross rails on top for proper support. Next, assemble the corner blocks and install them with ⁵/₁₆ x 3½-in. lagscrews and glue.

Finishing the Job

After the table has been assembled, trim the bead molding to fit the rabbets in the end and side apron pieces. Secure with glue and ½-in. brads. Let the glue dry and scrape off squeeze-out. Using 120-grit sandpaper, ease the sharp corners on all table parts. Then sand the entire table with 120-grit, followed by 220-grit sandpaper and prepare for finishing by cleaning the table with a tack cloth.

We used red mahogany stain on the table to give the wood a deep traditional color. Follow the stain with three coats satin polyurethane, thinning the first coat six parts varnish to one part thinner. Between coats, lightly sand with 220-grit sandpaper and clean with a tack cloth.

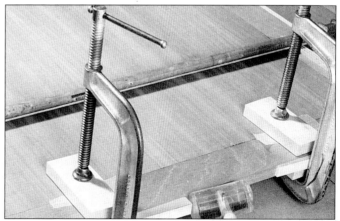

Fig. 6 C-clamps and wedges bring the end frame pieces into position. After the glue has set, trim a 10° bevel on tabletop edges.

Strong Coffee

Forget that showpiece couch; this coffee table will be the highlight of your living room.

As with so many attention-getting pieces, the design of this coffee table has its roots in the Arts & Crafts tradition. With its strong yet simple lines, this table of curly maple complements a wide variety of furniture styles. Should you need an end table, kitchen table, or worktable, the dimensions of the legs, aprons, and top can be easily modified to suit different needs. And, because the table is a reasonably simple design, it is an ideal project for a woodworker with intermediate-level skill, who has a well-equipped workshop that includes a table saw. Take your time, follow the instructions, and you will be rewarded. The challenge will be in bringing the rest of your furniture up to grade.

*Key*POINTS

TIME
Prep Time	7 hours
Shop Time	12 hours
Assembly Time	8 hours

EFFORT
Skill Level	intermediate

COST / BENEFITS
Expense: **moderate**

- **Rugged simple lines** make this piece an attractive addition to the living room.
- The table design is **extremely adaptable** for creating a kitchen or end table.

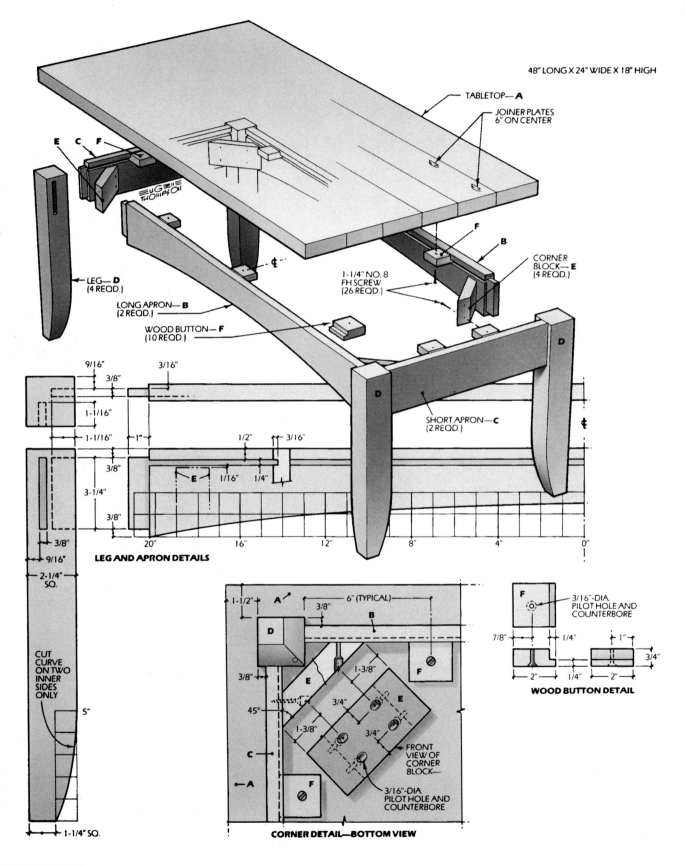

48" LONG X 24" WIDE X 18" HIGH

TABLETOP—**A**

JOINER PLATES
6" ON CENTER

E **C** **F**

LEG—**D**
(4 REQD.)

LONG APRON—**B**
(2 REQD.)

WOOD BUTTON—**F**
(10 REQD.)

F

B

CORNER
BLOCK—**E**
(4 REQD.)

1-1/4" NO. 8
FH SCREW
(26 REQD.)

¢

SHORT APRON—**C**
(2 REQD.)

D

D

¢

9/16"

3/8"

3/16"

1-1/16"

1-1/16" 1"

3/8"

3-1/4"

3/8"

3/8"

9/16"

2-1/4"
SQ.

CUT
CURVE
ON TWO
INNER
SIDES
ONLY

5"

1-1/4" SQ.

1/2" 3/16"

E 1/16" 1/4"

20" 16" 12" 8" 4" 0"

LEG AND APRON DETAILS

1-1/2" **A** 6" (TYPICAL)

3/8"

D **B**

3/8"

E

F

1-3/8"

45° 3/4" **E**

1-3/8" 3/4"

C

A **F**

FRONT
VIEW OF
CORNER
BLOCK—

3/16"-DIA.
PILOT HOLE AND
COUNTERBORE

CORNER DETAIL—BOTTOM VIEW

F

3/16"-DIA.
PILOT HOLE AND
COUNTERBORE

7/8" 1/4" 1"

2" 1/4" 2" 3/4"

WOOD BUTTON DETAIL

This table's top is glued-up and forms a solid panel. Its legs are cut from thick slabs of curly maple. The easy-to-apply finish consists of three coats of hand-rubbed oil, which builds up to a thin coating. It produces a soft sheen and brings out the figure in the curly maple, as well as imparting a slightly amber tone to the wood.

Making the Top

Begin by selecting the 5/4 stock for the tabletop. Note that the top is glued-up from six 4-in.-wide strips. In selecting the wood for the top, try to match the pieces for color and grain pattern so the piece will have a uniform appearance.

Joint the edge of each board, rip each one to about 4⅛ in., then joint the boards again to remove the saw marks and crosscut them about 2 in. longer than the finished dimension (**Fig. 1**). Check to be sure that each joint is tight and square along its entire length. Mark the stock for joining plates spaced about 6 to 8 in. on center, then cut the slots with the plate joiner (**Fig. 2**). Use a flat tabletop or a saw table as a work surface. Be sure to hold both the workpiece and joiner tightly to the table as you cut the slots.

Spread glue on the board edges and in the plate grooves, insert the joining plates and assemble the top. Use bar clamps to pull the joints tight. After about 20 to 30 minutes, scrape off any excess glue squeeze-out from the surfaces of the panel, then let the glue cure completely.

Trim the tabletop to length, using either a sliding table jig on the table saw, or a circular saw with a straightedge clamped to the top.

Next, hold the top between bench dogs and lightly plane the top to remove any small irregularities left from gluing the stock together (**Fig. 3**). Use a razor-sharp plane and work diagonally across the panel. As figured woods have a tendency to tear out, take a very light cut. If you still have trouble with

Materials List

Key	No.	Size and description (use)
A	1	1⅛ x 24 x 48" maple (top)
B	2	¾ x 4 x 42½" maple (long apron)
C	2	¾ x 4 x 18½" maple (short apron)
D	4	2¼ x 2¼ x 16⅞" maple (leg)
E	4	1⅛ x 2¾ x 5½" maple (corner block)
F	10	¾ x 2 x 2" maple (button)

Misc.: 1¼" No. 8 fh screws; No. 20 joining plates; white glue; 120-, 220-, and 320-grit sandpaper; 4/0 steel wool; transparent finish.

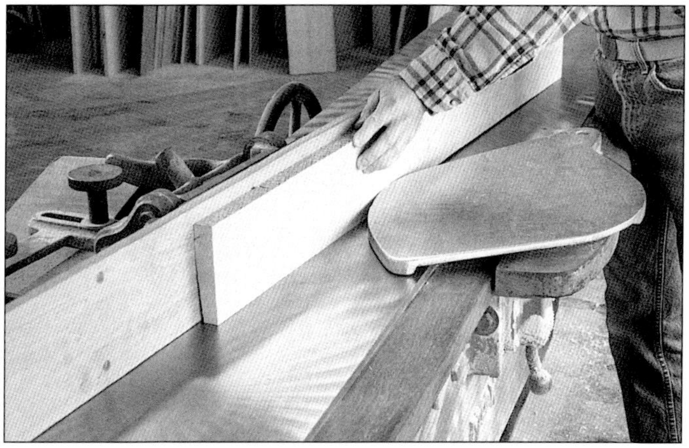

Fig. 1 ***Joint one edge of each board used in the top. Rip the board slightly over width, then joint the sawn edges smooth and straight.***

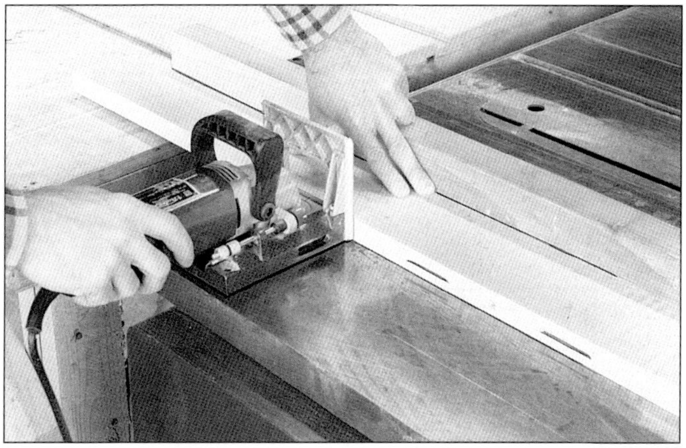

Fig. 2 ***Cut the joining plate slots in the edge of each board. Work on the table saw or another clean, flat surface.***

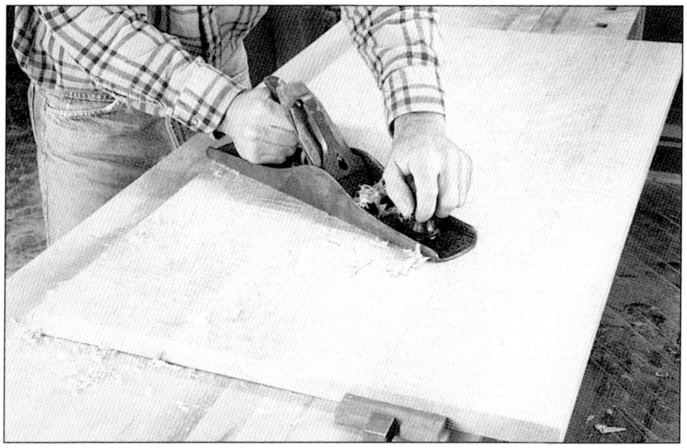

Fig. 3 ***After glue-up, use a razor-sharp plane to remove irregularities on the top. Work diagonally or across the top.***

Fig. 4 *Before sanding the top, use a cabinet scraper to remove small areas of tearout left behind by the hand plane.*

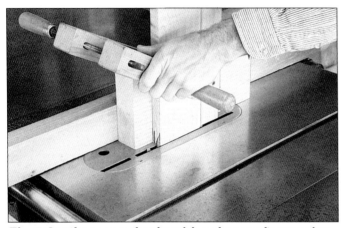

Fig. 5 *Cut the tenon cheeks with a shopmade tenoning jig, after test-cutting a piece of scrap. Use a parallel jaw clamp to hold the apron to the jig.*

Fig. 6 *Saw the tenon shoulders with a miter gauge and extension fence. Note the parallel jaw clamp that acts as a stop.*

tearout, you can plane directly across the panel's width, although this will require more sanding later.

Use a freshly sharpened cabinet scraper to finish smoothing the tabletop (**Fig. 4**).

Making the Aprons

Rip and crosscut the stock for the table aprons to finished size. Although the tenons can be cut in a number of ways, including using dado blades and by hand with a backsaw, we chose to use a shopmade tenoning jig on the table saw. Numerous commercial jigs are available, but most operate on the same principle of passing the workpiece vertically over the saw blade to cut the tenon cheeks.

The jig consists of a block of wood with a long, narrow piece of scrap screwed to it. The block rides against the table saw fence and the long, narrow piece acts as a backrest for the piece being sawn. The backrest is screwed to the block at a 90° angle. The dimensions of the pieces used to make the jig aren't important as long as they provide adequate support for the workpiece. This means that the block should be long enough to accommodate the apron and backrest, and wide enough to provide an adequate bearing surface for a clamp to secure the workpiece.

It is important that the two pieces that form the jig have square edges. Any deviation from square in the jig will result in a tenon that does not fit the mortise properly.

Make a test cut on scrap before sawing the tenons. To do this, clamp a piece of scrap against the jig so that its end rests on the saw table and its back edge butts to the backrest. Adjust the saw blade height carefully, and run the test piece over the blade. If the saw cuts are correctly located, parallel, and to the right depth, you can cut the tenons (**Fig. 5**). If the test cuts are out of parallel, it means the jig is out of square. Any other adjustments can be made by moving the saw fence or changing the blade height.

Fig. 7 *Cut the small shoulders with the apron on edge. Cut the waste piece off the tenon with a dovetail saw or band saw.*

Before cutting the shoulder cuts on the aprons, screw a long piece of straight scrap to the miter gauge to form an extension fence. Fasten a clamp to the extension fence to act as a stop, and test the setup on a piece of scrap before making the shoulder cuts. Saw the tenon shoulder first (**Fig. 6**), then saw across the apron's edge (**Fig. 7**).

Sawing the narrow shoulder in this way leaves a small piece of waste attached to the tenon. Remove this by cutting with a dovetail saw, or cut off the waste on the band saw.

Make a template from cardboard or hardboard of the curved bottom profile on the long aprons. Trace the shape on the apron, and use the band saw or a sabre saw to cut the curved shape (**Fig. 8**). Keep the saw blade barely to the waste side of the line as you cut.

We cleaned off the saw marks on this edge and refined the curve by clamping the apron upright on the bench and taking short strokes with a sharp spokeshave (**Fig. 9**). If you are careful, you can accomplish the same thing using a sanding drum on a drill press. Use light pressure on the drill press to avoid burning the wood or leaving crescents. Take fine cuts if you are using the spokeshave to avoid gouging. With either method, work down to the line in several passes.

Using a dado blade in the table saw, cut the groove on the top inside surface of the apron pieces (**Fig. 10**). This groove will house the lip on the wood buttons for fastening the top to the base. Even a narrow dado blade has a tendency to push a workpiece off the saw table, especially if the blade is dull. To avoid this, feed the workpiece slowly, and use a pushstick at the end of the cut to keep your hand clear of the dado blade. And, off course, use a sharp blade.

If you find that the workpiece is riding up despite these steps, try cutting the groove in two shallow passes.

Making the Legs

The table legs are unusual in that they are made from stock far thicker than that at an average lumberyard. You may be able to order curly maple for the rest of this project at a local lumberyard that sells hardwood, but chances are such a yard will have difficulty finding curly maple that is this thick. Note that the stock will arrive with rough-sawn surfaces. You need to have the stock planed to thickness at a lumberyard or plane it yourself.

If you plane the stock by machine, put a set of sharp knives in your planer. If you use hand planes, get ready for some exercise and sharpen your tools well before and during the operation. Either way, take very shallow cuts. The less you tear out the maple while planing it to thickness, the less cleanup you will have later with scrapers and sandpaper.

If you have the stock planed at a lumberyard, expect to pay a premium for this work—the yard may have to install a fresh set of knives and take extra time with the stock.

Once the stock is the correct thickness, rip and joint the leg blanks to 2¼ in. wide and crosscut them to length. Draw

Fig. 8 *Mark the curve on the long aprons, and saw just outside the line using a band saw or sabre saw.*

Fig. 9 *Remove the saw marks and smooth the apron's curve with a sharp spokeshave, or use a sanding drum on a drill press.*

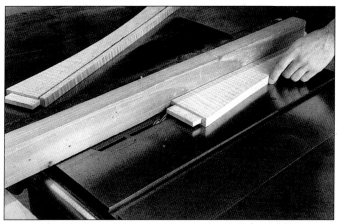

Fig. 10 *Cut the groove in the aprons with a dado blade in the table saw. The small lip on each button fits the groove.*

Fig. 11 *Cut the mortises with a plunge router and fence. Place a scrap piece next to the leg blank to support the router.*

Fig. 12 *Square the mortise ends with a chisel. If the mortise is bored on the drill press, its sides must be pared flat.*

Fig. 13 *Cut the leg blanks to shape on the band saw. The curved profile is cut on the inside surfaces of each leg, staying just to the inside of the waste side.*

Fig. 14 *Crosscut the buttons on the table saw using the miter gauge. A piece of masking tape on the saw table acts as a guide.*

the position of the mortises on the leg blanks using a sharp pencil and square, or use a mortise gauge.

Hold a leg securely between bench dogs, and use your plunge router and edge guide to cut the mortises (**Fig. 11**). If you like, you can also bore out the bulk of the mortise on a drill press, then pare the sides flat with a chisel. Either method will require that you also pare the mortise ends square (**Fig. 12**).

Make a template of the curved section of the leg and trace the curve on each leg. Note that the legs curve only on the inside faces. Cut the legs to shape on a band saw, staying just to the waste side of the line (**Fig. 13**). Clean up the curved face with a plane or a belt sander.

Assembly

To begin assembly, rip a strip of ¾-in.-thick stock to 2 in. wide, and crosscut it at least 24 in. long for making the wood

buttons that fasten the tabletop to the base. Use a dado blade in the table saw to cut a ¼-in.-wide x ½-in.-deep rabbet along one edge of the strip. As was the case with cutting the groove in the aprons, the workpiece may have a tendency to move away from the blade. If necessary, cut the rabbet in two passes.

Crosscut each button to length using an extension fence on the miter gauge (**Fig. 14**). Mark the length of the buttons with a strip of tape on the table saw table. Carefully and slowly slide the workpiece up to the edge of the tape and move it over the saw blade.

Bore and counterbore pilot holes in the buttons for the screws that attach them to the top.

Test and fit the legs to the aprons without glue. If a joint is too tight, pare the tenon to fit with a sharp chisel, or use a chisel and block plane. If a joint is too loose, glue a veneer shim to the tenon cheek.

Once all the joints fit correctly, begin the assembly of the table base by joining the short aprons to the legs. Apply glue to both mortises and tenons and use a bar clamp to pull the joints snug. Compare opposite diagonal measurements of the assembly to check that it is square, and adjust the clamps if necessary (**Fig. 15**).

After the glue has cured, glue and clamp the two ends to the long aprons. Be sure to do this on a flat surface in order to avoid imparting any twist to the base.

Cut pieces of 5/4 stock for the corner blocks. Use either the table saw and miter gauge or a miter box to cut the 45° angle on the block ends.

Bore and counterbore pilot holes in the blocks on the drill press (**Fig. 16**). It makes the process easier if you clamp a fence, 45° base, and stop block to the drill press table.

Next, screw the corner blocks to the aprons with 1¼-in.-long No. 8 fh screws (**Fig. 17**). The screws will go in easier if you lubricate them with a little wax.

Carefully sand all the parts with 120-grit sandpaper, followed by 220-grit, and finished with 320-grit sandpaper. Then dust off everything thoroughly with a tack cloth.

We applied three coats of transparent finish to the table. Apply the finish with a clean rag, allowing only a thin film to remain on the surface.

After overnight drying, scuff the finish lightly with 320-grit sandpaper, wipe it off thoroughly with a tack cloth, and apply the next coat. Repeat the process on the next coat. When the last coat has finally cured, rub it out with 4/0 steel wool and polish it with a soft, clean cloth.

To assemble the table, place the top upside down on a padded surface, then place the inverted base over it. Adjust the base for an equal overhang on all sides, then install the wood buttons and bore pilot holes in the top. Attach the base to the top by screwing through the buttons with 1¼-in.-long No. 8 fh screws (**Fig. 18**).

Fig. 16 *Clamp a stop block and backrest to the drill press. Bore, then counterbore, the pilot holes in the corner blocks.*

Fig. 17 *Lubricate the screws that hold the corner blocks to the aprons with a little wax. Screw the corner blocks to the aprons.*

Fig. 15 *Glue and clamp the short aprons to the legs. Measure to opposite diagonals to check the assembly for square.*

Fig. 18 *Invert the leg-apron assembly on the top with equal spacing all around. Screw the buttons into the top.*

Chopping Block

No matter how you cut it, this beautiful butcher block table really stands up.

We're fond of a hardy stews, canning and the type of cooking that requires a rugged work surface. That was the initial reason we built this butcher block table. But if we knew how good-looking it would turn out, we would have designed the project a long time ago. It's been in the kitchen for only a short while, but it's already the room's focal point, both visually and for preparing food. Generations of good cooks have relied on tables like this, and ours is built along those same, time-tested traditional lines. The work surface will last for decades, and the design has longevity too. Much as you may love its charm, however, the looks didn't come at the expense of its durability.

*Key*POINTS

TIME
Prep Time .... **6 hours**
Shop Time .... **11 hours**
Assembly Time .... **6 hours**

EFFORT
Skill Level .... **advanced**

COST / BENEFITS
Expense: **moderate**
- **This durable workhorse** offers the cook's kitchen an always-needed extra work surface, and the added bonus of an attractive piece for any style of kitchen.

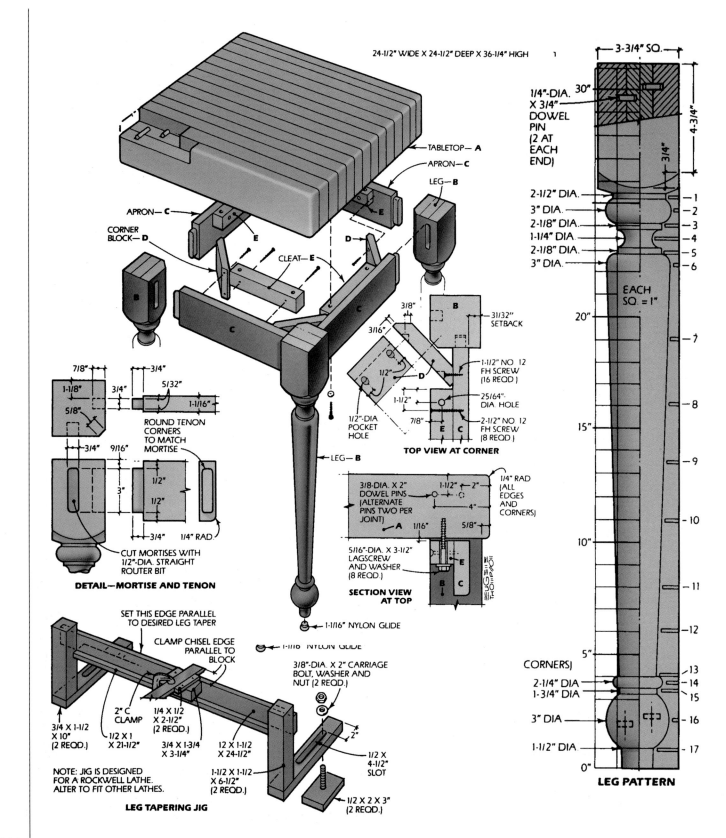

24-1/2" WIDE X 24-1/2" DEEP X 36-1/4" HIGH

TABLETOP — A

APRON — C

LEG — B

APRON — C

CORNER BLOCK — D

E

CLEAT — E

D

C

C

E

D

C

LEG — B

LEG — B

7/8"
3/4"
1-1/8"
3/4"
5/32"
5/8"
1-1/16"
ROUND TENON CORNERS TO MATCH MORTISE
3/4"
9/16"
3"
1/2"
1/2"
3/4"
1/4" RAD.
CUT MORTISES WITH 1/2"-DIA. STRAIGHT ROUTER BIT

DETAIL—MORTISE AND TENON

3/8"
3/16"
B
31/32" SETBACK
1/2"
D
1-1/2" NO. 12 FH SCREW (16 REQD.)
1-1/2"
25/64"- DIA. HOLE
7/8"
2-1/2" NO. 12 FH SCREW (8 REQD.)
E   C
1/2"-DIA POCKET HOLE

TOP VIEW AT CORNER

3/8-DIA. X 2" DOWEL PINS (ALTERNATE PINS TWO PER JOINT)
1-1/2"   2"
1/4" RAD (ALL EDGES AND CORNERS)
4"
A   1/16"
5/8"
5/16"-DIA. X 3-1/2" LAGSCREW AND WASHER (8 REQD.)
E
B   C

SECTION VIEW AT TOP

1-1/16" NYLON GLIDE

1-1/16" NYLON GLIDE

SET THIS EDGE PARALLEL TO DESIRED LEG TAPER

CLAMP CHISEL EDGE PARALLEL TO BLOCK

2" C CLAMP

3/4 X 1-1/2 X 10" (2 REQD.)

1/2 X 1 X 21-1/2"

1/4 X 1/2 X 2-1/2" (2 REQD.)

3/4 X 1-3/4 X 3-1/4"

12 X 1-1/2 X 24-1/2"

1-1/2 X 1-1/2 X 6-1/2" (2 REQD.)

3/8"-DIA. X 2" CARRIAGE BOLT, WASHER AND NUT (2 REQD.)

2"

1/2 X 4-1/2" SLOT

1/2 X 2 X 3" (2 REQD.)

NOTE: JIG IS DESIGNED FOR A ROCKWELL LATHE. ALTER TO FIT OTHER LATHES.

LEG TAPERING JIG

3-3/4" SQ.

1/4"-DIA. X 3/4" DOWEL PIN (2 AT EACH END)
30"
4-3/4"
3/4"
2-1/2" DIA. — 1
3" DIA. — 2
2-1/8" DIA. — 3
1-1/4" DIA. — 4
2-1/8" DIA. — 5
3" DIA. — 6
EACH SQ. = 1"
20"
7
15"
8
9
10"
9
10
10
5"
11
12
CORNERS)
13
2-1/4" DIA — 14
1-3/4" DIA — 15
3" DIA — 16
1-1/2" DIA — 17
0"

LEG PATTERN

This table called for hefty dimensions and tough materials. Its top, therefore, is a 5-in.-thick lamination of rocky maple, and the poplar legs are likewise beefy. The legs are enameled to stay good-looking, even if you slop onto them with a mushy floor mop or spill while cooking.

Making the Top

Make the top by gluing up 14 pieces of 8/4 maple face to face. Buy lumber that is S2S (surfaced two sides). Select carefully, culling out warped, cracked, cupped, or bowed pieces.

Crosscut the boards slightly over length, cutting off any sniped ends (**Fig. 1**). A snipe is a crescent-shaped cut in the board's face when it was planed to finished thickness. A snipe interferes with face gluing the boards.

Joint an edge on each piece. Make a shallow test cut to determine which direction the grain runs. If the jointer tears out the grain, joint the board from the opposite direction. Mark each jointed edge with an arrow pointing the way the grain runs. Rip each piece to 5 in. wide on the table saw. Joint the sawn edge, and mark it for planing direction.

Next, cut the stock to finished length. Stack the pieces on the table saw with the edge arrows facing the same direction. If possible, shift the boards so they are paired with the annual rings opposing each other, but keep the arrows pointing the same way. Number the pieces 1 through 14.

We used a pair of ⅜-in.-dia. x 2 in.-long dowel pins between each board to align the boards during glue-up. Offset the dowels on both sides of each board so the holes don't meet. Bore a pair of dowel holes on one face of each board on the drill press, but not on the last board (No. 14). Place a batch of boards, in sequence, on the table saw. Insert dowel center plugs in the paired holes, butt the boards against the rip fence, and, using the miter gauge to keep the pieces square to the fence, press them together to transfer the dowel center marks (**Fig. 2**). Bore holes on the marks.

We used water-resistant plastic resin glue, which is nontoxic when cured, to join the boards. The glue dries quickly, so glue the pieces together in stages. We glued together two batches of seven boards, but three batches (5-4-5) will work too.

Before gluing the boards together, set up six bar or pipe clamps to prevent fumbling once the glue is applied. Use protective wood pads behind the clamp heads. Apply the glue to both surfaces using a short-bristled, 2-in.-wide brush (**Fig. 3**). Allow the glue to dry overnight before joining the subassemblies (**Fig. 4**).

Use a paint scraper to remove hardened glue, and use a very sharp plane to level and smooth the top and bottom surfaces (**Fig. 5**). Smooth the end grain with a belt sander and

Fig. 1 *Beware of sniped areas on board ends. These will interfere with face gluing the top, so mark them and then cut them off.*

Materials List

Key	No.	Size and description (use)
A*	1	4⁷⁄₈ x 24¹⁄₂ x 24¹⁄₂" maple (top)
B	4	3³⁄₄ x 3³⁄₄ x 31¹⁄₄" poplar (legs)
C	4	1¹⁄₁₆ x 4 x 17¹⁄₄" poplar (apron)
D	4	1¹⁄₁₆ x 3³⁄₄ x 6¹⁄₈" poplar (corner block)
E	4	1³⁄₄ x 1³⁄₄ x 9³⁄₄" maple (cleat)

Misc.: 8-⁵⁄₁₆ x 3¹⁄₂" lagscrews and washers; 16-1¹⁄₂" No. 12 fh screws; 8-2¹⁄₂" No. 12 screws; 16-¹⁄₄"-dia. x ³⁄₄" dowel pins; 26-³⁄₈"-dia. x 2" dowel pins; plastic resin glue; gray primer; evergreen spray enamel

*14 pieces, 1³⁄₄ in. thick glued up.

Fig. 2 *To mark the dowel centers, align grain on the boards, butt them to the table saw fence and push them together using a miter gauge.*

Fig. 3 *Quickly spread plastic resin glue on the boards using a short-bristled brush. Glue and clamp together the top in at least two groups.*

Fig. 4 *Once the glue is dry, glue and clamp the two groups of boards. Keep clamps off the top by using thin strips of wood.*

Fig. 5 *Aligning edge grain pays off during surface planing. Scrape off the hardened glue, and surface the top with a sharp smooth plane.*

Fig. 6 *Clamp the mortise template to the leg. Cut the mortise using a plunge router equipped with a guide bushing and straight bit.*

progressively finer belts in an 80-, 100-, and 120-grit sequence. Round the corners with a router and a ¼-in.-rad. rounding bit. Work the vertical corners first, then round the top and bottom ends, and finish by cutting with the grain.

The Legs

Make the leg blanks by gluing together three pieces of 6/4 stock x 3⅜-in.-wide (like the top, position the edge grain facing the same way on the leg blanks). This results in a blank 3¹⁵⁄₁₆ in. thick. Trim the blanks to 3¾ in. square on the jointer.

Cut the mortises in the blanks before turning the legs. Mark the mortises with a square and a sharp pencil or a marking gauge. We cut them with a plunge router equipped with a template guide bushing and a ½-in.-dia. straight bit (**Fig. 6**). The template is made from lauan plywood and a couple of scrap blocks. Make the template to suit your router setup. Clamp it to the leg tops, and flip it end for end to cut

Fig. 7 *To make turning the large leg blanks easier, make stopped bevel cuts on the table saw. Cut off the scrap strips with a handsaw.*

the off-center mortises. Next, mark the center on both ends of the blanks, and set the table saw blade at 45°. Make stopped cuts at each corner, to within 10 in. of the leg top (**Fig. 7**). Cut off the waste with a handsaw.

Cut the small bevel on the inside of the legs, where the corner brace butts against it.

Tape a full-size pattern of the leg on a piece of cardboard. Mark the pattern as shown in the drawing, with depth grooves corresponding to the leg profile. Tack the pattern to the wall behind the lathe as a guide.

Make the legs' rounded shoulder cuts using a skew chisel. Make a starting nick at the upper end of the shoulder holding the skew with its long end (the toe) down and the heel up.

Slowly allow the toe to make contact. Then, rest the skew flat on the toolrest with the toe to the right, and push it gently into the leg (**Fig. 8**). Finish the shoulder by pivoting the skew.

Next, shape the leg into a cylinder with a gouge. Pivot the gouge to the right and take a thin cut as you move left to right down the toolrest (**Fig. 9**). Stop the lathe, and measure from your left to make pencil marks on the blank corresponding with the depth grooves on the pattern. Start the lathe, and touch the pencil to the blank on the marks (**Fig. 10**). Set an outside caliper to about ⅛ in. more than the diameter at each depth groove location. Cut the depth grooves with the parting tool, and check them with the calipers (**Figs. 11 and 12**). Back off from the cut periodically to avoid overheating the tool's tip.

With the depth grooves completed, shape the leg's beads and coves with round-nose and spear-point tools pivoted as required (**Figs. 13 and 14**).

The leg's long taper is shaped in a 3-step process. First, get it as close as you can to finished shape with the gouge. Next, using the skew, turn two narrow bands to finished diameter at opposite ends of the taper. Finally, use a leg-tapering jig to bring the taper to final shape (**Fig. 15**). This jig fits a

Fig. 9 *Rough the leg into a cylinder. Pivot the gouge to the right, and keep its bevel placed securely against the spinning workpiece.*

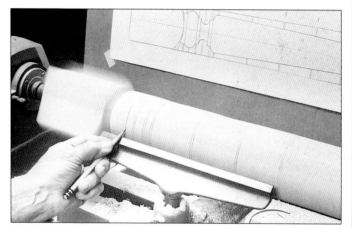

Fig. 10 *First, mark the depth groove locations with the leg stopped. Then, to darken the marks, touch the pencil to the leg while the leg is spinning.*

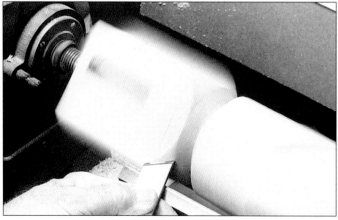

Fig. 8 *Shape the shoulder in two steps. First, use a skew vertically, with the toe forward. Then hold the skew as shown, taking a thin cut.*

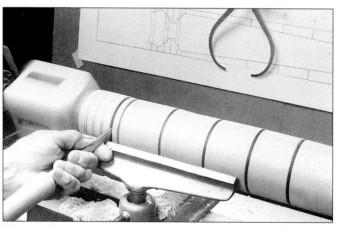

Fig. 11 *Cut on the pencil markings using a parting tool. To prevent overheating the tool's tip, back off periodically and let it cool.*

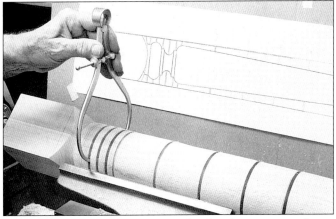

Fig. 12 *Check the diameter at the depth grooves using an outside caliper. Set the caliper width a little larger than the grooves on the drawing.*

Fig. 13 *Cut beads and coves using the depth grooves as guides. Cut the cove with a round-nose chisel held straight and pivoted.*

Fig. 14 *Use a spear-point chisel to shape the convex curve at the top of the leg. Move the tool with its point leading into the waste.*

Fig. 15 *After the taper is roughed down with a gouge, trim it to final size and smoothness using a skew chisel on a sliding jig.*

Fig. 16 *Cut the apron tenons with a dado blade mounted in the table saw. Butt each apron against the stop to cut the face and edge.*

Fig. 17 *Glue and clamp the aprons to the legs. Use wood blocks under the clamp heads, and position the clamps inside and outside of the legs.*

Rockwell-Delta lathe. You may have to alter the design to fit your machine. The jig consists of a block that slides on a long toolrest. The toolrest height is equal to the leg's centerline, and it is sloped to parallel the leg's taper. The skew chisel is positioned at an angle on the block by two strips of wood. To ensure it won't overcut, the skew is set for a thin cut and held in place with a C-clamp. Finish sand the legs first with 120-, then 180-, and finally 220-grit sandpaper torn into strips.

Aprons, Assembly, and Finish

Cut the aprons to dimension. Use a dado blade in the table saw and a stop block on the miter gauge to cut the apron tenons (**Fig. 16**). Use a chisel to round the tenons to fit the mortise. Glue and clamp two pairs of legs, each spanned by an apron. When the glue is dry, glue and clamp them with the other two aprons (**Fig. 17**).

Rip and miter the corner blocks. Bore pocket holes in them on the drill press using the fixture shown. To make the fixture, cut two 45° mitered guide blocks, and nail the large guide block on a scrap piece of plywood. It's important that the large guide block be 1¾ in. thick. Next, mark a centerline across the larger guide block's width. Measure ⅝ in. from the guide block's edge, and mark a second line so it crosses the centerline. Bore on the intersection of the lines with a ½-in.-dia. bit.

Slide a corner block against the guide block. To determine the position of the second (and smaller) guide block, mark the corner block's mitered thickness on the plywood base. Nail the second guide block to the base with its edge on the line.

Mark each corner block's long face with two lines, each ½ in. from the block's edge. Slide a corner block into the fixture. Match the line on the corner block with the line on the guide block, and bore the pocket and pilot holes (**Fig. 18**).

Hold the corner blocks to the aprons with a clamp and a notched block on the leg (**Fig. 19**). Bore the pilot holes in the aprons, and attach the corner blocks. Rip and crosscut the cleats, and bore holes for fastening the cleats to the aprons and the top. Clamp the cleats in place to bore the pilot holes in the aprons. Glue and screw the cleats to the aprons.

Place the top upside down slightly overhanging the bench on two adjoining sides to permit clamping the leg assembly on it. Center mark the lagscrew holes in the top by pressing the point of the ²⁵⁄₆₄-in. drill bit through the holes in the cleat and boring a shallow hole (**Fig. 20**).

Remove the leg assembly, and use a drill guide to bore the ¹⁷⁄₆₄-in.-dia. holes for the lagscrews in the top. Finish for the top is optional. We applied several coats of salad bowl finish with a lint-free cloth. We finished the legs and aprons with two coats of green spray enamel over a basecoat of gray primer. These oil-based paints contain Teflon.

When all the parts are finished, lagscrew the top to the leg assembly. The clearance between the ⁵⁄₁₆-in. lagscrews and the ²⁵⁄₆₄-in. holes in the cleats allows the top to expand and contract with changes in humidity.

Fig. 18 *Bore holes in the corner blocks using the fixture. Note that the line on the corner block is continuous with the one on the fixture.*

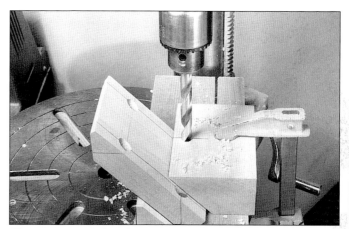

Fig. 19 *Extend the pilot holes through the corner blocks into the aprons. Hold the corner block with a fast-action clamp and a notched block.*

Fig. 20 *Fasten the cleats to the aprons with glue and screws. Center mark the pilot holes in the top with a ²⁵⁄₆₄-in. drill bit.*

Double Duty

This durable chest fills two roles. Not only does it provide a rugged table, it works as a file cabinet.

Set this file chest next to your favorite easy chair and it serves the usual end table purposes—a place to put a drink and chips during the game. Then, when you lift the hinged, stay-open top, your personal papers are at your disposal. The chest is sized to accommodate both legal-size and letter-size papers and hanging files. Aside from its filing capacity, this chest's generous proportions permit it to swallow anything from a couple of small pillows to a blanket—or just about anything else lying around and cluttering the view of your family room. Likewise, its size and styling make it suitable as an elevated blanket chest in a bedroom or loft. Simple and versatile, you may need to make another to meet your storage needs.

*Key*POINTS

TIME
Prep Time	4 hours
Shop Time	10 hours
Assembly Time	8 hours

EFFORT
Skill Level	beginner

COST / BENEFITS
Expense: **low**
- **Rugged durability** marks this piece as a long-lasting workhorse.
- Useful **office function** makes this a great addition to home office or living room.

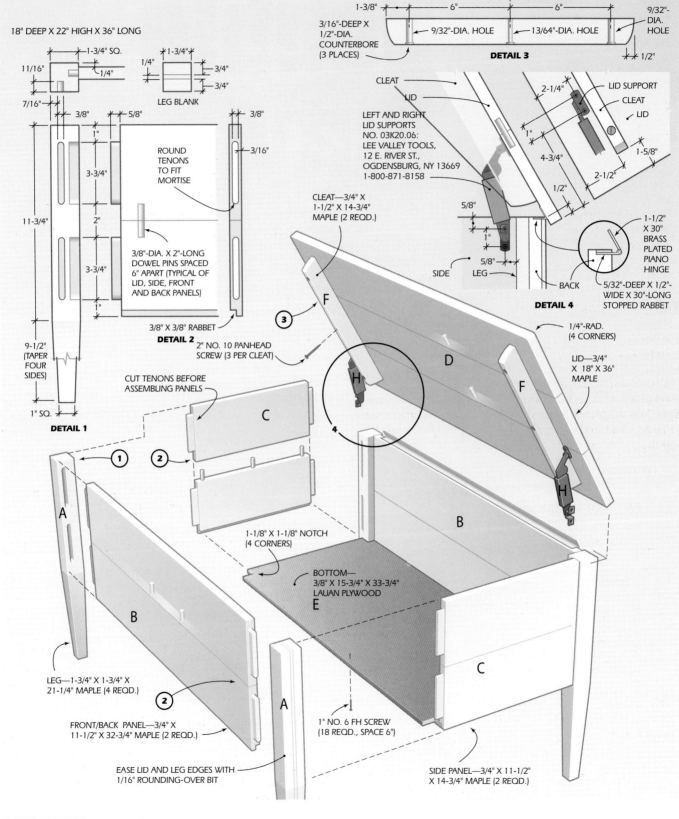

18" DEEP X 22" HIGH X 36" LONG

1-3/4" SQ.

11/16"
1/4"
7/16"

1-3/4"
1/4"
3/4"
3/4"

LEG BLANK

3/8"
1/4"
3/16"
3/16"

3/8"
5/8"
1"
3-3/4"
2"
3-3/4"
1"

ROUND TENONS TO FIT MORTISE

3/8"-DIA. X 2"-LONG DOWEL PINS SPACED 6" APART (TYPICAL OF LID, SIDE, FRONT AND BACK PANELS)

3/8" X 3/8" RABBET

DETAIL 2

11-3/4"

9-1/2" (TAPER FOUR SIDES)

1" SQ.

DETAIL 1

1-3/8"
6"
6"
9/32"-DIA. HOLE

3/16"-DEEP X 1/2"-DIA. COUNTERBORE (3 PLACES)

9/32"-DIA. HOLE
13/64"-DIA. HOLE

1/2"

DETAIL 3

CLEAT
LID

LEFT AND RIGHT LID SUPPORTS NO. 03K20.06: LEE VALLEY TOOLS, 12 E. RIVER ST., OGDENSBURG, NY 13669 1-800-871-8158

2-1/4"
LID SUPPORT
CLEAT
LID

1"
4-3/4"
1-5/8"
1/2"
2-1/2"

CLEAT—3/4" X 1-1/2" X 14-3/4" MAPLE (2 REQD.)

5/8"
1"

SIDE
LEG

BACK

5/8"

1-1/2" X 30" BRASS PLATED PIANO HINGE

5/32"-DEEP X 1/2"-WIDE X 30"-LONG STOPPED RABBET

DETAIL 4

F
3

2" NO. 10 PANHEAD SCREW (3 PER CLEAT)

H

4

D

F

1/4"-RAD. (4 CORNERS)

LID—3/4" X 18" X 36" MAPLE

CUT TENONS BEFORE ASSEMBLING PANELS

C

1
2

A

B

2

LEG—1-3/4" X 1-3/4" X 21-1/4" MAPLE (4 REQD.)

FRONT/BACK PANEL—3/4" X 11-1/2" X 32-3/4" MAPLE (2 REQD.)

EASE LID AND LEG EDGES WITH 1/16" ROUNDING-OVER BIT

1-1/8" X 1-1/8" NOTCH (4 CORNERS)

BOTTOM— 3/8" X 15-3/4" X 33-3/4" LAUAN PLYWOOD

E

B

H

C

A

1" NO. 6 FH SCREW (18 REQD., SPACE 6")

SIDE PANEL—3/4" X 11-1/2" X 14-3/4" MAPLE (2 REQD.)

I f your shop is modestly equipped, you'll like the fact that this table is easy to build. The simple construction belies durable good looks.

Making the Panels

To get started, rip and crosscut the stock for the front, back, and side panels to the sizes indicated in the drawing. For the top, cut all three boards about 1 in. oversize in length. The two outside boards are cut about ½ in. oversize in width, while the center board is cut to the 6-in. finished width. This allows for trimming the top to size.

Arrange the boards back to back in a vise and, using a square, mark the dowel centerlines across both edges. Then, always working the same side of a doweling jig to the face of the workpieces, bore the dowel holes (**Fig. 1**).

The end tenons on the side panels must be cut before the paired boards are edge glued. For best results, add an auxiliary fence to the saw's miter gauge, and clamp a stop block to the fence to ensure that the rabbet cuts are of uniform size. Using a dado blade, make a cut on the face of the workpieces. Then raise the blade to project 1 in., and pass each board over the blade on edge to form the tenon (**Fig. 2**).

Prepare for edge gluing by readying three bar or pipe clamps, four small clamps, and four cauls. Apply paste wax to the cauls so that they don't get glued to the panel. Tap the dowel pins into their holes and then apply glue to the panel edges. Join the pieces. Then alternately apply pressure to the bar clamps and to the caul clamps to close the joint and to keep the panel from buckling (**Fig. 3**). Use a belt and finish

Materials List

Key	No.	Size and description (use)
A	4	1¾ x 1¾ x 21¼" maple (leg)
B*	2	¾ x 11½ x 32¾" maple (front/back panel)
C*	2	¾ x 11½ x 14¾" maple (side panel)
D	1	¾ x 18 x 36" maple (lid)
E	1	⅜ x 15¾ x 33¾" lauan plywood (bottom)
F	2	¾ x 1½ x 14¾" maple (cleat)
G	1	30"-long x 1½" brass plated piano hinge
H	2	Left and right lid supports
I	30	⅜ x 2" long dowel pins
J	18	1" No. 6 fh screws

Misc.: 120-, 150-, 180-, and 220-grit sandpaper; satin polyurethane varnish; yellow ochre universal color pigment (available at art stores).

*Two boards for each panel.

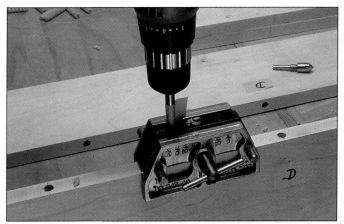

Fig. 1 *Use a dowel jig to bore the holes in the panel edges. A piece of tape positioned on the drill bit serves as a depth stop.*

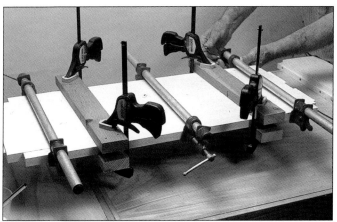

Fig. 2 *Cut the tenons using a dado blade, and use a stop block clamped to the auxiliary fence on the miter gauge.*

Fig. 3 *Cross cauls keep the panel from bowing as you apply clamping pressure. The glue will not stick to the waxed cauls.*

Fig. 4 *Using a dado head and an auxiliary fence on the table saw, cut the rabbet into which the bottom panel fits.*

Fig. 5 *Resaw the center piece for the leg blanks carefully. To do this safely, use a featherboard and a kerf splitter.*

Fig. 6 *Mark the grain direction on the leg blank pieces. Then glue and clamp these pieces using nails as alignment pins.*

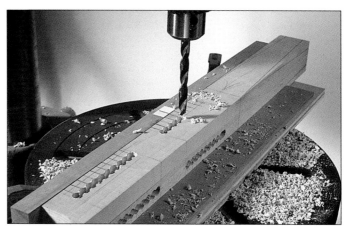

Fig. 7 *Bore the mortise holes in the leg blanks on the drill press. The leg blank is positioned for drilling by two fences.*

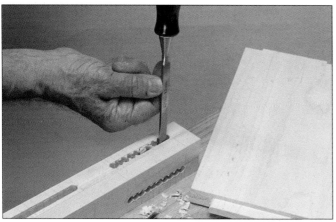

Fig. 8 *Chisel the waste from the leg mortises. The mortise ends are round and match the shape of the tenons.*

Fig. 9 *Cut the leg tapers using a jig on the table saw. The jig's notched block is repositioned after two cuts.*

sander to dress the panel faces. Then use a 4-in. hand file or a chisel to round the tenons. To complete the panels, cut the rabbets for the bottom (**Fig. 4**). Next, use a router with a straight bit to cut the hinge rabbet. Then switch to a ¹⁄₁₆-in. rounding-over bit to ease the panels' exposed edges.

Making the Legs

Make the legs from two 45-in.-long blanks, which you'll later cut into four finished lengths. The legs require that three pieces of wood be glued together. The center piece is sawn from a thicker piece. Be sure to use a smooth cutting blade, the saw's anti-kickback splitter, a featherboard, and a pushstick for this operation (**Fig. 5**).

Glue and clamp the leg pieces (**Fig. 6**). To keep the pieces from sliding out of alignment during clamping, bore two ³⁄₃₂-in. holes in the ends of the blanks, and use 2-in.-long finishing nails as alignment pins. The pins are inserted in an area to be cut off.

Mark the mortise locations on each leg, and be sure to arrange the legs so that the surfaces showing the glue joint face the chest's ends. Mark each leg mortise with centerlines ⅜ in. apart, and then bore the mortise holes (**Fig. 7**). Trim the mortise to finished dimension (**Fig. 8**).

Use a jig to cut the leg tapers. Place the leg between the rear stop and the front notched block, and make two cuts. The notched block is tack nailed so it projects 1 in. from the guide board. Make a taper cut on two adjacent faces, and then reposition the block so the notch projects 1⅜ in. Cut the remaining tapers (**Fig. 9**). Then use a router to ease their corners (**Fig. 10**).

Assembly

Before gluing the parts together, make a dry assembly to prepare the necessary cauls. Check the clamp adjustments and the fit of parts.

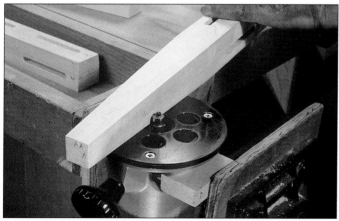

Fig. 10 *Use a router table, or clamp the router in a vise, and use a rounding-over bit to ease the sharp edges on the legs.*

Fig. 11 *Glue and clamp the subassemblies and panels. The clamps on the ends ensure proper alignment.*

Fig. 12 *Attach the lid supports securely to the side panels first, then to the box lid itself. The cleats are attached last.*

Do the gluing in two stages. Apply glue only on the short end panels and legs. Then make a temporary complete assembly. When the glue has dried, remove the clamps. Then glue and clamp the long side panels to the preglued end subassemblies (**Fig. 11**).

Cut the bottom panel to size and attach it with screws. Trim the top to size. Rip and crosscut its cleats, and bore the holes in them. The two outside holes are oversize to permit the lid to move with changing humidity.

Bore the pilot holes for the hinge, lid supports, and cleats. First, install the hinge at the back, then lay the table on its back to join the second leaf of the hinge to the lid. Attach the lid support in the same manner (**Fig. 12**). Attach the cleat with screws only, not glue.

After finish sanding, we applied three coats of clear satin polyurethane. The first coat was tinted with yellow ochre universal color, available at art supply stores.

Beautiful Legs

Here's the classic solution for saving space
—a handsome drop-leaf table in solid cherry.

While attitudes change, and styles come and go, there are certain ideas that remain as useful and appropriate today as they were 200 years ago. And, when it comes to furniture, there's little question that the enduring drop-leaf table falls into this category. Our solid cherry version is based on the Queen Anne style of furniture design popular in the 18th century. When fully open, its spacious circular top easily accommodates up to six adults in comfort and style. After your guests have gone, simply fold down the leaves for an elegant side table—and more space in your dining area. You'll do the work for one table, and end up with two.

*Key*POINTS

TIME

Prep Time	4 hours
Shop Time	14 hours
Assembly Time	10 hours

EFFORT

Skill Level	advanced

COST / BENEFITS

Expense: **expensive**

- **Classic function** combines with classic beauty in this timeless table.
- **A multi-room piece** that can be used in a number of different ways.

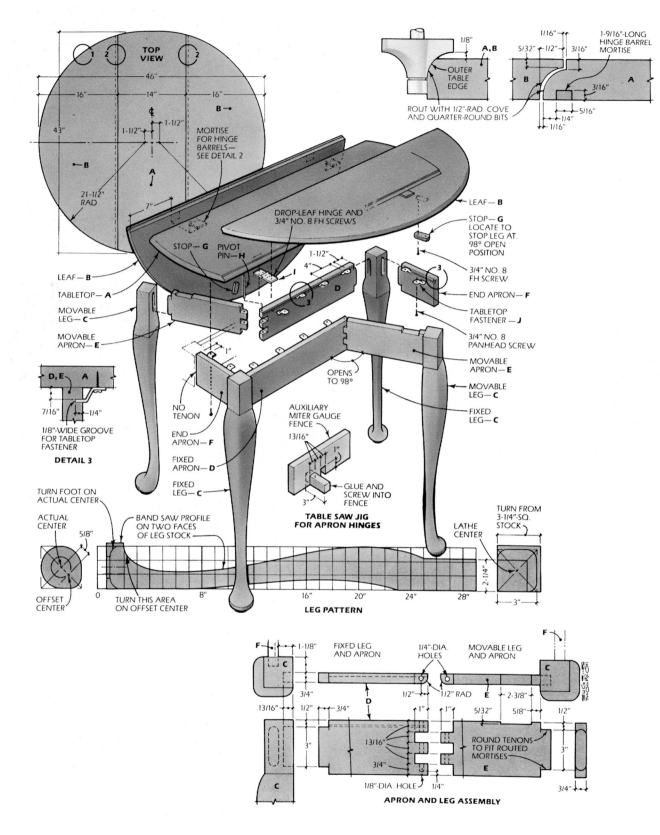

TOP VIEW

1 2 2

46"

16" 14" 16"

43"

1-1/2"
1-1/2"

MORTISE
FOR HINGE
BARRELS—
SEE DETAIL 2

B

A

B

21-1/2"
RAD

7"

1/8"

OUTER
TABLE
EDGE

A, B

ROUT WITH 1/2"-RAD. COVE
AND QUARTER-ROUND BITS

1/16"
5/32" 1/2" 3/16"

1-9/16"-LONG
HINGE BARREL
MORTISE

B A

3/16"

1/4" 5/16"

1/16"

LEAF — **B**

STOP — **G**
LOCATE TO
STOP LEG AT
98° OPEN
POSITION

3/4" NO. 8
FH SCREW

END APRON — **F**

TABLETOP
FASTENER — **J**

3/4" NO. 8
PANHEAD SCREW

MOVABLE
APRON — **E**

MOVABLE
LEG — **C**

FIXED
LEG — **C**

DROP-LEAF HINGE AND
3/4" NO. 8 FH SCREWS

STOP — **G** PIVOT
PIN — **H**

1-1/2"

4"

D

3

3

I

LEAF — **B**

TABLETOP — **A**

MOVABLE
LEG — **C**

MOVABLE
APRON — **E**

D, E   **A**

7/16"   1/4"

1/8"-WIDE GROOVE
FOR TABLETOP
FASTENER

DETAIL 3

1"

NO
TENON

END
APRON — **F**

FIXED
APRON — **D**

FIXED
LEG — **C**

OPENS
TO 98°

AUXILIARY
MITER GAUGE
FENCE

13/16"

1"

3"

GLUE AND
SCREW INTO
FENCE

**TABLE SAW JIG
FOR APRON HINGES**

TURN FOOT ON
ACTUAL CENTER

ACTUAL
CENTER

5/8"

OFFSET
CENTER

BAND SAW PROFILE
ON TWO FACES
OF LEG STOCK

TURN THIS AREA
ON OFFSET CENTER

0   8"   16"   20"   24"   28"

LEG PATTERN

TURN FROM
3-1/4"-SQ.
STOCK

LATHE
CENTER

2-1/4"

3"

FIXED LEG
AND APRON

1-1/8"

C

3/4"

13/16"   1/2"   3/4"

3"

C

1/4"-DIA.
HOLES

1/2"   1/2" RAD

D

1"   1"

13/16"

3/4"

1/8"-DIA. HOLE   1/4"

MOVABLE LEG
AND APRON

F

C

E   2-3/8"

5/32"   5/8"

ROUND TENONS
TO FIT ROUTED
MORTISES

E

1/2"

3"

3/4"

APRON AND LEG ASSEMBLY

With the leaves down, the four handsomely carved cabriole legs are positioned at the corners—exactly where they'd be in an ordinary table. However, the legs at two opposing corners actually swing out on traditional wooden hinges when the table is opened.

The Tabletop

We used ¾-in.-thick boards to make each tabletop section. When choosing the stock, try to match the boards for color and grain pattern. Also, plan to join the boards so that the direction of the annual rings on the board ends alternates from one board to the next. This tends to even out any cupping that may occur.

Lay the stock out as it will be assembled and mark the adjacent pieces so they won't be mixed up. Crosscut each piece roughly to length and true all mating surfaces.

Although the boards can be glued with no additional joinery, it helps to use dowels or splines to ensure good alignment. We used a plate joiner, which cuts accurately positioned slots for standard, No. 20 compressed-wood plates (**Fig. 1**). Make sure to locate the joints so they won't appear on the table edge when the top is cut to shape. Test fit the components before gluing (**Fig. 2**).

To keep the tops flat when they're clamped up, prepare four cauls from scrap stock. These are clamped in pairs above and beneath the assembly at each end. Wrap the cauls in wax paper to keep them from becoming glued to the work.

Apply glue to the mating surfaces of the first section and assemble. Lightly clamp the cauls in place and draw the

Fig. 1 *We used a plate joiner and No. 20 plates to join the tabletop pieces. Place plates 6 in. apart and located to miss the finished edge.*

Fig. 2 *Dry assemble each top section to check for alignment. Apply glue in plate slots and on stock edges. Clamp until the glue sets.*

components together with bar or pipe clamps. Double-check that the work is flat, and assemble the remaining two sections in the same way.

Use a belt sander to smooth the surfaces. Follow with an orbital finishing sander using 120- and then 220-grit sandpaper. Then trim the excess from both edges of the center section. Joint these edges and the inner edges of the leaves.

The rule joint is shaped with a router. Use a ½-in.-rad. quarter-round bit for the center-section edges and then switch to a ½-in.-rad. cove bit for the inside edges of the leaves. Begin with the center section. Make a trial pass on scrap stock to ensure that the depth of cut will produce the profile shown in the drawing. Note that a strip tacked to the underside of the stock along the edges is required to guide the pilot on the bit (**Fig. 3**). Then cut the cove halves of the rule joint on the leaves.

The shape of the tabletop is not a true circle, but rather

Materials List

Key	No.	Size and description (use)
A	1	¾ x 15 x 43" cherry (top)
B	2	¾ x 16 x 43" cherry (leaf)
C	4	3¼ x 3¼ x 28¼" cherry (leg)
D	2	¾ x 4 x 19½" cherry (fixed apron)
E	2	¾ x 4 x 13" cherry (movable apron)
F	2	¾ x 4 x 7½" cherry (end apron)
G	2	½ x ¾ x 2½" cherry (stop)
H	2	¼"-dia. x 3¾" steel pin (pivot)
I	2 pr.	1½ x 3⅛" drop-leaf hinge
J	12	¾ x 1¼" tabletop fastener

Misc.: 24-¾" No. 8 fh screws; 12-¾" No. 8 panhead screws; 4-¾" No. 8 fh screws; 120- and 220-grit sandpaper; cherry gel stain; semi-gloss polyurethane varnish.

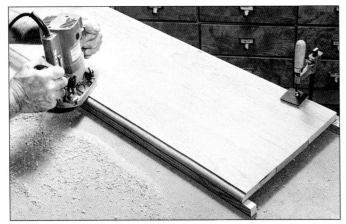

Fig. 3 *Tack strips flush with the center section edges to guide ½-in.-dia. quarter-round bit. A cove bit routs the rule joint on the leaves.*

Fig. 4 *Use dual centers, spaced 3 in. apart, to lay out the tabletop shape. A block taped to the top holds the pin end of a shopmade compass.*

Fig. 7 *Rout the mortises in the center section for the drop-leaf hinge knuckles. Router edge guide and strips tacked to the stock will guide the cut.*

Fig. 8 *Mark the hinge screw hole positions and bore the screw pilot holes to correct depth. The drill guide ensures perpendicular holes.*

two half circles set 3 in. apart. First prepare a strip of wood to act as a compass. Install a pushpin or nail at one end and bore a small hole for your pencil 21½ in. away. Lay out the tabletop pieces and tape a small block of wood at the center to receive the point of the compass (**Fig. 4**). After drawing each circular half, connect the lines using a flexible stick bent tangent to the arcs as a guide for your pencil.

Band saw to the line (**Fig. 5**) and sand the edges smooth. Securely clamp the pieces together and to your workbench for routing the edge profile with a ½-in.-rad. quarter-round bit as shown (**Fig. 6**).

To install the drop-leaf hinges, first rout the hinge knuckle mortises on the underside of the center section as shown (**Fig. 7**). Then, clamp the pieces together—top side up—with 1/16-in.-thick spacers in between the sections. Flip the assembly over, position the hinges, and mark and bore the screw pilot holes. Then install the hinges (**Fig. 8**).

Shaping the Legs

The legs are made from square 16/4 (4x4) stock. You can also glue together thinner boards to produce the leg blanks. Joint each piece to 3¼ in. sq. and cut them to finished length. Then make two band saw cuts on the top of each leg to form the recessed cheek surfaces (**Fig. 9**). These cuts are placed 1 in. in from adjacent faces and extend 4 in. deep, as shown.

Then cut the 13/16-in.-deep mortises for joining the aprons. Note that two legs have a mortise on each inner face and the other two have only one mortise apiece. The legs with only one mortise are the pivoting legs—be sure to lay out the mortise on the same face on each.

The mortises can be cut with a router equipped with an edge guide and ¾-in.-dia. straight bit. However, preboring a series of ½-in.-dia. holes makes the job easier and saves wear and tear on the bit. The mortise ends are left round and the tenons will be shaped to fit (**Fig. 10**). The next step is to band

Fig. 5 *After the curve is drawn, band saw the top sections to the line. Then smooth them with a stationary belt sander or by hand sanding.*

Fig. 6 *Clamp the top together with C-clamps and long boards that span the joints. Rout the edge profile with a ½-in.-dia. quarter-round bit.*

Fig. 9 *Band saw 4-in.-deep cuts, 1 in. from the surface of 3¼-in.-sq. leg blanks. These cuts form the leg cheeks on adjacent sides.*

Fig. 10 *Rout the mortises ¹³⁄₁₆ in. deep. Preboring ½-in. holes makes the job easier. Note the two swinging legs have only one mortise each.*

saw the leg profile on the same two adjacent faces where you made the 4-in.-deep cheek cuts. Using a template made from cardboard, lay out the curves on the stock. Before making the cuts, however, mark the true center of the blank on each end and the offset center at the foot end as shown in the drawing. Note that the foot profile is not sawn but left square.

Band saw the profile on one face of the first leg. Tape the waste back in place to provide support for cutting the adjacent side and to restore the cutting line. Then make the second profile cut and shape the remaining legs in the same way (**Fig. 11**). Sand the cheek surfaces and the convex knee area of each leg. Mount a leg in the lathe on its true centers for turning the foot. Run the lathe at slow speed and turn the foot profile as shown in the drawing (**Fig. 12**). Also, shape the convex back ankle area just above the foot.

After sanding at medium speed, shift the tailstock center to the offset center of the leg foot as shown in the drawing and

shape the concave section just above the foot at slow speed. Take very light shavings and check the work frequently to avoid removing too much wood (**Fig. 13**).

During all the turning operations, be very careful to keep your hands clear of the rotating leg. Most of the leg is eccentric and its corners are indistinct and difficult to see.

After the foot area has been turned, lock the leg in position using the indexing pin on the lathe and shape the remaining sections with rasps, files, and spokeshave (**Fig. 14**). Then sand the leg smooth.

Apron Joinery

First cut the stock to width and oversize in length. Mount a dado blade in the table saw and set for a ¹³⁄₁₆-in.-wide, 1-in.-deep cut. Prepare a 4x12-in. auxiliary miter gauge fence and cut two notches in it exactly ¹³⁄₁₆ in. apart. Glue and screw a guide pin to the outermost notch as shown in the drawing.

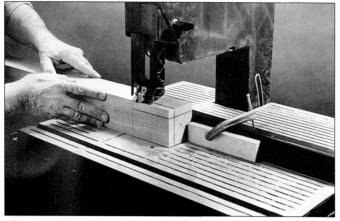

Fig. 11 *Lay out the profile on two sides of the stock and band saw one face to line. Reattach the waste with masking tape, and band saw the adjacent face.*

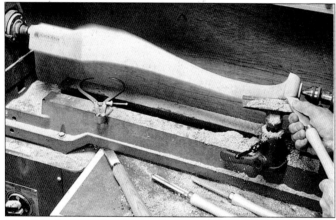

Fig. 12 *Mount a leg in the lathe on the actual stock centers. Turn the convex foot section to the profile shown. Also, begin to round the back of the ankle.*

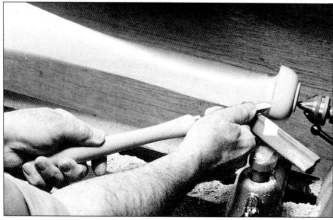

Fig. 13 *Turn the inside concave area above the foot on offset center. Use a round-nose turning tool. Stay safely away from the knee area.*

Then secure the assembly to the miter gauge so the remaining notch lines up with the dado blade.

Place a fixed (long) apron against the fence with its face out and its edge against the guide pin. Cut a notch in the apron end (**Fig. 15**). Without removing this piece, place a pivoting (short) apron against the first piece—face in—so that its edge lines up with the outer edge of the last notch. Clamp both pieces to the fence and make the cut. Shift both pieces over the guide pin for the second cut (**Fig. 16**). Repeat the procedure for the third cut.

Engage each knuckle joint and bore a ¼-in.-dia. hinge pinhole from the top edge that stops ¼ in. from the bottom. Bore the last ¼ in. with a ⅛-in. bit. This keeps the pin in place, but allows it to be driven out when necessary. Round the corners of the hinge fingers as shown.

With the pins installed, mark the apron lengths and cut to size. Prepare the end aprons and cut all tenons with the dado blade. Then round the tenon ends to match the mortises. This can be done by hand, or you can use a template and guide bushing with your router. Cut a groove in each apron piece for the tabletop fasteners and notch the movable aprons so they clear the drop-leaf hinges as shown in the drawing.

Assembly and Finish

Gluing the aprons to the legs is done in two stages. First, dry assemble the long hinged aprons to the appropriate legs. Lay these subassemblies upside down and in position on the inverted top. Place wax paper between the top and legs. These subassemblies hold the legs in position for gluing and clamping the short end aprons. Apply glue to the end mortise-and-tenon joints and draw the joints tight with bar or pipe clamps. Check for square and adjust if necessary (**Fig. 17**).

After the glue has dried, remove the clamps and apply glue to the long apron mortise-and-tenon joints. Use C-clamps and scrap stock to hold the hinged aprons rigid and straight.

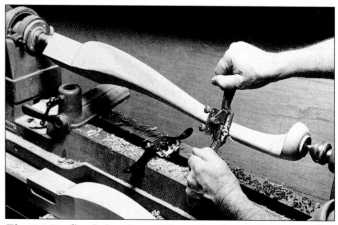

Fig. 14 *Do final shaping with spokeshaves, rasps, and files. Use an index pin on the lathe head to keep the leg in place. Smooth by hand sanding.*

Fig. 15 *Cut the wood hinges with a dado blade and auxiliary miter gauge fence. Begin by cutting a 1-in.-deep notch in the long apron.*

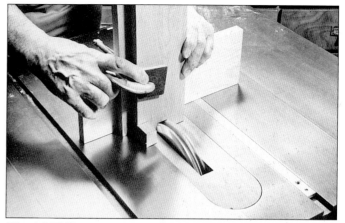

Fig. 16 *Shift aprons over the guide pin, clamp, and cut. The third pass requires a scrap block behind the top apron to prevent tearout.*

Fig. 17 *Begin assembly by dry fitting the long aprons to the legs for support. Then glue and clamp the short aprons to the legs and let the glue dry.*

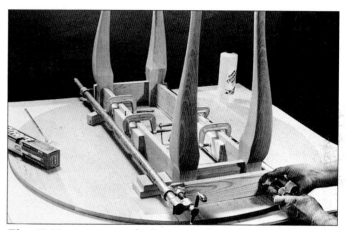

Fig. 18 *Use scrap stock clamped alongside the aprons to hold the hinges straight. Apply glue and draw the remaining joints tight.*

Then draw the joints tight with pipe clamps, check for square, and let the glue set (**Fig. 18**). Finish sand all the components with 220-grit sandpaper.

It's easiest to finish the table before installing the top and with the hinged aprons and leaves disassembled. We used cherry gel stain followed by three coats of semi-gloss polyurethane varnish.

When choosing a stain, keep in mind that the cherry wood will darken naturally over time. Sand lightly between each coat of varnish.

The bottom surface of the center top section need not be stained. However, it's a good idea to apply the same number of coats to both surfaces of every piece to help prevent warping.

Finally, reassemble the tabletop and hinged aprons. Lay the base subassemblies in position on the inverted top and install the tabletop fasteners (**Fig. 19**). Then screw in place the two small blocks that limit the travel of the swinging legs.

Fig. 19 *After applying the finish, secure the tabletop to the base assemblies with metal fasteners. Prebore screw holes to correct depth.*

Play Time

Your children—and their children —will have hours of fun with this set.

This table and chair set is child-size, but it's built to be as sturdy as any adult furniture. This is as it should be, because little children are known to use furniture for more than gentle fun and games. Specifically, the components have been fastened together with sturdy, long-lasting mortise-and-tenon joints. This construction provides the extra measure of durability that classifies these pieces as furniture, not toys. We've also added reinforcement with tabletop fasteners and solid maple wood. Even the finish should hold up to play time spills, crayon marks, banging, and more. That makes this set tough enough to withstand more than one generation of use, so that your children's children will enjoy it.

*Key*POINTS

TIME

Prep Time	10 hours
Shop Time	12 hours
Assembly Time	10 hours

EFFORT

Skill Level	basic

COST / BENEFITS

Expense: low
- **Attractive durability** is perfect for the kids' room.
- A gift **for multiple generations**, with added bonus as a memory maker.

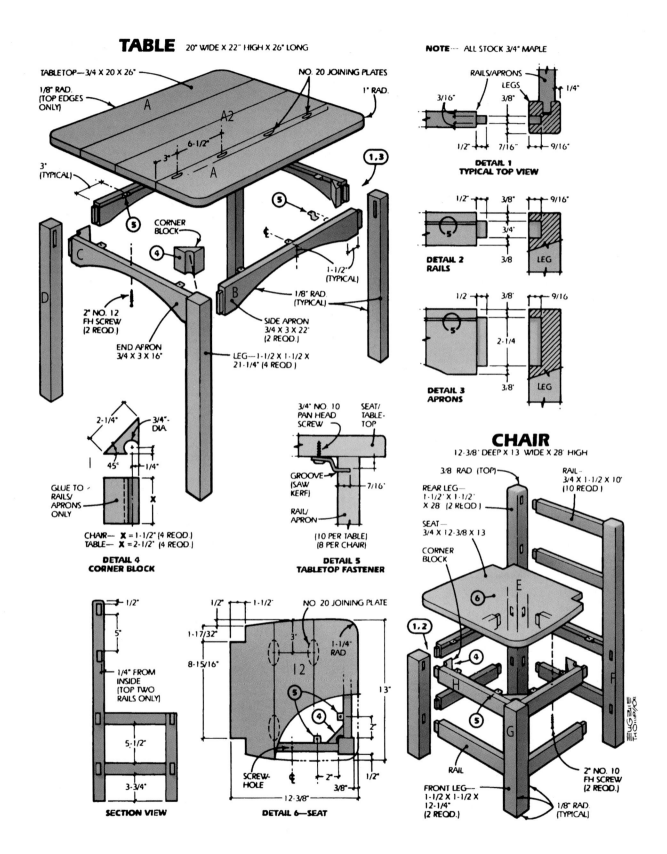

TABLE   20" WIDE X 22" HIGH X 26" LONG

TABLETOP—3/4 X 20 X 26"

1/8" RAD. (TOP EDGES ONLY)

NO. 20 JOINING PLATES

1" RAD.

A

A2

6-1/2"

3"

A

3" (TYPICAL)

CORNER BLOCK

4

5

5

1,3

5

¢

1-1/2" (TYPICAL)

C

D

2" NO. 12 FH SCREW (2 REQD.)

END APRON 3/4 X 3 X 16"

B

1/8" RAD. (TYPICAL)

SIDE APRON 3/4 X 3 X 22" (2 REQD.)

LEG—1-1/2 X 1-1/2 X 21-1/4" (4 REQD.)

NOTE— ALL STOCK 3/4" MAPLE

RAILS/APRONS

LEGS

3/16"

3/8"

1/4"

1/2"

7/16"

9/16"

DETAIL 1
TYPICAL TOP VIEW

1/2"

3/8"

9/16"

5

3/4"

3/8"

LEG

DETAIL 2
RAILS

1/2

3/8"

9/16

5

2-1/4

LEG

3/8"

DETAIL 3
APRONS

2-1/4"

3/4" DIA.

45°

1/4"

X

GLUE TO RAILS/ APRONS ONLY

CHAIR— **X** = 1-1/2" (4 REQD.)
TABLE— **X** = 2-1/2" (4 REQD.)

DETAIL 4
CORNER BLOCK

3/4" NO. 10 PAN HEAD SCREW

SEAT/ TABLE-TOP

GROOVE (SAW KERF)

RAIL/ APRON

7/16"

(10 PER TABLE)
(8 PER CHAIR)

DETAIL 5
TABLETOP FASTENER

CHAIR   12-3/8" DEEP X 13" WIDE X 28" HIGH

3/8" RAD. (TOP)

RAIL— 3/4 X 1-1/2 X 10" (10 REQD.)

REAR LEG— 1-1/2" X 1-1/2" X 28" (2 REQD.)

SEAT— 3/4 X 12-3/8 X 13

CORNER BLOCK

6

E

1,2

4

H

5

F

G

RAIL

FRONT LEG— 1-1/2 X 1-1/2 X 12-1/4" (2 REQD.)

2" NO. 10 FH SCREW (2 REQD.)

1/8" RAD. (TYPICAL)

1/2"

5"

1/4" FROM INSIDE (TOP TWO RAILS ONLY)

5-1/2"

3-3/4"

SECTION VIEW

1/2"

1-1/2"

NO. 20 JOINING PLATE

1-17/32"

3"

1-1/4" RAD.

8-15/16"

12

13"

5

4

2"

SCREW-HOLE

¢

2"

1/2"

12-3/8"

3/8"

DETAIL 6—SEAT

EUGENE THOMPSON

O ur choice of wood is solid maple, a smooth and sturdy material that accepts radiused edges well. The corners of each piece are rounded for safety, and we cover the pieces with a clear finish. But there's no reason the project couldn't be finished with a stain or varnish, or a playfully colored paint. It's a fun project to build, but it's twice as much fun to see kids play with it.

Making the Parts

Rip and crosscut the stock for the tabletop and chair seats. For the tabletop, rip two pieces 5 in. wide for the center and two pieces about 5¼ in. wide for the outsides. Rip and crosscut stock for the chair seats (you'll want more than the one we've specified here). Make the center boards 4⅛ in. wide, and the two outside boards 4⅜ in. wide. The extra width on the outside boards allows you to trim off clamp marks after the workpiece has been glued together.

Now rip and crosscut the stock for the chair and table legs, the table aprons, and the chair rails. The important first step when preparing boards to be glued together is to determine the grain direction of each. The direction should be similarly oriented to allow the glued-together assembly to be planed, if necessary, without tearing out grain on some of the pieces. If you're not sure of the grain direction, make a light test cut on each piece using a block plane (**Fig. 1**). Mark an arrow on each piece to indicate grain direction.

To make a panel for the tabletop or chair seat, place the boards on a work surface, align the boards' grain directions, and mark the locations of joining plates (or dowels) on each panel face. Use a plate joiner to cut the slots in each piece, and apply glue to the slots, edges, and plates (**Fig. 2 and 3**).

Apply pressure to the panel with bar clamps, and use cauls and C-clamps to keep the panel flat as the glue sets. A handy trick for keeping the panel centered on the clamp jaws is to lay a strip of wood along each clamp. The strip keeps the panel at the right height. Later, use a scraper to shave off beads of dried glue,

then smooth the panel surface with a belt sander (**Fig. 4**). Rip the tabletop panel to finished dimension. Next, crosscut the panels to length. We did this using a guide strip that was lightly tack nailed to the bottom of the panel. The strip slides snugly in the miter-gauge slot and is positioned perpendicular to the panel's edge.

Cut the panel twice. The first cut removes excess stock at one end of the panel. From the cut edge, measure and mark the finished length. Position the guide strip accordingly, and crosscut the panel to its finished dimension (**Fig. 5**). Rip and crosscut the chair-seat panels to the finished dimension. Cut out the corner notches for the back legs on the table saw before making the curved

Fig. 1 *Before gluing together the boards for the tabletop and the chair seats, test the grain direction using a block plane.*

Fig. 2 *Place the boards on a flat work surface and butt them to a stop block. Cut the biscuit slots at the locations you marked.*

Materials List

Key	No.	Size and description (use)
A1	2	³/₄ x 5¹/₄ x 26" maple (tabletop outside board)
A2	2	³/₄ x 5 x 26" maple (tabletop inside board)
B	2	³/₄ x 3 x 22" maple (table side apron)
C	2	³/₄ x 3 x 16" maple (table end apron)
D	4	1¹/₂ x 1¹/₂ x 21¹/₄" maple (table leg)
E	1	³/₄ x 12³/₈ x 13" maple (chair seat)
F	2	1¹/₂ x 1¹/₂ x 28" maple (chair back leg)
G	2	1¹/₂ x 1¹/₂ x 12¹/₄" maple (chair front leg)
H	10	³/₄ x 1¹/₂ x 10" maple (chair rail)
I1	4	2¹/₄ x 2¹/₂" maple (table corner block)
I2	4	2¹/₄ x 1¹/₂" maple (chair corner block)

Misc.: 18 tabletop fasteners (10 per table, 8 per chair); 2-2" No. 12 fh screws; 2-2" No. 10 fh screws; 12 No. 20 joining plates.

Fig. 3 *Glue and clamp the panel. A spacer strip positioned below the boards centers the panel on the clamp jaws and keeps them at correct height.*

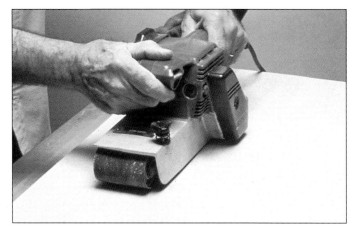

Fig. 4 *Scrape off the glue beads with a spokeshave, then sand the panel. Be careful not to tip the belt sander near the panel's edge.*

edge cuts. Next, cut the tenons on the aprons and chair rails using a dado blade in the table saw and a stop block on the miter gauge. (**Fig. 6**). Butt the workpiece against the stop block, and make one pass to cut the tenon cheek and shoulder.

Repeat the procedure on the opposite face. Raise the saw blade, stand the workpiece on edge, and finish the cuts. Be sure to keep sawdust out of the corner between the auxiliary fence on the miter gauge and the stop block. Sawdust will prevent the workpiece from butting snugly to the stop block, and this will produce inaccurate tenons.

Cut the grooves in the table aprons, then cut the curves on the aprons using a sabre saw or band saw. Remove saw marks using a spokeshave (**Fig. 7**). Cut the grooves in the chair rails as well. To cut the mortises in the table and chair legs, bore a series of overlapping holes, then pare away any waste using a chisel (**Fig. 8**). To avoid making it too large, test fit the matching tenon into the mortise.

Assembly

Before assembly, round all corners using a ⅛-in.-rad. rounding-over bit in a router table (**Fig. 9**). Also, bore screw holes in the aprons and chair rails, and finish sand them. Finally, dry fit all parts.

Apply slow-setting hide glue on the table rail and apron tenons. Then, glue and clamp together two subassemblies consisting of a pair of legs and an apron. For the chairs, glue and clamp a pair of legs and rails.

To complete the table base, glue and clamp the subassemblies with a pair of aprons. To finish up the chairs, insert four rails into the front leg-rail subassembly, then glue and clamp this together with the rear legs and rails (**Fig. 10 and 11**).

Install the corner blocks on the table base, then finish sand and install the tabletop. Finish sand and install the seats. Both are attached with wrought-steel fasteners (**Fig. 12**). Finish all with a satin-finish polyurethane.

Fig. 7 *Cut the curves on the aprons as shown in the drawing, then smooth out the curves, and remove saw marks using a spokeshave.*

Fig. 10 *First, dry fit all of the pieces. Then glue and clamp the front chair legs and rails, followed by the side rails.*

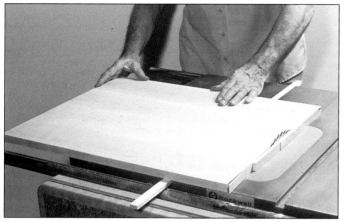

Fig. 5 *To accurately crosscut the panel, tack a guide strip to it. The strip slides snugly in the saw's miter-gauge slot.*

Fig. 6 *Use a stop block, a miter gauge with an auxiliary fence, and a dado blade in the table saw to cut all the tenons.*

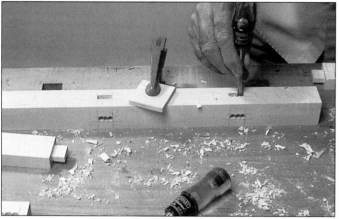

Fig. 8 *Remove the bulk of each mortise by boring a series of overlapping holes to remove the waste. Finish the mortises with a sharp chisel.*

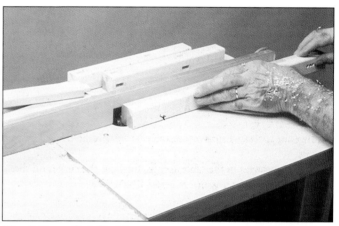

Fig. 9 *For a finished look, use a 1/8-in.-rad. rounding-over bit in the router table to cut the curve on all leg and rail edges.*

Fig. 11 *Glue and clamp the chair's subassemblies. Lay a steel square on the bench to ensure that the parts are in line.*

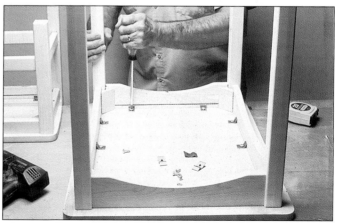

Fig. 12 *Align the top, or seat, over the base. Install the fasteners in their grooves, and drive the screws into the panel.*

Big Top

This maple coffee table is more than just a surface on which to put your magazines—it's extra storage!

A coffee table is a useful thing, even if it's never used to take a coffee break. And we think our hinged-top storage model is much more useful than most. It's big enough to accommodate several magazines and even a couple of books on top. But when unexpected company drops by, just lift the top and stash the accumulation. Or you can simply store often-used items like board games, photo albums, and catalogs in the compartment. Another nice feature of this project is its simple design, which works just as well in elaborate living rooms as it does in simple family rooms. It can even fit at the end of your bed for storing linens.

*Key*POINTS

TIME
Prep Time	4 hours
Shop Time	10 hours
Assembly Time	8 hours

EFFORT
Skill Level	basic

COST / BENEFITS
Expense: **moderate**
- **Sturdy, simple design** makes this a pleasing piece for many different rooms.
- The storage compartment is a **perfect hideaway** for frequently used items.

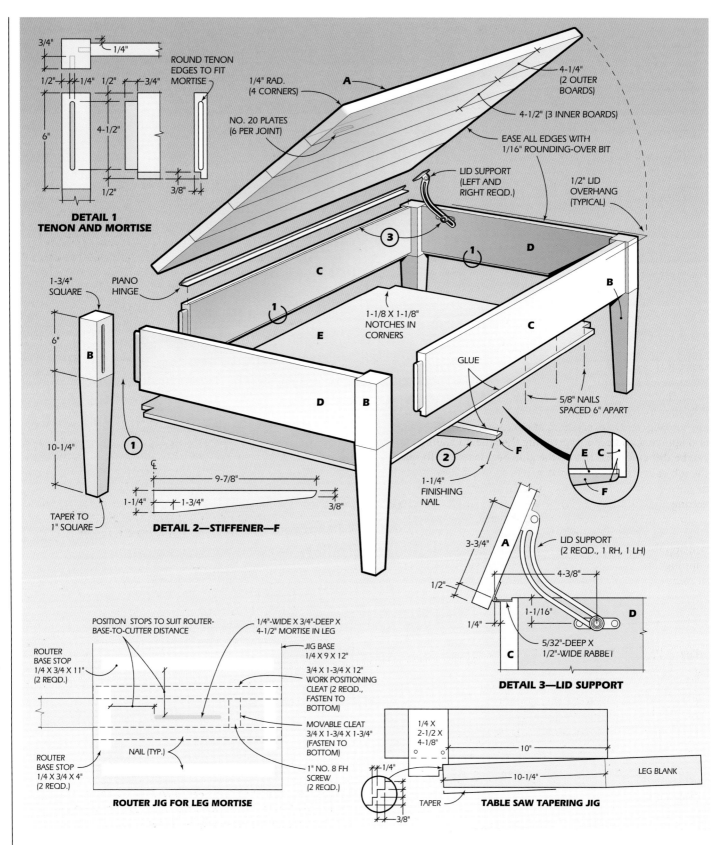

DETAIL 1
TENON AND MORTISE

3/4"
1/4"
ROUND TENON EDGES TO FIT MORTISE
1/2" 1/4" 1/2" 3/4"
6"
4-1/2"
1/2"
3/8"

1/4" RAD.
(4 CORNERS)

NO. 20 PLATES
(6 PER JOINT)

A

4-1/4"
(2 OUTER BOARDS)

4-1/2" (3 INNER BOARDS)

EASE ALL EDGES WITH
1/16" ROUNDING-OVER BIT

1/2" LID OVERHANG (TYPICAL)

LID SUPPORT
(LEFT AND RIGHT REQD.)

③

D

B

1

C

B

1-3/4" SQUARE

PIANO HINGE

6"

B

1-1/8 X 1-1/8"
NOTCHES IN CORNERS

E

1

C

10-1/4"

1

D

B

GLUE

F

②

5/8" NAILS
SPACED 6" APART

E   C

TAPER TO
1" SQUARE

9-7/8"

1-1/4"   1-3/4"

3/8"

DETAIL 2—STIFFENER—F

1-1/4"
FINISHING NAIL

F

ROUTER JIG FOR LEG MORTISE

POSITION STOPS TO SUIT ROUTER-BASE-TO-CUTTER DISTANCE

1/4"-WIDE X 3/4"-DEEP X 4-1/2" MORTISE IN LEG

ROUTER BASE STOP
1/4 X 3/4 X 11"
(2 REQD.)

JIG BASE
1/4 X 9 X 12"

3/4 X 1-3/4 X 12"
WORK POSITIONING CLEAT (2 REQD., FASTEN TO BOTTOM)

MOVABLE CLEAT
3/4 X 1-3/4 X 1-3/4"
(FASTEN TO BOTTOM)

ROUTER BASE STOP
1/4 X 3/4 X 4"
(2 REQD.)

NAIL (TYP.)

1" NO. 8 FH SCREW
(2 REQD.)

3-3/4"

A

LID SUPPORT
(2 REQD., 1 RH, 1 LH)

1/2"

4-3/8"

1/4"

1-1/16"

D

C

5/32"-DEEP X
1/2"-WIDE RABBET

DETAIL 3—LID SUPPORT

1/4 X
2-1/2 X
4-1/8"

10"

1/4"

10-1/4"

LEG BLANK

TAPER

3/8"

TABLE SAW TAPERING JIG

This simple table project is straightforward and requires little more than a few power tools and a table saw—equipment most small home workshops would have. This is a good project to tackle for the beginner or intermediate craftsman with a long weekend of free time. We built our table out of maple, but you can use any other commonly available furniture-grade wood and get great results.

The Top and Legs

The panel for the tabletop is assembled by edge-gluing five boards together. Begin construction of the tabletop by ripping and crosscutting the stock slightly oversize, 4½ in. wide x 35 in. long.

If you have a plate joiner, use it to cut the slots for six joining plates for each edge joint. Carefully arrange the boards to produce the most attractive grain pattern. And make sure the endgrain growth ring directions alternate between the boards.

Mark centerlines for the slot positions along each joint line, then clamp each board to a flat benchtop while the slots are cut (**Fig. 1**). Do everything at once—inserting the plates and applying and evenly spreading the glue on eight edges can be difficult to do before the glue begins to set. To make the job easier, preglue the plates in each board. Use a small-nozzle squeeze bottle to apply glue in the slots without getting any on the edges (**Fig. 2**).

To assemble the panel, you'll need four or five long clamps, six smaller clamps, and six cauls. This arrangement will apply even pressure across the panel to prevent it from cupping. Rub paste wax on each caul's contact surface to prevent it from sticking to the boards.

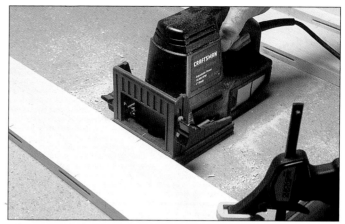

Fig. 1 *Begin by ripping and jointing the edges of the boards for the tabletop, and cut the slots in them to receive the joining plates.*

Fig. 2 *Save glue application time by pregluing the joining plates in their slots. A small-nozzle bottle is handy here.*

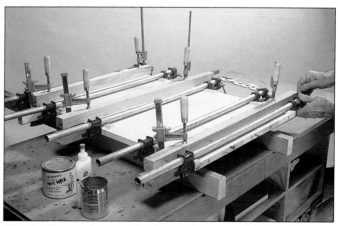

Fig. 3 *Glue and securely clamp the top using cauls above and below the tabletop. Wax the cauls to prevent glue from sticking to them.*

Materials List

Key	No.	Size and description (use)
A	1	³/₄ x 22 x 34" maple (lid)
B	4	1³/₄ x 1³/₄ x 16¹/₈" maple (leg)
C	2	³/₄ x 5¹/₂ x 31" maple (apron)
D	2	³/₄ x 5¹/₂ x 19" maple (apron)
E	1	¹/₄ x 19³/₄ x 31³/₄" lauan plywood (bottom)
F	1	³/₄ x 1¹/₄ x 19³/₄" maple (stiffener)

Misc.: Curved friction lid supports; brass 1¹/₂-in.-wide x 48-in.-long piano hinge.

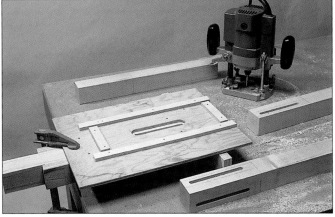

Fig. 4 *Use a jig as shown with your plunge router to cut the leg mortises. The stops are positioned to suit the router's base.*

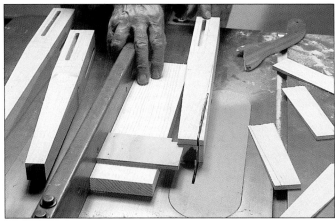

Fig. 5 *Use a stepped jig on the table saw to precisely cut the leg tapers. Each step positions the leg to cut two tapers.*

Fig. 6 *Round the bottom of the leg corners on the router table. Don't round the top of the leg where it abuts the apron.*

Apply glue to edges and plates, slide the boards together, then apply pressure to the cauls and the long clamps (**Fig. 3**).

Remove the hardened glue that has squeezed out from the joint using a scraper, belt sander, and finishing sander, in that order. Next, crosscut the panel to finished size.

Rip and crosscut the legs to size and joint their four faces so that they are square to one another and smooth. Lay out the mortise positions on adjacent faces and install a ¼-in.-dia. straight bit in your plunge router for cutting the mortises. You can use a router edge guide to make the cuts, but the simple jig shown in the photos here enables you to do the job much more quickly and easily. The jig is made of ¼-in. plywood with cleats attached to the bottom to secure the leg. A removable end cleat allows the leg to be repositioned so that one jig can be used to cut the mortises on both leg faces. Placed on top of the jig, four strips guide the router and stop its travel. Make mortise cuts in several passes (**Fig. 4**). When the first mortise has been cut on each leg, reposition the jig's end cleat, insert the blank from the other end, and proceed to cut the mortise on the adjacent face.

The tapers are cut on the table saw with the aid of a simple step jig. The taper is cut on two adjacent faces with the leg positioned in the first step of the jig. The end of the leg is placed in the second step to cut the two remaining tapers (**Fig. 5**).

Smooth the inner leg surfaces using a sander, but sand the mortised faces gently by hand to avoid distorting the surface surrounding the mortise. The mortise surface has to remain flat and square.

To complete the legs, set up a ¹⁄₁₆-in.-rad. rounding-over bit in a router table and round the corners (**Fig. 6**).

Aprons and Assembly

Rip and crosscut the aprons, then set up a dado blade on the table saw to cut the apron tenons. Clamp a stop block to the

Fig. 7 *Use a stop block clamped to the table saw's miter gauge and a dado blade in the table saw to cut the apron tenons.*

miter gauge fence, elevate the blade for a ½-in.-deep cut, and cut the tenon in four passes (**Fig. 7**). Next, cut the rabbets for the bottom panel on the inside edges of the four aprons.

After you use a sharp chisel to round the ends of the tenons to match the mortises, the table is ready for assembly.

Use four clamps and four cauls to assemble the legs and aprons (**Fig. 8**). Apply glue sparingly to the tenons, and draw the assembly together. Check the assembly for square by measuring the diagonals. If necessary, adjust the clamps to make the assembly square.

After the glue has set, use the router with a straight bit to cut the hinge rabbet. To do this, clamp two pieces of scrap flush with the apron's top edge to provide a stable surface for the router. Set the router to make a ⁵⁄₃₂-in.-deep cut (**Fig. 9**). You need to note that the rabbet's ½-in. width is critical. It positions the hinge so that the top can tilt without striking the leg's corner.

Next, crosscut the piano hinge to fit the rabbet and install it temporarily. Do this by placing the lid on the workbench with the bottom facing up. Then place the table, bottom up, onto the lid and mark the position of the hinge on the lid. Remove the hinge, mark the screw centers, and bore the screw pilot holes. Attach the hinge to the table first, then to the lid.

Once the hinge is installed, mark and bore the screw pilot holes for lid supports. Attach the supports to the aprons first, then the lid (**Fig. 10**).

Cut the plywood bottom to size and install it with glue and nails. Also, glue the stiffener strip to the bottom. Remove the lid to allow finishing.

We finished the table with three coats of polyurethane lightly tinted with a few drops of yellow ochre to give it a warm honey color.

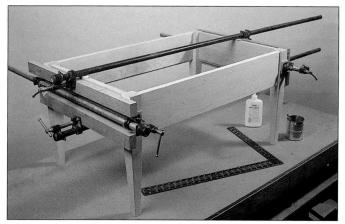

Fig. 8 *Glue and securely clamp the aprons and legs. The heavy cauls distribute clamping pressure equally across each apron.*

Fig. 9 *Clamp a scrap piece to the rear apron to provide a base for the router, then cut the hinge rabbet using a straight bit.*

Fig. 10 *The assembly sequence is important when attaching the top's support hardware. Attach it to the apron first, then the top.*

TECH *Tips*

Cutting Wide Panels

When straight or angle sawing of oversize plywood panels prevents you from using a miter gauge or rip fence, you can still handle the panels easily and safely. Cut a strip of wood to suit the miter-gauge groove in the saw table and about 2 ft. longer than the panel. Secure the strip to the underside of the work with brads, letting it project beyond the panel by 1 ft. at both ends. Fasten the strip so that it runs in the table's groove as you feed the work. Wax the strip if needed.

Perfect Pair

Two graceful and unique tables make for a dynamic duo in just about any room of the house.

If you're having trouble getting a weekend alone in your shop, then we've got the solution. Just leave the book open to this page on the kitchen table. Once the rest of the family gets an eyeful of our two solid cherry tables, they're liable to lock you in the shop until the tables are done. Both are interesting departures from the norm. The 3-legged table is ideal for the hall, foyer, or against a living room wall. If you're looking for more surface area, the unique 5-legged table will provide an exciting accent to any room. Both feature similar construction techniques and joinery. So, once you've built one, the second will go that much easier. The question is whether your family will let you stop at just two.

*Key*POINTS

TIME

Prep Time	10 hours
Shop Time	12 hours
Assembly Time	12 hours

EFFORT

Skill Level	intermediate

COST / BENEFITS

Expense: **expensive**

- **Fabulous matched set** provides a wonderful combination of accent tables that can create a design theme in the house.

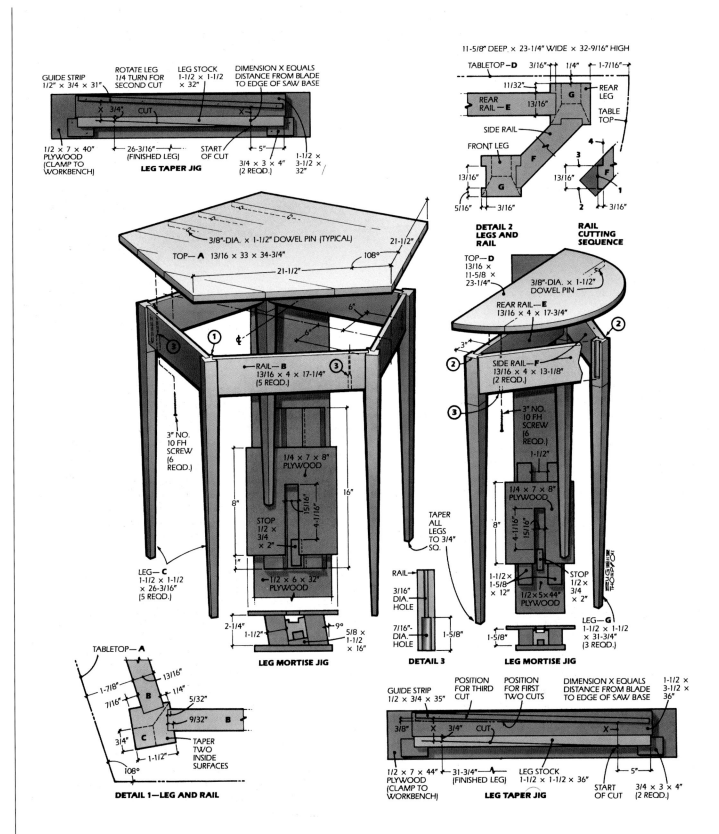

The tabletops and rails of these two tables are all made from nominal 1-in. stock. This type of stock typically measures ¹³⁄₁₆ in. thick. However, be sure to check the actual thickness of your material and adjust our specifications if necessary. The legs are shaped from 1½-in.-sq. cherry. Buy 2-in. lumber for these and, if possible, have your dealer plane the stock to 1½ in. thick. If this isn't possible through your local lumberyard or dealer, then square the stock to size with your circular saw.

Fig. 1 *Plane one edge of each tabletop board straight and square before ripping. Use the longest plane you have for the best results.*

The 5-Legged Table

Prepare the 1-in. stock for the tabletop and rails by using a hand plane to trim one edge of each board straight and true (**Fig. 1**). Clamp a straightedge guide parallel to the trued edge of each workpiece to serve as a guide for your circular saw. Rip the tabletop stock to roughly 5 in. wide and rip the rails exactly to width (**Fig. 2**). Smooth all edges.

The top is made by edge-gluing seven boards. Draw a full-size outline of the top on paper and lay out the positions of the boards to determine their lengths. Crosscut each board slightly longer than necessary.

Next, position the pieces edge-to-edge on your worktable. Because this top is large and you can expect wood to shrink slightly after it adjusts to the dry air in your home, the top is held to the rails by only six screws near the central glue joint (**see drawing**).

This allows the remaining surface area to move freely. Place the boards so that the wood's annual rings—seen on the board

Fig. 2 *Use a straightedge tacked in the board's waste area—parallel to the finished edge—to guide the circular saw when ripping to width.*

Materials List

Key	No.	Size and description (use)
A	1	¹³⁄₁₆ x 33 x 34¾" cherry (5-leg top)
B	5	¹³⁄₁₆ x 4 x 17¼" cherry (5-leg rail)
C	5	1½ x 1½ x 26³⁄₁₆" cherry (5-leg leg)
D	1	¹³⁄₁₆ x 11⅝ x 23¼" cherry (3-leg top)
E	1	¹³⁄₁₆ x 4 x 17¾" cherry (3-leg rear rail)
F	2	¹³⁄₁₆ x 4 x 13⅛" cherry (3-leg side rail)
G	3	1½ x 1½ x 31¾" cherry (3-leg leg)

Misc.: 12 3" No. 10 fh wood screws; ³⁄₈"-dia. x 1½" dowel pins; glue; wax paper; cherry penetrating stain; satin finish polyurethane.

Fig. 3 *After crosscutting the boards oversize, lay them edge-to-edge, and mark for identification. Chalk marks are easy to remove.*

Fig. 4 *Keep the same side of the doweling jig on the working face of each board to ensure good alignment. The tape on the bit acts as a depth gauge.*

Fig. 5 *Assemble the top in two stages. Lightly clamp flat, sturdy cauls across the joints with wax paper placed between the cauls and the tabletop.*

Fig. 7 *Tack a straight cutting guide to the top so that it is parallel to—and correctly spaced from—the outline. Use a sharp blade.*

ends—point upward. In this way, any drying out will cause the boards to press tightly against the rails.

Lay out the outline with chalk and letter the boards for identification when assembling (**Fig. 3**). Mark the dowel positions on each joint and use a doweling jig to bore the holes (**Fig. 4**). Glue the top together in two stages (**Fig. 5**).

After the glue has dried, place the top good side down on your worktable and mark the cutting outline. Use your circular saw guided by a straightedge to cut to the outline (**Fig. 7**). Then, smooth both top surfaces with a hand plane or belt sander and clean up the saw marks (**Fig. 8**).

Making the Legs

Construct the leg-tapering jig as shown in the drawing. Crosscut the 1½-in.-sq. leg blanks 6 in. longer than their finished dimension (**Fig. 9**).

Place a leg blank in the jig, tape back the blade guard on

Fig. 6 *Make a cardboard template of the 108° corner angle to aid in laying out the table outline on the underside of the tabletop.*

Fig. 8 *Smooth the tabletop surfaces with a belt sander or hand plane for a good connection to rails, and a smooth, flat top surface.*

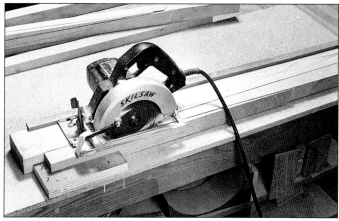

Fig. 9 *Cut the leg tapers with a circular saw. The stock is held in the jig and the saw is guided by a straight strip. Stop cutting about 6 in. from the end.*

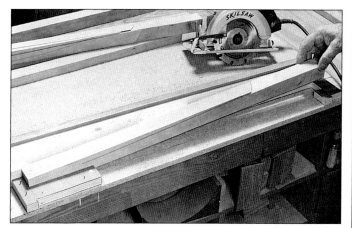

Fig. 10 *Rotate the leg blank to cut the second taper. Note that the blade guide is taped in a retracted position. Work with extra care.*

Fig. 11 *A T-shaped right-angle guide aids in cutting the legs squarely to length. Clamp two legs together and cut them in one pass.*

Fig. 12 *The angled mortise is cut on this jig. A plywood template guides width and length of cut. Use a ½-in. bit and template guide.*

your circular saw so that it won't interfere with the cut, and adjust the blade depth. Don't forget that the guard has been fixed in this position when you finish each cut, and exercise a great deal of caution when working like this. Do not move the saw until the blade completely stops rotating.

Make the first taper cut, stopping short of the leg end as shown in the drawing. This leaves the waste in place for support when the next cut is made. Then rotate the blank and repeat the cut (**Fig. 10**). After cutting two tapers on each leg, use a right-angle guide to cut the legs to length (**Fig. 11**). Smooth the sawn surfaces.

Construct the jig for routing the angled mortises in the legs from 2x4 stock (**Fig. 12**). Keep the beveled cutoffs to use later as clamping cauls and for a support shim for this jig. The jig shown is dimensioned for use with a ¹⁄₁₆-in. offset template guide and a ½-in.-dia. straight bit. Rout angled mortises on one face of each leg.

Fig. 13 *The corner template helps position the legs. Draw an outline of each leg end and measure the correct rail lengths between legs.*

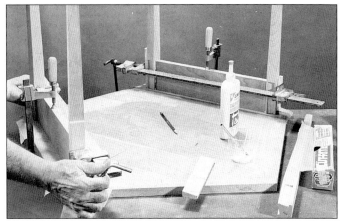

Fig. 14 *Glue two opposing leg assemblies first, using the marked side of the top as a guide. Use wax paper to keep excess glue off the top.*

Fig. 15 *After adding the connecting rail, glue and clamp the fourth rail and last leg to the assembly. Finally, add the remaining rail.*

Fig. 3b *The top is prepared by gluing two boards edge-to-edge. Use a sabre saw with a circle-cutting guide to cut the tabletop shape.*

Fig. 4b *Clean up the rough-sawn edge with a cabinet scraper. Finish by sanding with a palm sander or with sandpaper and block.*

Then remove the plywood template and stop and secure them at the other end of the jig for routing the remaining mortises.

Table Assembly

First, cut a template to hold each leg in position at the corners (**Fig. 13**). Tack the template at one corner, hold a leg in place, and trace the outline of the leg end on the underside of the top.

After marking each leg position in this manner, measure the exact rail lengths and cut each rail to size. Then bore and counterbore the screw holds for fastening the top.

Next, glue two legs to one rail. Use the cutoffs from the mortising jig as clamping pads and place wax paper under the assembly to prevent excess glue from securing the legs and rail to the top. Then glue up a leg assembly for an opposing side (**Fig. 14**).

After the glue has set on the first two units, glue the third connecting rail in place and clamp. Let the glue set and then glue and clamp the fifth leg and fourth rail in position (**Fig. 15**). Finally, add the last rail in the same manner. Mark the centers for the screw pilot holes in the top and bore. Then screw the top in place.

We finished the table with a coat of cherry penetrating stain followed by two coats of satin finish varnish. The underside of the top was given a coat of sanding sealer.

The 3-Legged Table

This piece bears a resemblance to the first table in leg detailing and construction. It differs, however, in the leg-to-rail joint and the fact that the legs are tapered on three sides.

Begin by gluing up the top as shown in the drawing. After the glue is dry, belt sand or plane the top smooth and flat and use a sabre saw to cut the arc. Most ordinary circle cutting

Fig. 1b *The mortising jig for the 3-legged table produces square cuts. Use a ¹⁄₁₆-in. offset template guide and ½-in.-dia. bit.*

Fig. 2b *After cutting the bevel and slot, set the blade depth for cutting the notch, and guide the saw with a strip tacked squarely to the rail.*

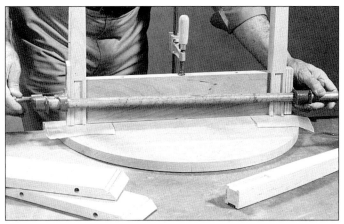

Fig. 5b *Assemble the rear rail and two legs with glue, and clamp until dry. Use a layout drawn on the underside of the top as a guide.*

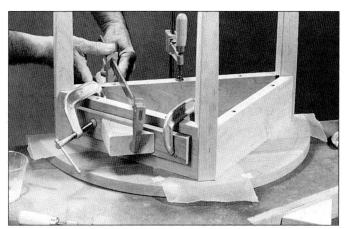

Fig. 6b *Angled clamping jigs secured to the front rails with small clamps aid when drawing the rail and the leg joints together.*

guides are not large enough to handle this radius. You can make your own guide from a length of mild steel. Hammer the strip of steel over at one end to produce an L-shape and bore a pivot hole in the folded end in line with the cutting edge of the blade (**Fig. 3b**).

Use a sharp blade with adequate set for this cut. You can also cut the arc by following a line scribed with trammel points or a large compass. Smooth the curved edge with a cabinet scraper and sandpaper (**Fig. 4b**).

Construct the leg tapering jig for the 3-legged table as shown in the drawing. First, cut one side taper, then rotate the blank 180° and cut the second taper on each leg.

Next, readjust the guide strip for the outward facing taper and cut each leg. Crosscut the legs to length with a circular saw and right-angle cutting guide.

Set up the leg mortising jig and equip your router with a ½-in.-dia. straight bit and ¹⁄₁₆-in. offset template guide. Then

cut the ³⁄₁₆ x ¹³⁄₁₆-in. mortises in the legs (**Fig. 1b**).

Set your circular saw to 45° and adjust the depth for crosscutting both ends of the two angled rails. Make a T-square guide and clamp or nail it to the rails to ensure square cuts. After the first cut, readjust the T-square guide and make the second cut as shown in the drawing. The third and fourth cuts are slots that combine to form the notch in the rail end. Make sure the blade depth is set appropriately for these cuts.

Bore the screw holes in the rails for attaching the top. Glue the rear rail to two legs and temporarily clamp the assembly in position on the tabletop with wax paper in between (**Fig. 5b**). After the glue has set, join the two front rails to the rear legs and remaining front leg using angle cauls to provide uniform clamping pressure (**Fig. 6b**).

Finally, mark and bore the screw pilot holes in the top and secure it to the leg assembly. Install with 3-in. No. 10 fh screws. Apply the same finish as on the 5-leg table.

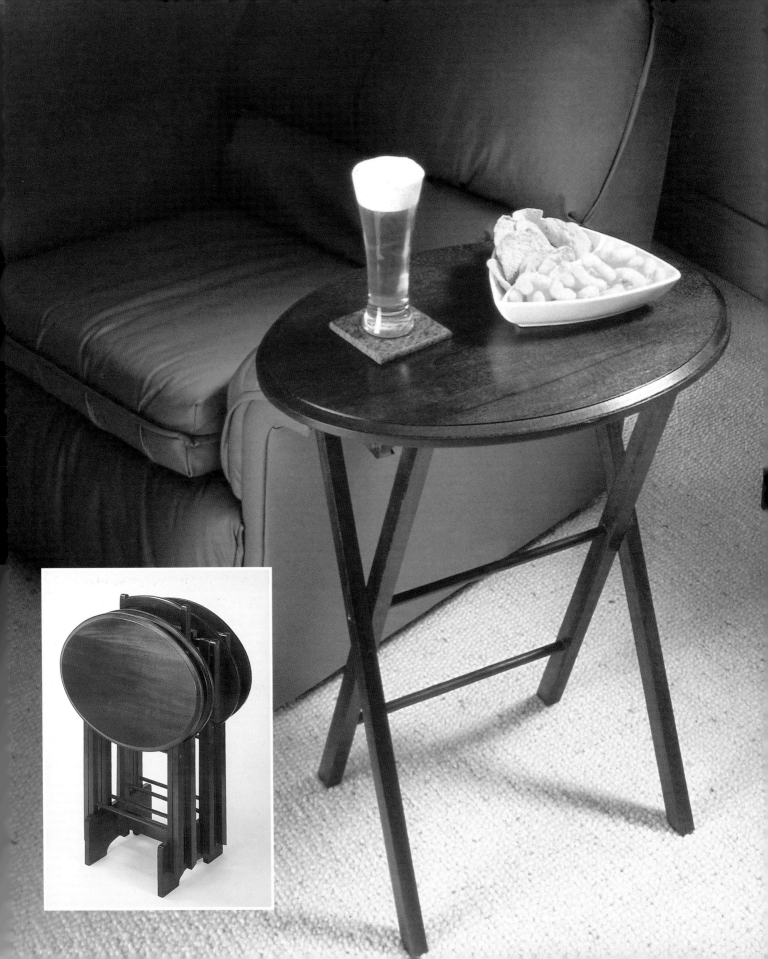

Spare Elegance

These low-space tables are durable mahogany to stand up to any use, in any room, at any time.

Most households need extra table space when company comes. Typically, folding card or tray tables are pressed into service and are later put away in the closet. Our folding tables, however, are attractive enough to be stored out in the open and can be used for company or TV watching. Considerably more elegant than a card table or sheet metal tray tables, these are made from mahogany, although other hardwoods, such as cherry, walnut, or oak will also look attractive. Being able to store these in the open not only frees up closet space, but makes them more convenient. You'll never have to dig in a closet again to get at a folding table. In fact, you just may opt to eat in front of the TV more often.

*Key*POINTS

TIME

Prep Time	3 hours
Shop Time	15 hours
Assembly Time	12 hours

EFFORT

Skill Level	intermediate

COST / BENEFITS

Expense: **moderate**

- **Durable and handy** surfaces for everything from homework to TV dinners.
- Attractive wood and finish makes for **simple and easy storage**.

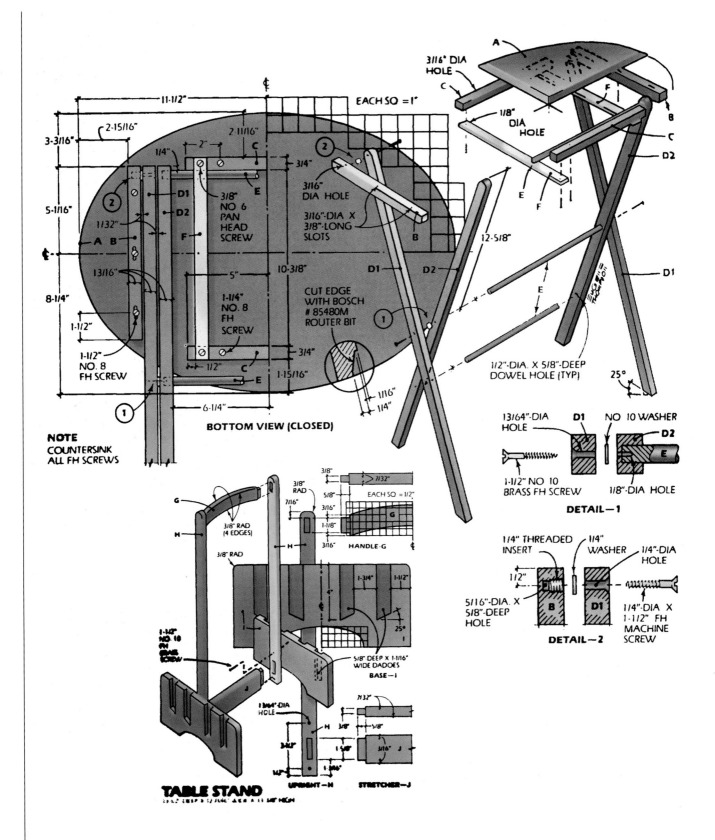

EACH SQ = 1"

3-3/16"
11-1/2"
2-15/16"
2-11/16"
1/4"
2"
3/4"
5-1/16"
1/32"
8-1/4"
13/16"
1-1/2"
1-1/2"
NO. 8
FH SCREW
6-1/4"
5"
10-3/8"
1/2"

A B
D1
D2
F
E
C

3/8"
NO 6
PAN
HEAD
SCREW

3/16"
DIA HOLE

3/16"-DIA. X
3/8"-LONG
SLOTS

B

1-1/4"
NO. 8
FH
SCREW

CUT EDGE
WITH BOSCH
85480M
ROUTER BIT

3/4"
1-15/16"
1/16"
1/4"

BOTTOM VIEW (CLOSED)

NOTE
COUNTERSINK
ALL FH SCREWS

A
3/16" DIA
HOLE
C
1/8"
DIA
HOLE
F
B
C
D2
E
F

12-5/8"
D1
D2
E

1/2"-DIA. X 5/8"-DEEP
DOWEL HOLE (TYP)

25°

13/64"-DIA
HOLE
D1
NO 10 WASHER
D2
E
1-1/2" NO 10
BRASS FH SCREW
1/8"-DIA HOLE

DETAIL—1

1/4" THREADED
INSERT
1/4"
WASHER
1/4"-DIA
HOLE
1/2"
B
D1
5/16"-DIA. X
5/8"-DEEP
HOLE
1/4"-DIA X
1-1/2" FH
MACHINE
SCREW

DETAIL—2

3/8"
3/8"
RAD
7/32"
7/16"
5/8"
3/16"
1-1/8"
3/16"
G
EACH SQ = 1/2"
HANDLE·G

3/8" RAD
(4 EDGES)
G
H
3/8" RAD
1-3/4"
1-1/2"
25°
1-1/2"
NO. 10
FH
BRASS
SCREW
5/8"-DEEP X 1-1/16"
WIDE DADOES
BASE—1

13/64"-DIA
HOLE
7/32"
H
3/8"
5/8"
1/16" **J**

TABLE STAND

UPRIGHT—H
STRETCHER—J

These tables are fairly simple in construction, but to work properly, they must be constructed precisely. When put together well, the method of construction along with the choice of mahogany as the material for the tables ensures their longevity, even given many years of hard use.

The Top

Begin by making a template of the top from ¼-in.-thick plywood. Saw out the template, then smooth it to final shape by filing, sanding, or using a block plane. Then rip and crosscut four pieces of plywood, one for each tabletop, measuring 4¼ in. wide x 24¹³⁄₁₆ in. long. Joint their edges to form a good glue joint.

Lay out the pieces for each top and trace the oval shape from the template on them. We used jointing plates (also called biscuits) to align the pieces during glueup, but dowels serve just as well.

Lay out the location of the plates, keeping them at least 3 in. from the top's edge (**Fig. 1**) and about 6 to 8 in. on center. Cut the slots with a plate joiner, making sure that joiner and workpiece are held firmly to the bench (**Fig. 2**). The bench should be free of debris to ensure the joiner and workpiece are on the same plane.

Fig. 1 *Lay out the joining plate positions on the top. Keep the plates 3 in. back from the top's edge and space the plates 6 to 8 in. on center.*

Fig. 2 *Cut the plate slots in the boards. To ensure that the joiner and boards are on the same plane, the work surface should be free of debris.*

Fig. 3 *Apply glue sparingly to the plates and plate slots. Insert the plates in the slots and bring the pieces together with hand pressure.*

Materials List

Key	No.	Size and description (use)
A	1	¹³⁄₁₆ x 16½ x 23" mahogany (top)
B	2	¹³⁄₁₆ x 1 x 10⅛" mahogany (leg cleat)
C	2	¾ x ¹³⁄₁₆ x 10" mahogany (stop cleat)
D1	2	¹³⁄₁₆ x 1 x 27" mahogany (outside leg)
D2	2	¹³⁄₁₆ x 1 x 27" mahogany (inside leg)
E	3	½"-dia. x 13⅜" mahogany dowel (stretcher)
F	2	.028-gal. x ¾ x 11⅞" steel (restraint)
G	1	¹³⁄₁₆ x 2¼ x 10¹¹⁄₁₆" mahogany (handle)
H	2	¹³⁄₁₆ x 1⅛ x 31½" mahogany (upright)
I	2	¹³⁄₁₆ x 6 x 13½" mahogany (base, stand)
J	1	¹³⁄₁₆ x 2 x 10¹¹⁄₁₆" mahogany (stretcher)

Misc.: 2¼"-dia. threaded inserts; 2 ¼"-dia. x 1½" fh machine screws; 2 ¼" washers; 6 1½" No. 10 fh brass screws; 2 No. 10 washers; 6 1¼" No. 8 fh screws; 4 1¼" No. 8 fh screws; 4 ⅜" No. 6 panhead screws; 120- and 220-grit sandpaper; glue; tack cloth; medium-brown mahogany stain; retarder; varnish.

Fig. 4 *Bring the edge joints tight with bar or pipe clamps. Scrape off the excess glue after 20 to 30 minutes, before it dries and hardens.*

Fig. 5 *Tap the threaded inserts into the ⁵⁄₁₆-in.-dia. holes in the top cleats. These inserts allow for the folding leg assembly to screw to the top.*

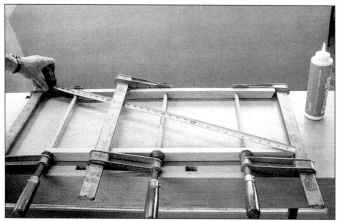

Fig. 7 *Glue and clamp together the legs and dowels. Measure the diagonals to ensure that the leg assembly is square, and let the glue dry.*

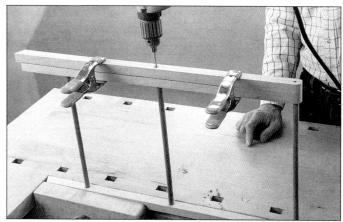

Fig. 8 *Use spring or C-clamps to hold the outside legs to the leg assembly. Bore the pilot hole for the screw at the pivot point.*

Apply glue to the edges of each piece, to the plates themselves, and to the plate slots (**Fig. 3**). Pull the pieces together with pipe clamps (**Fig. 4**), and scrape off glue squeeze out after 20 to 30 minutes, while the glue is firm but still soft enough to remove easily.

When the glue is completely dry, smooth the surface of the boards with a cabinet scraper. Retrace the top outline on the blank and cut out the top with a band saw or jigsaw. Cut on the waste side of the guideline and remove saw marks and refine the outline with a sharp block plane. Sand the edges smooth using 120- and 220-grit sandpaper.

We cut the top's decorative edge with a panel-raising router bit and an edge guide in our router. Clamp the top so half of its edge overhangs the bench. Cut the molding on half the top, then reclamp as before and finish routing the edge. Be sure the bit is razor sharp and advance the router slowly to avoid tearout.

Rip and crosscut the legs and cleats. Plane or sand away any saw marks, then cut the radiused ends on them and rasp each piece to shape. Sand them smooth using first 120-grit and then 220-grit sandpaper.

The two cleats that run crossgrain under the top are attached with three screws each. One screw fits in a round hole, while the other two fit into elongated holes to allow for expansion and contraction of the top with changes in humidity. Without the slotted holes, the cleats would restrict the top's movement and over time, it would split.

You will form the elongated holes by boring two holes side by side and completely chiseling out the waste using a sharp chisel. Then counterbore each hole for the screwhead. You should bore a ⁵⁄₁₆-in.-dia. hole in the side of each cleat as shown, and tap in a ¼-in. threaded insert (**Fig. 5**).

Place one of the tabletops upside down on your workbench, bore the pilot holes (**Fig. 6**), and attach the cleats.

Fig. 6 *Bore pilot holes into the top. The elongated screw holes in the cleats allow the top to expand and contract without cracking.*

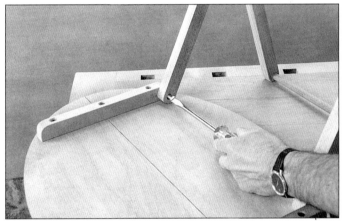

Fig. 9 *Attach the legs to the top with a machine screw. Place a washer between the leg and the cleat to reduce friction.*

Leg Assembly

The inside pairs of legs are securely joined together with ½-in.-dia. mahogany dowels (see the "Misc." section of the Materials List).

To seat the dowels properly, bore ½-in.-dia. holes, ⅝ in. deep in each leg at the locations shown in the plan. Crosscut the dowels to length, and pre-sand them with 120- and 220-grit sandpaper.

Cut a 25° angle at each leg bottom, arranging the legs in pairs so that the angles match properly.

Spread the glue in the dowel holes and on the dowel ends, and join them to the inner legs. Pull the assembly tight with clamps, and cross measure it to check it for square (**Fig. 7**).

Clamp the outside legs to the inside legs (**Fig. 8**) and bore a ⅛-in.-dia. pilot hole into the inner leg. Attach the legs with a washer between them.

With the tabletop upside down, screw the leg assembly to

the top, driving the machine screw into the cleat's threaded insert (**Fig. 9**). Separate the leg and cleat with a washer.

Bore and counterbore pilot holes in the cleats that run with the grain and attach them to the top. Cut strips of sheet steel to length using tin snips, debur them with a file, and bore a ⅛-in.-dia. pilot hole in the end of each strip. Attach strips to the cleats.

Open and close each table to check for smooth action and then sand the parts to eliminate any friction between them.

Table Stand

Rip and crosscut the pieces for the stand base, and lay out the dadoes and curved bottom edge. Cut the curved bottom edge with a jigsaw, and smooth the cut with a rasp (**Fig. 10**). Rout the dadoes in them using an edge guide and a ¾-in.-dia. straight bit (**Fig. 11**). Guide the cut with a straightedge clamped to the workpiece, and chisel the cut square.

SKILL*Builder*

GLUE CLEANUP
Because it's better to apply a little too much glue than not enough, some glue will always squeeze out around a joint and between pieces. Failure to clean this glue up can lead to a less-than-perfect finishing on your pieces.

Some glue manufacturers recommend removing the excess with a cloth and warm water. Unless the surface is to receive an opaque finish, such as paint or lacquer, this practice should be avoided. Even after you've wiped away the apparent glue, a diluted glue residue will remain on the wood and will fill the pores of coarse-grained woods such as oak. The residue will interfere with the absorption of stains and remain apparent under clear coatings.

The best way to remove glue is to first let it set until it begins to thicken (but not dry entirely). Then run a sharp chisel along the joint to neatly peel off the glue bead. Glue that has completely dried is also removed with a sharp chisel followed by sanding.

In some situations, however, such as a tight corner or confined space, a dampened cloth may be the best way to remove the excess glue. In these cases, carefully remove most of the excess with a small stick or other pointed tool to reduce the amount of glue to be wiped up. Follow with the cloth and warm water, and the let the surface dry. Then hand sand.

Fig. 10 *Lay out the dadoes and the curved cutout on the stand base. Make the curved cut with a jigsaw. Remove any saw marks with a rasp, then sand.*

Fig. 11 *Clamp base pieces to the bench and run your router against a fence clamped to the base. Finish the dadoes by chiseling them square.*

Rip and crosscut a block 6 in. wide x 10¹¹⁄₁₆ in. long. From this, cut the handle and bottom stretcher. Use the dado blade in the table saw to cut the tenons on this (**Fig. 12**).

Rip the stretcher off the block, then cut out the handle (**Fig. 13**). Smooth saw marks off the handle, and cut the shoulders at the top and bottom edge of each tenon with a backsaw. Round the handle's edges with a ⅜-rad. rounding-over bit in your router.

Rip and crosscut the uprights to size and cut their curved ends. Bore out the bulk of the stretcher mortises on the drill press. Then carefully chisel the mortise ends square and smooth their walls (**Figs. 14 and 15**). Bore and counterbore

TECH *Tips*

Grain Filling

All hardwoods have pores that result from cutting across the grain structure of the wood. Pores appear most dramatically on the ends of the stock, but are also apparent along the surface, due to the fact that the grain is never exactly parallel to the saw cut. In some woods, such as maple and birch, the pores are so small that they have little effect on finishing—a surface coating of varnish will lay flat and smooth. Other woods, such as oak, walnut, and mahogany, have large pores. When a surface coating is applied, it seeps into the pores instead of creating a flat surface. To create a smooth, glasslike finish on these woods, the pores are first filled with paste wood filler to level the surface. Grain filling is not necessary on softwoods, such as pine and fir.

Wood filler is available in a natural (buff) color that may be used as is or tinted to match a stain or wood color. It usually comes in a pastelike form with the consistency of peanut butter, and must be thinned with a solvent before use. Some brands come ready to use. Always follow the manufacturer's directions supplied with the product for best results.

Apply the filler with a stiff brush and work it well into the pores. First brush with the grain, and then across the grain. Work only a small area of the surface at one time to prevent the excess filler from drying to quickly and becoming difficult to remove.

Allow the filler to set for about 30 minutes, or until it dulls over. Then wipe across the grain with a coarse cloth to pack the filler into the pores while removing the excess filler. Follow by wiping gently with a soft cloth in the direction of the grain. Use a cloth over a pointed stick to remove excess filler from inside corners. Allow the filler to dry for at least 24 hours and then sand lightly to remove any residual filler from the surface.

Next, apply a coat of sealer, and follow with a light sanding. If the work is to be stained, apply the stain first, then seal, and follow with the filler. To match darker woods or stains, tint the paste wood filler with an appropriate Japan color. After grain filling, apply a compatible surface coating.

Fig. 12 *Rip a 6-in.-wide x 10¹¹/₁₆-in.-long piece and cut the tenons on both ends. From this, rip the stretcher and handle.*

Fig. 13 *Cut out the curved handle on a band saw or with a jigsaw. Smooth away saw marks with a rasp or spokeshave, then finish sand.*

Fig. 14 *With a ³/₈-in.-dia. bit in the drill press, bore overlapping holes to remove waste from the mortises in the stand uprights.*

Fig. 15 *Use a sharp chisel to square the mortise ends and smooth its walls. Test fit mortise-and-tenon joints for a snug fit.*

pilot holes in the uprights for attaching them securely to the base. Sand all the base parts with one sanding of 120-grit, followed by a sanding of 220-grit sandpaper, and then wipe the pieces clean with a tack cloth.

Glue and clamp together the uprights, stretcher and handle, and check for square. After the glue sets, screw the uprights to the base.

Finish the stand unassembled, and be sure to remove the leg assembly from the tops and separate the outer legs from the inner leg assembly. Finish sand the parts, wipe them with a tack cloth, and apply stain.

We used a medium-brown mahogany stain. If you apply this stain by brush or rag, use a high-quality retarder to prevent lap marks caused by rapid drying. When the stain has dried, wipe each part with a tack cloth and finish it with a good quality varnish. Reassemble the tables when finishing is completed.

Super Countersink

Common nails are a great choice to use in much of woodworking because they are superior to finishing nails in holding strength. Unfortunately, they are difficult to countersink without raising splinters on the work surface. But this isn't true if you use a hollow leather punch to mark the nail location.

Use a punch of a diameter that roughly matches the nail head size. You can then drive and set the nails as though they were the finishing type. You can buy a leather punch set at most large crafts supply stores.

Picture Credits

ROCK STAR (Pg. 10):
Lead Photo: John Griebsch;
Illustration: Eugene Thompson;
Step Photos: Neal Barrett.

HIGH CLASS (Pg. 20):
Lead Photo: Neal Barrett;
Illustration: Eugene Thompson;
Step Photos: Neal Barrett.

SITTING PRETTY (Pg. 28):
Lead Photo: J.R. Rost;
Illustration: Eugene Thompson;
Step Photos: Rosario Capotosto.

BENCH MARK (Pg. 36):
Lead Photo: Neal Barrett;
Illustration: Eugene Thompson;
Step Photos: Neal Barrett.

CHOICE SEATING (Pg. 44):
Lead Photo: J.R. Rost;
Illustration: Eugene Thompson;
Step Photos: Rosario Capotosto.

TWO GOOD (Pg. 54):
Lead Photo: J.R. Rost;
Illustration: Eugene Thompson;
Step Photos: Peggy Caswell.

PRETTY PERCH (Pg. 62):
Lead Photo: Neal Barrett;
Illustration: Eugene Thompson;
Step Photos: Neal Barrett.

OTTOMAN EMPIRE (Pg. 70):
Lead Photo: J.R. Rost;
Illustration: Eugene Thompson;
Step Photos: Neal Barrett.

RESERVED SEATING (Pg. 80):
Lead Photo: Neal Barrett;
Illustration: Eugene Thompson;
Step Photos: Neal Barrett.

EASY STREET (Pg. 88):
Lead Photo: J.R. Rost;
Illustration: Eugene Thompson;
Step Photos: Rosario Capotosto.

SUPER SOFA (Pg. 96):
Lead Photo: John Griebsch;
Illustration: Eugene Thompson;
Step Photos: Neal Barrett.

TABLE MANNERS (Pg. 108):
Lead Photo: Neal Barrett;
Illustration: Eugene Thompson;
Step Photos: Neal Barrett.

ELEGANT EATING (Pg. 118):
Lead Photo: Neal Barrett;
Illustration: Eugene Thompson;
Step Photos: Neal Barrett.

BEDSIDE MANNER (Pg. 126):
Lead Photo: Neal Barrett;
Illustration: Eugene Thompson;
Step Photos: Neal Barrett.

CHINA BOUND (Pg. 136):
Lead Photo: J.R. Rost;
Illustration: Eugene Thompson;
Step Photos: Neal Barrett.

WRITE ON (Pg. 144):
Lead Photo: J.R. Rost;
Illustration: Eugene Thompson;
Step Photos: Neal Barrett.

SIDE ORDER (Pg. 152):
Lead Photo: Neal Barrett;
Illustration: Eugene Thompson;
Step Photos: Neal Barrett.

SHAKER STYLE (Pg. 158):
Lead Photo: J.R. Rost;
Illustration: Eugene Thompson;
Step Photos: Neal Barrett.

ROOM & BOARD (Pg. 164):
Lead Photo: Neal Barrett;
Illustration: Eugene Thompson;
Step Photos: Neal Barrett.

COOL CONSOLE (Pg. 172):
Lead Photo: Neal Barrett;
Illustration: Eugene Thompson;
Step Photos: Neal Barrett.

FAIR GAME (Pg. 180):
Lead Photo: J.R. Rost;
Illustration: Eugene Thompson;
Step Photos: Rosario Capotosto.

FINE DINING (Pg. 188):
Lead Photo: J.R. Rost;
Illustration: Eugene Thompson;
Step Photos: Rosario Capotosto.

STRONG COFFEE (Pg. 194):
Lead Photo: John Griebsch;
Illustration: Eugene Thompson;
Step Photos: Neal Barrett.

CHOPPING BLOCK (Pg. 202):
Lead Photo: J.R. Rost;
Illustration: Eugene Thompson;
Step Photos: Rosario Capotosto.

DOUBLE DUTY (Pg. 210):
Lead Photo: Rosario Capotosto;
Illustration: Eugene Thompson;
Step Photos: Rosario Capotosto.

BEAUTIFUL LEGS (Pg. 216):
Lead Photo: J.R. Rost;
Illustration: Eugene Thompson;
Step Photos: Rosario Capotosto.

PLAY TIME (Pg. 224):
Lead Photo: J.R. Rost;
Illustration: Eugene Thompson;
Step Photos: Rosario Capotosto.

BIG TOP (Pg. 230):
Lead Photo: Spencer Jones;
Illustration: Eugene Thompson;
Step Photos: Rosario Capotosto.

PERFECT PAIR (Pg. 236):
Lead Photo: J.R. Rost;
Illustration: Eugene Thompson;
Step Photos: Rosario Capotosto.

SPARE ELEGANCE (Pg. 244):
Lead Photo: J.R. Rost;
Illustration: Eugene Thompson;
Step Photos: Neal Barrett.

Conversion Chart

U.S. STANDARD TO METRIC

U.S. Standard=Metric

Inches x 2.54 = centimeters

Feet x 30.48 = centimeters

Yards x .9144 = meters

Sq. in x 6.452 = square cm

Sq. ft. x 929 = square cm

Sq. yd x 8361 = square cm

Ounce x 28.85 = gram

Pound x .45 = kilogram

Common Approx. Conversions

$3/8$ in. = 1 cm

1 in. = 2.5 cm

2 in. = 5 cm

$2 1/2$ in. = 6.5 cm

1 ft. = 30 cm

Metric Conversion Tables

Metric Measurement	Imperial Equivalent	Imperial Measurement	Metric Equivalent
1mm	$1/32$ in.	$1/8$ in.	3.2mm
2mm	$1/16$ in.	$1/4$ in.	6.4mm
3mm	$1/8$ in.	$3/8$ in.	9.5mm
6mm	$1/4$ in.	$1/2$ in.	13mm
7mm	$9/32$ in. ($1/4$")	$5/8$ in.	16mm
10mm	$13/32$ in. ($3/8$")	$3/4$ in.	19cm
2cm (20mm)	$3/4$ in.	$7/8$ in.	2.2cm
3cm	$1^3/16$ in.	1 in.	2.5cm
4cm	$1^9/16$ in.	$1 1/4$ in.	3.2cm
5cm	2 in.	$1 1/2$ in.	3.8cm
6cm	$2^3/8$ in	$1 3/4$ in.	4.4cm
7cm	$2^3/4$ in.	2 in.	5.1cm
8cm	$3^1/8$ in.	$1 1/4$ in.	5.7cm
9cm	$3^1/2$ in.	$2 1/2$ in.	6.4cm
10cm	$3^{15}/16$ in. (4")	$2 3/4$ in.	7.0cm
15cm	$5^7/8$ in.	3 in.	7.6cm
20cm	$7^7/8$ in.	$3 1/4$ in.	8.3cm
25cm	$9^{13}/16$ in.	$3 1/2$ in.	8.9cm
30cm	$11^{13}/16$ in.	$3 3/4$ in.	9.5cm
35cm	$13^3/4$ in.	4 in.	10.2cm
40cm	$15^5/8$ in.	$4 1/2$ in.	11.4cm
42cm	$16^1/2$ in.	5 in.	14.0cm

Index

installing, 123, 161
tapers:
    cutting, 76, 146, 147, 153, 176–177, 239;
    jig, 31, 189, 190, 232, 239, 240, 241;
    lathe-turned, 205–206
tearout, preventing, 159–161, 160
templates:
    making, 13, 57, 102, 245;
    using, 32, 47, 57
            See also curves, compound
tenons:
    angled, cutting, 24–25, 74–75, 84, 85;
    fitting, 74, 75, 101, 111, 130;
    haunched, 167;
    jig, 75;
    laying out, 175;
    loose, 14, 15;
    rounding ends, 220;
    sawing technique, 66, 68, 75, 122, 166–167;
    shoulders, cutting, 85, 86;
    through, 74, 112;
    through, gluing, 78.
            See also mortise-and-tenon joints
thin strips, cutting, 16
threaded inserts, installing, 78, 246
tightening joints.
            See joints, closing
tongue-and-groove joints, 95
tool marks, removing
            See dressing rough surfaces
transferring shapes
            See templates
trimming to finished dimension, 83, 195
true, retaining while gluing joints
            See angles, truing
truing edges
            See edges, truing
tung oil varnish, applying, 19
turning, wood
            See lathe turning
twist, preventing
            See angles, truing
twisting of panels, preventing, 40

U

uniform lengths, cutting, 145, 147

V

varnish:
    applying, 141, 149;
    properties, 145
veneers:
    clamping, 68;
    cutting, 25, 68, 69, 119, 120, 128, 139;
    description, 138–139;
    fabrication, 139–140;
    gluing, 68, 68, 122, 123, 128–129, 140;
    joining sheets, 119–120;
    in plywood, 49;
    positioning sheets, 119;
    press, constructing, 120, 140
video cassettes, storage for, 150–155

W

waste wood, using, 67
wax finishes, 60
wedges, cutting, 58, 76
wenge, 65, 117, 119, 127
white glue, 27
white oak, quarter-sawn, 13, 99, 109
wide panels, cutting, 233
wood:
    drying, 74;
    filler, applying, 185, 248;
    manufactured, 49;
    properties, 104;
    screws, 133;
    waste, using, 67
wood turning
            See lathe turning
writing tables, 142–149

Y

yellow glue, 27